California

Science

Editorial Offices: Glenview, Illinois • Parsippany, New Jersey • New York, New York
Sales Offices: Boston, Massachusetts • Duluth, Georgia • Glenview, Illinois • Coppell, Texas • Sacramento, California • Mesa, Arizona

Series Authors

Dr. Timothy Cooney
Professor of Earth Science and Science Education
University of Northern Iowa (UNI)
Cedar Falls, Iowa

Dr. Jim Cummins
Professor
Department of Curriculum, Teaching, and Learning
University of Toronto
Toronto, Canada

Dr. James Flood
Distinguished Professor of Literacy and Language
School of Teacher Education
San Diego State University
San Diego, California

Barbara Kay Foots, M.Ed.
Science Education Consultant
Houston, Texas

Dr. M. Jenice Goldston
Associate Professor of Science Education
Department of Elementary Education Programs
University of Alabama
Tuscaloosa, Alabama

Dr. Shirley Gholston Key
Associate Professor of Science Education
Instruction and Curriculum Leadership Department
College of Education
University of Memphis
Memphis, Tennessee

Dr. Diane Lapp
Distinguished Professor of Reading and Language Arts in Teacher Education
San Diego State University
San Diego, California

Sheryl A. Mercier
Classroom Teacher
Dunlap Elementary School
Dunlap, California

Karen L. Ostlund, Ph.D.
UTeach Specialist
College of Natural Sciences
The University of Texas at Austin
Austin, Texas

Dr. Nancy Romance
Professor of Science Education & Principal Investigator
NSF/IERI Science IDEAS Project
Charles E. Schmidt College of Science
Florida Atlantic University
Boca Raton, Florida

Dr. William Tate
Chair and Professor of Education and Applied Statistics
Department of Education
Washington University
St. Louis, Missouri

Dr. Kathryn C. Thornton
Former NASA Astronaut
Professor
School of Engineering and Applied Science
University of Virginia
Charlottesville, Virginia

Dr. Leon Ukens
Professor Emeritus
Department of Physics, Astronomy, and Geosciences
Towson University
Towson, Maryland

Steve Weinberg
Consultant
Connecticut Center for Advanced Technology
East Hartford, Connecticut

ISBN: 0-328-18841-7

Copyright © 2008 Pearson Education, Inc.

6 7 8 9 10 V082 15 14 13 12 11 10 09 08

Contributing Author

Dr. Michael P. Klentschy
Superintendent
El Centro Elementary School District
El Centro, California

Consulting Author

Dr. Olga Amaral
Chair, Division of Teacher Education
San Diego State University
Calexico, California

Science Content Consultants

Dr. Herbert Brunkhorst
*Chair
Department of Science, Mathematics and Technology
College of Education*
California State University, San Bernardino
San Bernardino, California

Dr. Karen Kolehmainen
Department of Physics
California State University, San Bernardino
San Bernardino, California

Dr. Stephen D. Lewis
Earth and Environmental Sciences
California State University, Fresno
Fresno, California

Content Consultants

Adena Williams Loston, Ph.D.
Chief Education Officer
Office of the Chief Education Officer

Clifford W. Houston, Ph.D.
Deputy Chief Education Officer for Education Programs
Office of the Chief Education Officer

Frank C. Owens
Senior Policy Advisor
Office of the Chief Education Officer

Deborah Brown Biggs
Manager, Education Flight Projects Office
Space Operations Mission Directorate, Education Lead

Erika G. Vick
NASA Liaison to Pearson Scott Foresman
Education Flight Projects Office

William E. Anderson
Partnership Manager for Education
Aeronautics Research Mission Directorate

Anita Krishnamurthi
Program Planning Specialist
Space Science Education and Outreach Program

Bonnie J. McClain
Chief of Education
Exploration Systems Mission Directorate

Diane Clayton, Ph.D.
Program Scientist
Earth Science Education

Deborah Rivera
Strategic Alliances Manager
Office of Public Affairs
NASA Headquarters

Douglas D. Peterson
Public Affairs Office, Astronaut Office
Office of Public Affairs
NASA Johnson Space Center

Nicole Cloutier
Public Affairs Office, Astronaut Office
Office of Public Affairs
NASA Johnson Space Center

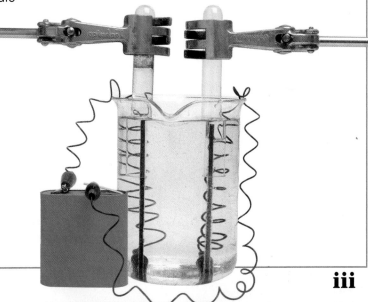

Reviewers

Elaine Chasse-DeMers
Teacher
Taylor Street School
Sacramento, California

Kevin Clevenger
Teacher
Oak Chan Elementary
Folsom, California

Kim Eddings
Teacher
Madison Elementary
Pomona, California

Joseph Frescatore
Teacher
Chavez Elementary
San Diego, California

Candace Gibbons
Teacher
Freedom Elementary
Clovis, California

Anne Higginbotham
Teacher
Arundel Elementary
San Carlos, California

Sean Higgins
Teacher
Monte Verde Elementary
San Bruno, California

Sharon Janulaw
Science Education Specialist
Sonoma County Office of
Education
Santa Rosa, California

Jeanne E. Martin
Teacher
John Gill School
Redwood City, California

Mark Allen Schultz
Teacher
Theodore Judah Elementary
Folsom, California

Corinne Schwartz
Teacher
Lincrest Elementary
Yuba City, California

Schelly T. Solko
Teacher
Loudon School
Bakersfield, California

Bobbie Stumbaugh
Teacher
Roy Cloud School
Redwood City, California

Kimberly Thiesen
Teacher
Freedom Elementary
Clovis, California

Carole Bialek Vargas
Teacher
Empire Oaks Elementary
Folsom, California

Bonita J. Walker-Davis
Teacher
Don Riggio School
Stockton, California

Debra Willsie
Teacher
Tarpey Elementary
Clovis, California

Olivia Winslow
Teacher
Earl Warren Elementary
Sacramento, California

Science *California*

What makes up everything around us?

Chapter 1 • Building Blocks of Matter

Chapter 2 • Changes in Matter

How do you use chemistry every day?

How do cells help an organism?

Chapter 3 • Basic Structures of Organisms

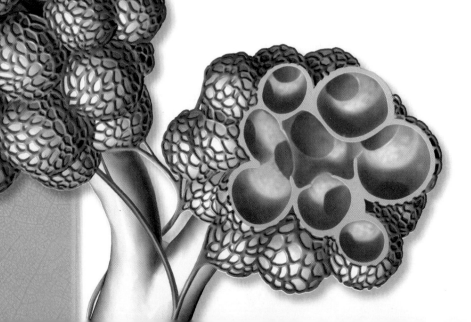

Chapter 4 • Human Body Systems

How do the systems in your body help keep you alive?

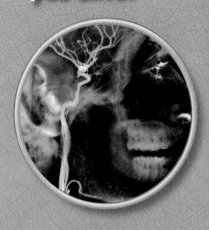

ix

How does water move through the environment?

Why does the weather change?

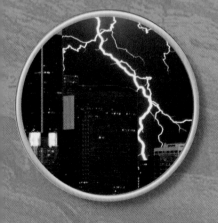

Chapter 7 • The Solar System

What objects in space make up the solar system?

Science Process Skills

Observe
A scientist who studies weather observes many things. You use your senses when you find out about other objects, events, or living things.

Classify
Scientists classify clouds according to their properties. When you classify, you arrange or sort objects, events, or living things.

Estimate and Measure
Scientists estimate how much rain will fall. Then they use tools to measure how much rain fell.

Investigating Weather

Scientists use process skills when they investigate places or events. You will use these skills when you do the activities in this book. Which process skills might scientists use when they investigate weather?

Infer
Scientists infer what they think is happening during a storm based on what they already know.

Predict
Scientists predict how weather will change. Then people know how to prepare for the change.

Make and Use Models
Scientists make and use models such as pictures, maps, and computer simulations. Models are like real events in some ways but are different in other ways.

Science Process Skills

Investigate and Experiment

As scientists observe storms, they investigate and experiment to test a hypothesis.

Form Questions and Hypotheses

Think of a statement that you can test to solve a problem or answer a question about storms or other kinds of weather.

Identify and Control Variables

As scientists perform an experiment, they identify and control the variables so that they test only one thing at a time.

If you were a scientist, you might want to learn more about storms. What questions might you have about storms? How would you use process skills in your investigation?

Collect Data
Scientists collect data from their observations of weather. They put the data into charts or tables.

Interpret Data
Scientists use the information they collected to solve problems or answer questions.

Communicate
Scientists use words, pictures, charts, and graphs to share information about their investigation.

Using Scientific Methods for Science Inquiry

Scientists use scientific methods as they work. Scientific methods are organized ways to answer questions and solve problems. Scientific methods include the steps shown here. Scientists might not use all the steps. They might not use the steps in this order. You will use scientific methods when you do the **Full Inquiry** activity at the end of each unit. You also will use scientific methods when you do Science Fair Projects.

Ask a question.
You might have a question about something you observe.

What material is best for keeping heat in water?

State your hypothesis.
A hypothesis is a possible answer to your question.

If I wrap the jar in fake fur, then the water will stay warmer longer.

Identify and control variables.
Variables are things that can change. For a fair test, you can change just one variable. You must keep all other variables the same.

Test other materials. Put the same amount of warm water in other jars that are the same size and shape.

Test your hypothesis.
Make a plan to test your hypothesis. Collect materials and tools. Then follow your plan.

Collect and record your data.
Keep good records of what you do and find out. Use tables and pictures to help.

Interpret your data.
Organize your notes and records to make them clear. Make diagrams, charts, or graphs to help.

State your conclusion.
Your conclusion is a decision you make based on your data. Communicate what you found out. Tell whether or not your data supported your hypothesis.

Fake fur did the best job of keeping the water warm.

Go further.
Use what you learn. Think of new questions to test or better ways to do a test.

Ask a Question

State Your Hypothesis

Identify and Control Variables

Test Your Hypothesis

Collect and Record Your Data

Interpret Your Data

State Your Conclusion

Go Further

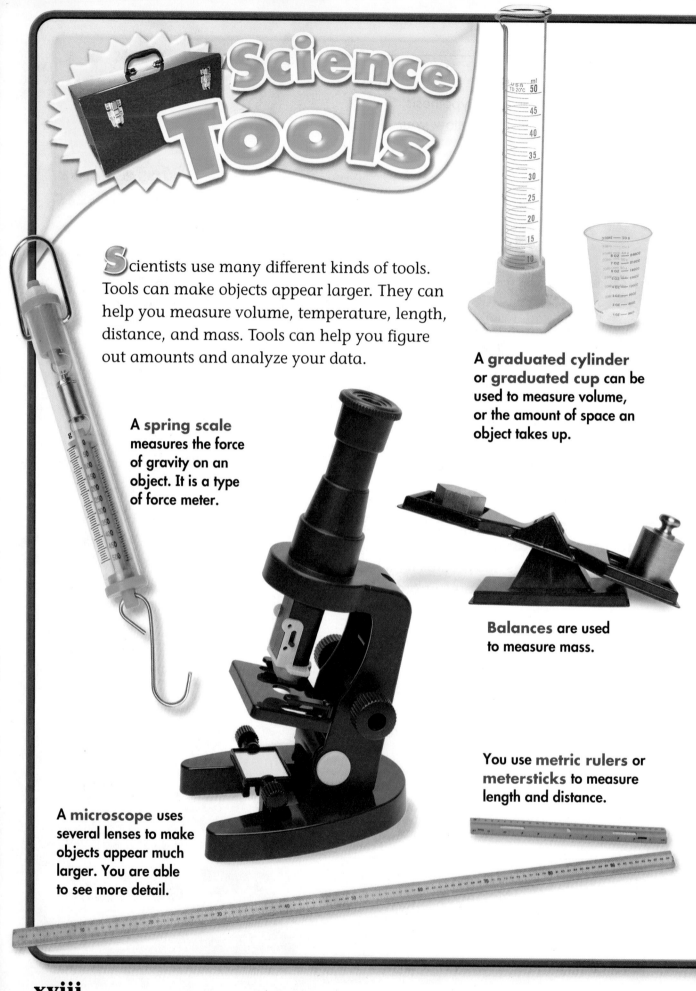

Science Tools

Scientists use many different kinds of tools. Tools can make objects appear larger. They can help you measure volume, temperature, length, distance, and mass. Tools can help you figure out amounts and analyze your data.

A **graduated cylinder** or **graduated cup** can be used to measure volume, or the amount of space an object takes up.

A **spring scale** measures the force of gravity on an object. It is a type of force meter.

Balances are used to measure mass.

You use **metric rulers** or **metersticks** to measure length and distance.

A **microscope** uses several lenses to make objects appear much larger. You are able to see more detail.

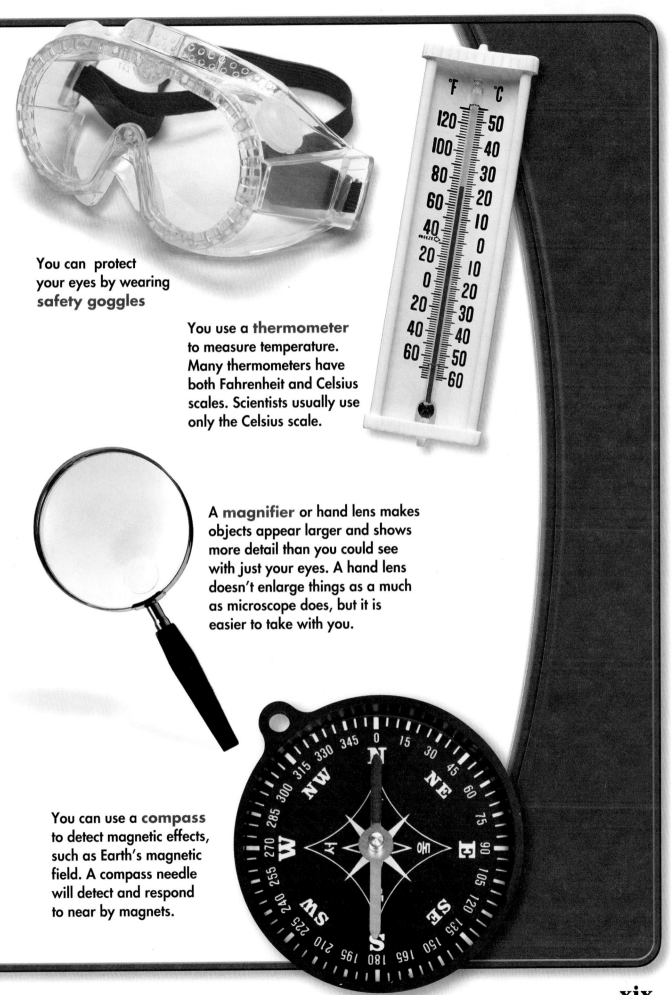

You can protect your eyes by wearing **safety goggles**

You use a **thermometer** to measure temperature. Many thermometers have both Fahrenheit and Celsius scales. Scientists usually use only the Celsius scale.

A **magnifier** or hand lens makes objects appear larger and shows more detail than you could see with just your eyes. A hand lens doesn't enlarge things as a much as microscope does, but it is easier to take with you.

You can use a **compass** to detect magnetic effects, such as Earth's magnetic field. A compass needle will detect and respond to near by magnets.

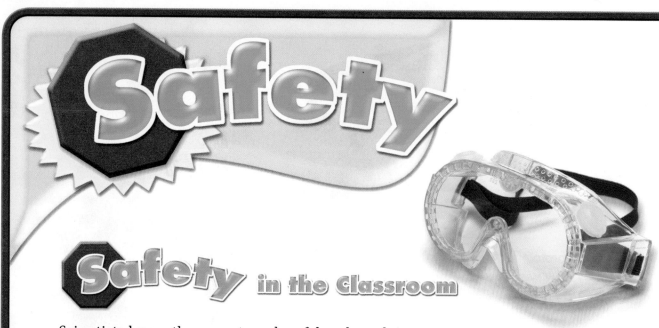

Safety

Safety in the Classroom

Scientists know they must work safely when doing experiments. You need to be careful when doing science activities too. Follow these safety rules:

- Read the activity carefully before you start.
- Listen to the teacher's instructions. Ask questions about things you do not understand.
- Wear safety goggles when needed.
- Keep your work area neat and clean.
- Clean up spills right away.
- Never taste or smell substances unless directed to do so by your teacher.
- Handle sharp items and other equipment carefully.
- Use chemicals carefully.
- Help keep plants and animals that you use safe.
- Tell your teacher if you see something that looks unsafe or if there is an accident.
- Put materials away when you finish.
- Dispose of chemicals properly.
- Wash your hands well when you are finished.

Safety at Home

Safety Tips

- Put toys, clothing, shoes, and books away. Do not leave anything lying on the floor.
- Do not play with sharp objects such as knives.
- Wash your hands with soap and warm water before you eat.
- Clean up all spills right away.
- Turn on a light before walking into a dark room.
- Do not run indoors.
- Do not jump down stairs.

Safety

Science Safety Tips

- Think about safety tips that you follow in your classroom.
- Do science activities only when an adult is with you.
- Never taste, or touch, or smell anything unless your teacher or an adult in your family tells you it is okay.

Fire Safety Tips

- Never use matches or lighters.
- Never use the stove or oven without the help of an adult.
- Get out quickly if a building you are in is on fire.
- Stop, drop, and roll if your clothing catches on fire. Do not run.
- Know two ways to get out of your home.
- Practice fire escape routes with your family.

Stop

Drop

Roll

Electrical Safety Tips

- Do not touch electrical outlets. When they are not in use, cover them with safety caps.
- Always unplug appliances by pulling on the plug instead of the cord. Pulling on the cord can damage the wires.
- A cord that has damaged insulation should be replaced immediately.
- Never touch a power line with your body or any object. Stay far away from downed power lines. If you see one, call 911.
- Never touch an electrical appliance, switch, cord, plug, or outlet if you or the appliance is touching water.
- Do not use cord-operated radios or other electrical appliances near a bathtub, pool, or lake. Use battery-operated devices instead.

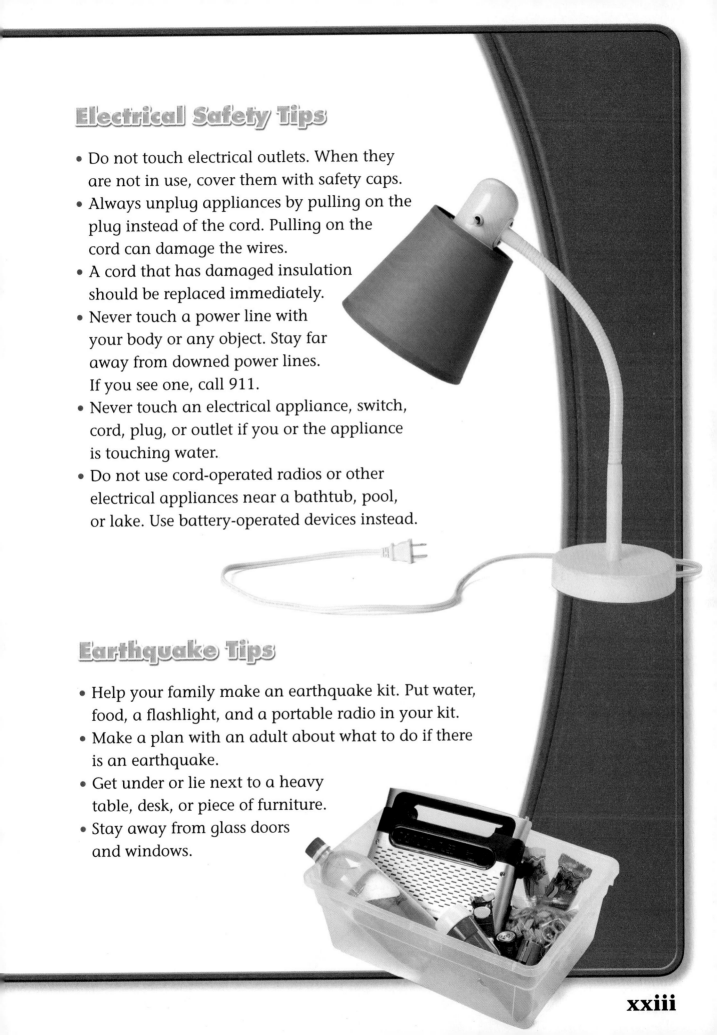

Earthquake Tips

- Help your family make an earthquake kit. Put water, food, a flashlight, and a portable radio in your kit.
- Make a plan with an adult about what to do if there is an earthquake.
- Get under or lie next to a heavy table, desk, or piece of furniture.
- Stay away from glass doors and windows.

Metric and Customary Measurement

The metric system is the measurement system most commonly used in science. Metric units are sometimes called SI units. SI stands for International System. It is called that because these units are used around the world.

These prefixes are used in the metric system:

kilo- means *thousand*
1 kilometer equals 1,000 meters

milli- means *one-thousandth*
1,000 millimeters equals 1 meter or 1 millimeter = 0.001 meter

centi- means *one-hundredth*
100 centimeters equals 1 meter or 1 centimeter = 0.01 meter

Length and Distance
One meter is longer than 1 yard.

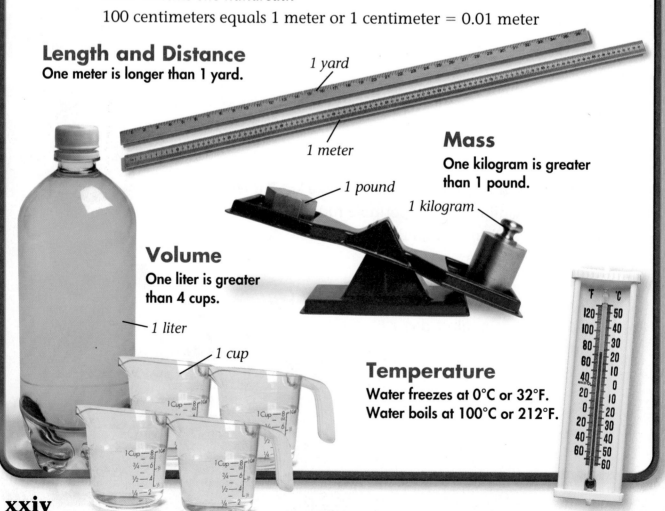

1 yard

1 meter

Mass
One kilogram is greater than 1 pound.

1 pound

1 kilogram

Volume
One liter is greater than 4 cups.

1 liter

1 cup

Temperature
Water freezes at 0°C or 32°F.
Water boils at 100°C or 212°F.

Physical Sciences

California Foundry History Museum

Sacramento, California

Where do fire hydrants come from? What about bells? They're made in foundries. Foundries are factories where metal is melted and molded, or cast, into all kinds of metal equipment. The California Foundry History Museum in Sacramento showcases this important industry.

Foundries have been important in California since the Gold Rush. The museum shows how foundries made equipment that miners needed to dig, carry, and purify gold and other metals. You can also see the wooden patterns used to make molds from sand or clay. Hot liquid metal was poured into the sand or clay mold, where it cooled and hardened.

Foundries are still important in California today. Most modern foundries use robots and computers. At the museum, you can see how metal is cast in modern foundries. You can try out a trolley bell, and then see exactly how it was made.

Find Out More

Research to find out more about how metal is used.

- **Research to learn about the process of metal casting. Prepare a poster or other display that shows the steps of the process.**

- **See whether there is a metal foundry in your area that you can visit. Interview a person who works with metal. Write a newspaper article about your visit and interview.**

Sacramento

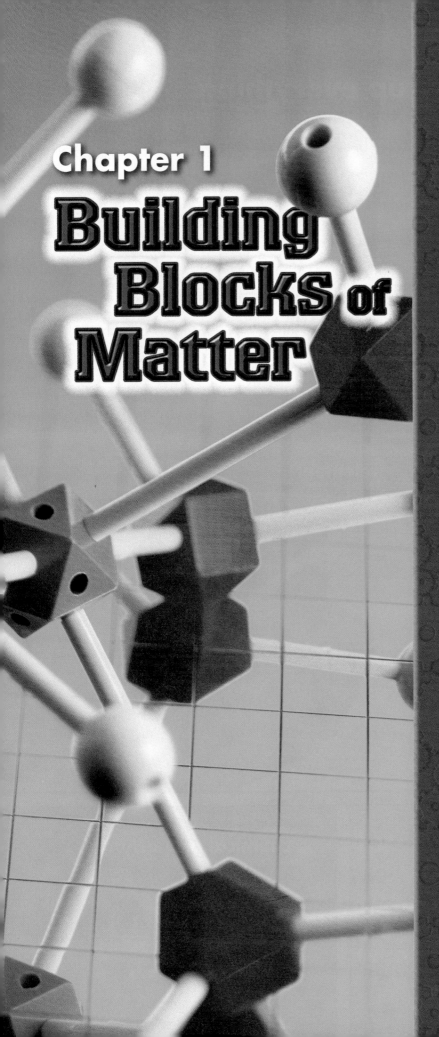

Chapter 1
Building Blocks of Matter

CALIFORNIA Standards Preview

5PS1.0 Elements and their combinations account for all the varied types of matter in the world. As a basis for understanding this concept:

5PS1.b Students know all matter is made of atoms, which may combine to form molecules.

5PS1.c Students know metals have properties in common, such as high electrical and thermal conductivity. Some metals, such as aluminum (Al), iron (Fe), nickel (Ni), copper (Cu), silver (Ag), and gold (Au), are pure elements; others, such as steel and brass, are composed of a combination of elemental metals.

5PS1.d Students know that each element is made of one kind of atom and that the elements are organized in the periodic table by their chemical properties.

5PS1.e Students know scientists have developed instruments that can create discrete images of atoms and molecules that show that the atoms and molecules often occur in well-ordered arrays.

5PS1.f Students know differences in chemical and physical properties of substances are used to separate mixtures and identify compounds.

5PS1.h Students know living organisms and most materials are composed of just a few elements.

5PS1.i Students know the common properties of salts, such as sodium chloride (NaCl).

5IE6.0 Scientific progress is made by asking meaningful questions and conducting careful investigations. As a basis for understanding this concept and addressing the content in the other three strands, students should develop their own questions and perform investigations. (Also **5IE6.b**, **5IE6.c**, **5IE6.f**, **5IE6.g**, **5IE6.h**)

Standards Focus Questions

- What are the properties of matter?
- What makes up matter?
- What are compounds?
- How can we separate mixtures?

What makes up everything around us?

element

physical property

chemical property

DIGITAL

Chapter 1 Vocabulary

solution

atom

atomic number

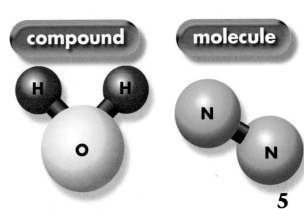

compound

H H

O

molecule

N N

Be careful!

Explore How can properties change during a chemical reaction?

Wear safety goggles. Do not taste the tablet or liquid.

Materials

safety goggles

warm water and ice-cold water

graduated cylinder

2 plastic cups

2 thermometers

4 fizzy antacid tablets

Use scientific evidence to help make **inferences** and draw conclusions. State if you need more evidence to support your conclusion.

What to Do

1 Put 100 mL of cold water and a thermometer in a cup. Put 100 mL of warm water and a thermometer in another cup.

cold water

warm water

2 After 1 minute record the temperatures.

3 Add 2 fizzy antacid tablets to each cup. **Observe** any changes.

Explain Your Results

1. How did some properties change?

2. **Infer** Draw a conclusion about the way temperature affected the speed of the reaction.

5PS1.a Students know that during chemical reactions the atoms in the reactants rearrange to form products with different properties. **5IE6.f** Select appropriate tools (e.g., thermometers, metersticks, balances, and graduated cylinders) and make quantitative observations. **5IE6.h** Draw conclusions from scientific evidence and indicate whether further information is needed to support a specific conclusion.

How to Read Science

Make Inferences

Learning to **make inferences** can help you evaluate what you read and observe. An inference is a conclusion based on facts, observations, experience, or knowledge.

- As you read, put together facts and then extend them to make an inference or form a conclusion.

- Sometimes you may be able to make more than one inference about the outcome of an event.

- Observations can help you make inferences.

Science Story

Choosing Materials

Rodney was building a model rocket for a competition. He was looking for the right material to use for the tailfins. He wanted the tailfins to be light, but the largest possible size. He had some pieces of plastic. Then he got some balsa wood at a craft shop. He cut pieces of both materials into triangles of the same size. When Rodney weighed the traingles, he found that the plastic was heavier.

Apply It!

Make a graphic organizer like this one. List facts from the science story to **make inferences** about Rodney's rocket.

Facts → **Inferences**

You Are There!

The time is the early 1900s. A set of tracks guides you through a narrow passage. As you go deeper, the air grows cool and damp. The bray of a mule and the clackety-clack of wheels alert you to an approaching cart. You step aside, allowing the mule and its load to pass. Light bounces from the cart's contents to reveal shiny yellow patches hidden in the rocks it carries. These lumps of rock from the Empire Mine in Nevada County hold one of the most valuable metals on Earth—gold! What other materials can you think of that come from Earth?

Standards Focus 5PS1.0 Elements and their combinations account for all the varied types of matter in the world. As a basis for understanding this concept: **5PS1.h** Students know living organisms and most materials are composed of just a few elements.

DIGITAL

Lesson 1

What are properties of matter?

All things around you are made with just a few kinds of matter. Each kind of matter has its own set of properties.

Gold

Elements

The gold that miners dug from the Empire Mine is one of more than 100 basic kinds of matter called elements. **Elements** are the building blocks of matter. They cannot be broken down into smaller pieces. These relatively few building blocks combine to make up all other kinds of matter.

Only a few elements, such as gold, exist in nature in pure form. Most living and nonliving things are made of just a few elements that combine in many ways. Living things contain mostly carbon, oxygen, hydrogen, nitrogen, sulfur, and phosphorus. More than 98 percent of the material in Earth's crust is made up of only eight elements—oxygen, silicon, aluminum, iron, calcium, sodium, potassium, and magnesium. These few elements in many combinations make up the nearly 3,500 known minerals on Earth.

Carbon, hydrogen, oxygen, and nitrogen make up 96 percent of the mass of the human body. Your body is more than 60 percent oxygen by mass. Oxygen is found in water, proteins, sugars, and fats in your body. Water is the most important substance to all living things.

1. ✓**Checkpoint** What are elements? Are most living things made up of pure elements or combinations of elements?

TARGET SKILL

2. **Make Inferences** How do so few elements make up so many substances?

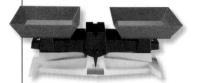

Balance

Spring scale

A balance is used to measure mass. A spring scale is used to measure weight.

Physical Properties of Matter

How would you describe the copper shown on the bottom of this page? Would you say that it is shiny and solid? These are both physical properties of copper. **Physical properties** are those that can be seen or measured without changing a material. Color, hardness, and state of matter are physical properties. You can observe all of these properties in the copper.

The copper also has mass and weight. People often confuse these two physical properties. Mass is a measure of the amount of matter in an object. You can use a balance to find the mass of an object. Weight is a measure of the pull of gravity on an object. Weight can be measured using a spring scale.

Unlike mass, weight changes if an object moves to a place where gravity is stronger or weaker. For example, your mass is the same on Earth as it is on the Moon. But your weight on Earth is six times greater than it would be on the Moon!

Other physical properties include whether a substance is magnetic or dissolves in other substances. The temperatures at which a substance boils and freezes are physical properties too.

Water freezes at 0°C. Ice melts at 0°C. The temperatures at which substances freeze and melt are physical properties.

Copper

10

Wood is flammable, as shown in the fireplace. Flammability is a chemical property of matter.

Whether a material changes when mixed with acid is a chemical property of the material. The zinc nail changes and forms bubbles in the beaker of acid. The gold chain does not.

Some Common Properties

Substance	Physical Property	Chemical Property
Wood	Does not conduct electricity	Flammable
Iron	Can be hammered into sheets	Combines with oxygen to form rust
Water	Colorless and odorless	Does not burn
Copper	Conducts electricity	Combines with oxygen to form the mineral cuprite

Chemical Properties of Matter

You can describe matter by its chemical properties as well as by its physical properties. A substance's **chemical properties** tell how the substance forms new substances when it mixes with something else. Look at the wood burning in the fireplace. As the wood burns, it changes into new materials—ash and gases. The ability of a material to burn is called flammability.

The chart lists some physical and chemical properties of matter. Notice that wood is flammable but that water will not burn. These are chemical properties of those substances.

✓ Lesson Review

1. What is the difference between physical and chemical properties?

2. **Make Inferences** Which material—wood or copper—would you infer to be best for use in making an electrical circuit?

3. **Writing in Science** **Descriptive** Choose an object and write a description of its physical properties.

11

Aluminum atom

Electron *Proton*

Neutron

Carbon atom

What makes up matter?

All matter is made of atoms. Atoms are particles of elements. Atoms combine to form molecules.

Atoms and Elements

An **atom** is the smallest particle of an element that has the same properties of the element. Atoms of one element are different from atoms of all other elements. The structure of an atom determines the properties of an element. It also determines how the element can combine with other elements.

If you could look at the structure of a pure metal such as aluminum, you would see that it is made from many tiny atoms. Each element is made of only one kind of atom, so elements are called pure substances. An element cannot be separated into simpler substances by ordinary physical or chemical methods.

Atoms are made up of smaller parts. Atoms are too small to be seen. Scientists use models, like the ones in the illustrations on this page, to represent atoms. The atom's center, or nucleus, has neutrons and protons. A neutron has no electrical charge. A proton has a positive charge. The number of protons in a nucleus is the element's **atomic number.** The atomic number of an element is its most important property. It identifies the element. For example, all carbon atoms have six protons. Carbon's atomic number is 6. No other kind of atom has six protons. Electrons surround an atom's nucleus. An electron has a negative charge.

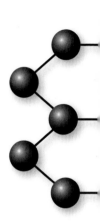

Standards Focus 5PS1.0 Elements and their combinations account for all the varied types of matter in the world. As a basis for understanding this concept:
5PS1.b Students know all matter is made of atoms, which may combine to form molecules.
5PS1.c Students know metals have properties in common, such as high electrical and thermal conductivity. Some metals, such as aluminum (Al), iron (Fe), nickel (Ni), copper (Cu), silver (Ag), and gold (Au), are pure elements; others, such as steel and brass, are composed of a combination of elemental metals.
5PS1.d Students know that each element is made of one kind of atom and that the elements are organized in the periodic table by their chemical properties.
5PS1.e Students know scientists have developed instruments that can create discrete images of atoms and molecules that show that the atoms and molecules often occur in well-ordered arrays.

Molecules

You have read that the smallest particle of a substance is an atom. But many substances are not made of single atoms of one element. Atoms can combine to form molecules. A **molecule** is the smallest part of a substance made from more than one atom that still has the properties of that substance.

A nitrogen molecule has two atoms.

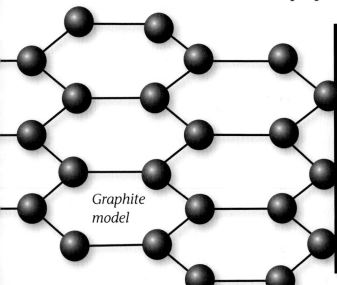

Graphite model

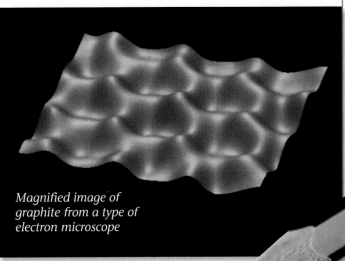

Magnified image of graphite from a type of electron microscope

Images of Molecules

Scientists have been thinking about atoms and molecules for a very long time. The first mention of the atom was about 2,500 years ago by a Greek philosopher named Democritus. He said that atoms were the smallest parts of matter. Later, other scientists wrote new ideas about what the atom might look like. Today, scientists often use the type of model shown in the illustrations on page 12.

Atoms and molecules are too small to be seen—even with a microscope! Scientists have developed technology that allows them to make images of atoms and molecules. This technology finds the shape of an atom or a molecule and then displays it on a computer screen. These images can show atoms as small, sphere-like objects. The images confirm that atoms and molecules often appear as a well-ordered array, or grid.

Carbon atoms join together to form graphite, which is used in pencils.

1. ✓**Checkpoint** Why are elements considered pure substances?

2. ✏️ **Writing in Science Expository** Write a paragraph to summarize what you know about atoms. Include the terms *atom*, *proton*, *neutron*, *electron*, and *nucleus*.

Elements and the Periodic Table

Elements are organized in a table called the periodic table of elements. The elements are arranged in order according to the atomic number. The atomic numbers increase from left to right. They also increase down line by line on the periodic table. Elements with similar properties, such as metals, are grouped together. The periodic table is arranged so that the elements in each column have similar chemical properties. You can predict the properties of an element if you know its column. For example, elements found in the last column on the right are gases at room temperature. These gases, called noble gases, do not usually combine with other elements.

Every element has a symbol of one or two letters. Only the first letter of the symbol is capitalized. Take a look at the periodic table. What elements have the symbols Na, Ag, and Ca?

Helium's atomic number is 2. All helium atoms have 2 protons and usually have 2 neutrons and 2 electrons.

Periodic Table of the Elements

Metals
Metalloids (semimetals)
Nonmetals

Elements that are metals can conduct electricity well.

Nonmetals do not conduct electricity well.

1	2	3	4	5	6	7	8	9	10	11	12	13	14	15	16	17	18
1 **H** Hydrogen																	2 **He** Helium
3 **Li** Lithium	4 **Be** Beryllium											5 **B** Boron	6 **C** Carbon	7 **N** Nitrogen	8 **O** Oxygen	9 **F** Fluorine	10 **Ne** Neon
11 **Na** Sodium	12 **Mg** Magnesium											13 **Al** Aluminum	14 **Si** Silicon	15 **P** Phosphorus	16 **S** Sulfur	17 **Cl** Chlorine	18 **Ar** Argon
19 **K** Potassium	20 **Ca** Calcium	21 **Sc** Scandium	22 **Ti** Titanium	23 **V** Vanadium	24 **Cr** Chromium	25 **Mn** Manganese	26 **Fe** Iron	27 **Co** Cobalt	28 **Ni** Nickel	29 **Cu** Copper	30 **Zn** Zinc	31 **Ga** Gallium	32 **Ge** Germanium	33 **As** Arsenic	34 **Se** Selenium	35 **Br** Bromine	36 **Kr** Krypton
37 **Rb** Rubidium	38 **Sr** Strontium	39 **Y** Yttrium	40 **Zr** Zirconium	41 **Nb** Niobium	42 **Mo** Molybdenum	43 **Tc** Technetium	44 **Ru** Ruthenium	45 **Rh** Rhodium	46 **Pd** Palladium	47 **Ag** Silver	48 **Cd** Cadmium	49 **In** Indium	50 **Sn** Tin	51 **Sb** Antimony	52 **Te** Tellurium	53 **I** Iodine	54 **Xe** Xenon
55 **Cs** Cesium	56 **Ba** Barium	57 **La** Lanthanum	72 **Hf** Hafnium	73 **Ta** Tantalum	74 **W** Tungsten	75 **Re** Rhenium	76 **Os** Osmium	77 **Ir** Iridium	78 **Pt** Platinum	79 **Au** Gold	80 **Hg** Mercury	81 **Tl** Thallium	82 **Pb** Lead	83 **Bi** Bismuth	84 **Po** Polonium	85 **At** Astatine	86 **Rn** Radon
87 **Fr** Francium	88 **Ra** Radium	89 **Ac** Actinium	104 **Rf** Rutherfordium	105 **Db** Dubnium	106 **Sg** Seaborgium	107 **Bh** Bohrium	108 **Hs** Hassium	109 **Mt** Meitnerium									

58 **Ce** Cerium	59 **Pr** Praseodymium	60 **Nd** Neodymium	61 **Pm** Promethium	62 **Sm** Samarium	63 **Eu** Europium	64 **Gd** Gadolinium	65 **Tb** Terbium	66 **Dy** Dysprosium	67 **Ho** Holmium	68 **Er** Erbium	69 **Tm** Thulium	70 **Yb** Ytterbium	71 **Lu** Lutetium
90 **Th** Thorium	91 **Pa** Protactinium	92 **U** Uranium	93 **Np** Neptunium	94 **Pu** Plutonium	95 **Am** Americium	96 **Cm** Curium	97 **Bk** Berkelium	98 **Cf** Californium	99 **Es** Einsteinium	100 **Fm** Fermium	101 **Md** Mendelevium	102 **No** Nobelium	103 **Lr** Lawrencium

The nonmetal neon (Ne) is used in colorful signs.

Mercury (Hg) is the only metal that is a liquid at room temperature.

Classifying Elements

Each element is made of one kind of atom. This atom has a unique number of protons. An element's set of protons, neutrons, and electrons give the element its properties. Scientists use these properties to place each element into one of three groups—metals, nonmetals, and metalloids.

Metals are usually solid, are good conductors of heat and electricity, and can be made into wires and hammered into sheets. You will learn more about metals later in this lesson. Nonmetals are usually brittle, are poor conductors of heat and electricity, and cannot be hammered into sheets or made into wires. Metalloids are elements that have some properties of both metals and nonmetals.

1. **√Checkpoint** Describe the periodic table and how it is organized.

2. **Make Inferences** Using the periodic table, how would you classify sulfur(S)—metal, metalloid, or nonmetal?

15

Information on the Periodic Table

If you want to learn about a word, you can go to a dictionary. If you want to learn about an element, you can go to the periodic table. The periodic table contains a great deal of information about the elements.

Each block in the periodic table contains information about one element. Look below at the block for chromium, an element commonly seen on appliances and car parts. It shows what information you can find about chromium. Each block on the periodic table on page 14 has similar information.

You can learn about an element's properties by looking at its location on the periodic table. The word *periodic* means "in a regular, repeated pattern." The properties of elements change in predictable ways as you move across a row, called a period, or down a column, called a group, in the periodic table.

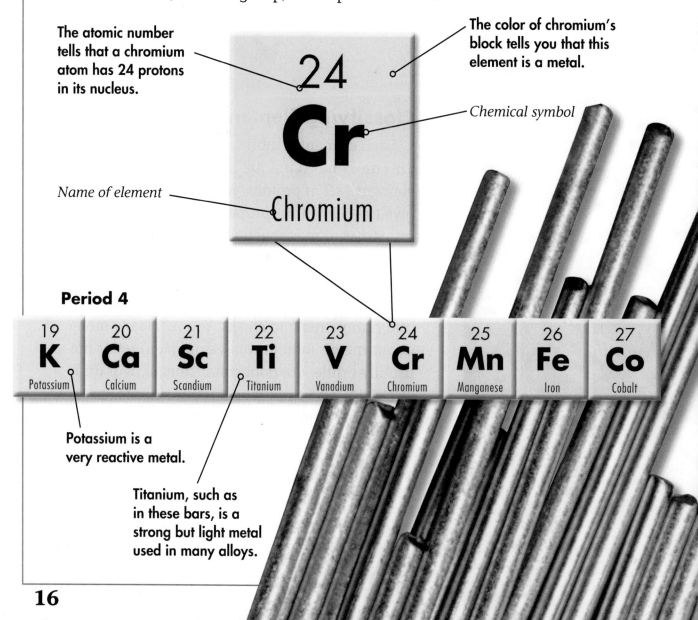

The atomic number tells that a chromium atom has 24 protons in its nucleus.

The color of chromium's block tells you that this element is a metal.

Chemical symbol

24

Cr

Chromium

Name of element

Period 4

19	20	21	22	23	24	25	26	27
K	**Ca**	**Sc**	**Ti**	**V**	**Cr**	**Mn**	**Fe**	**Co**
Potassium	Calcium	Scandium	Titanium	Vanadium	Chromium	Manganese	Iron	Cobalt

Potassium is a very reactive metal.

Titanium, such as in these bars, is a strong but light metal used in many alloys.

Groups and Periods

The periodic table has 18 columns. Each column is called a group or family. The groups are numbered from 1 to 18. The elements in a group have similar properties. They cause chemical changes, or react, with other substances in similar ways.

The elements in Group 18 are called inactive elements, or noble gases. These gases rarely react with other elements. All of the elements in Group 1 except for hydrogen are metals that combine, or react with water very easily. If these metals are mixed with water, they can catch on fire or even explode. Potassium is in Group 1. Hydrogen is an exception. It has very different properties than other elements in Group 1.

Each row in the periodic table is called a period. Unlike the elements in a group, the elements in a period have very different properties. The first element in a period is very reactive. The last element is inactive. Look at Period 4 below. The metallic elements change from very reactive to less reactive as you move from left to right. The elements in blue are metalloids. The last three elements are nonmetals.

Group 18

2								
He								
Helium								

| 10 |
| **Ne** |
| Neon |

| 18 |
| **Ar** |
| Argon |

Germanium and arsenic are metalloids.

Krypton is an inactive nonmetal. It is a gas.

28	29	30	31	32	33	34	35	36
Ni	**Cu**	**Zn**	**Ga**	**Ge**	**As**	**Se**	**Br**	**Kr**
Nickel	Copper	Zinc	Gallium	Germanium	Arsenic	Selenium	Bromine	Krypton

| 54 |
| **Xe** |
| Xenon |

| 86 |
| **Rn** |
| Radon |

1. ✓**Checkpoint** What chemical property is shared by the elements in Group 1 of the periodic table except hydrogen?

2. Is bromine a metal or a nonmetal? What is its chemical symbol?

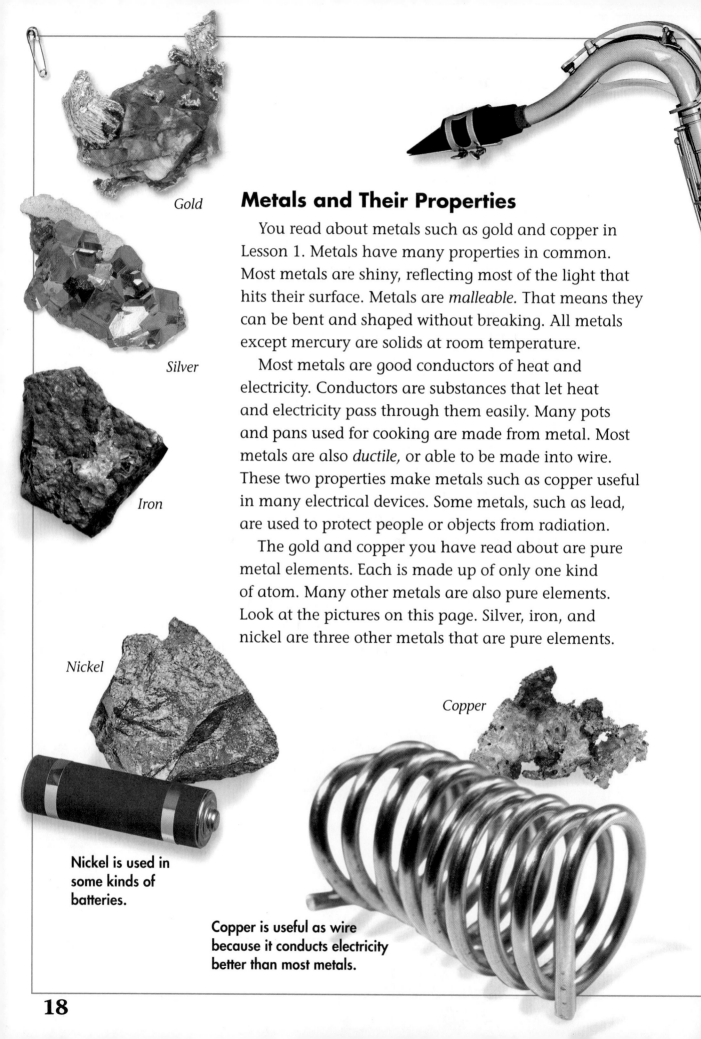

Gold

Silver

Iron

Metals and Their Properties

You read about metals such as gold and copper in Lesson 1. Metals have many properties in common. Most metals are shiny, reflecting most of the light that hits their surface. Metals are *malleable.* That means they can be bent and shaped without breaking. All metals except mercury are solids at room temperature.

Most metals are good conductors of heat and electricity. Conductors are substances that let heat and electricity pass through them easily. Many pots and pans used for cooking are made from metal. Most metals are also *ductile,* or able to be made into wire. These two properties make metals such as copper useful in many electrical devices. Some metals, such as lead, are used to protect people or objects from radiation.

The gold and copper you have read about are pure metal elements. Each is made up of only one kind of atom. Many other metals are also pure elements. Look at the pictures on this page. Silver, iron, and nickel are three other metals that are pure elements.

Nickel

Copper

Nickel is used in some kinds of batteries.

Copper is useful as wire because it conducts electricity better than most metals.

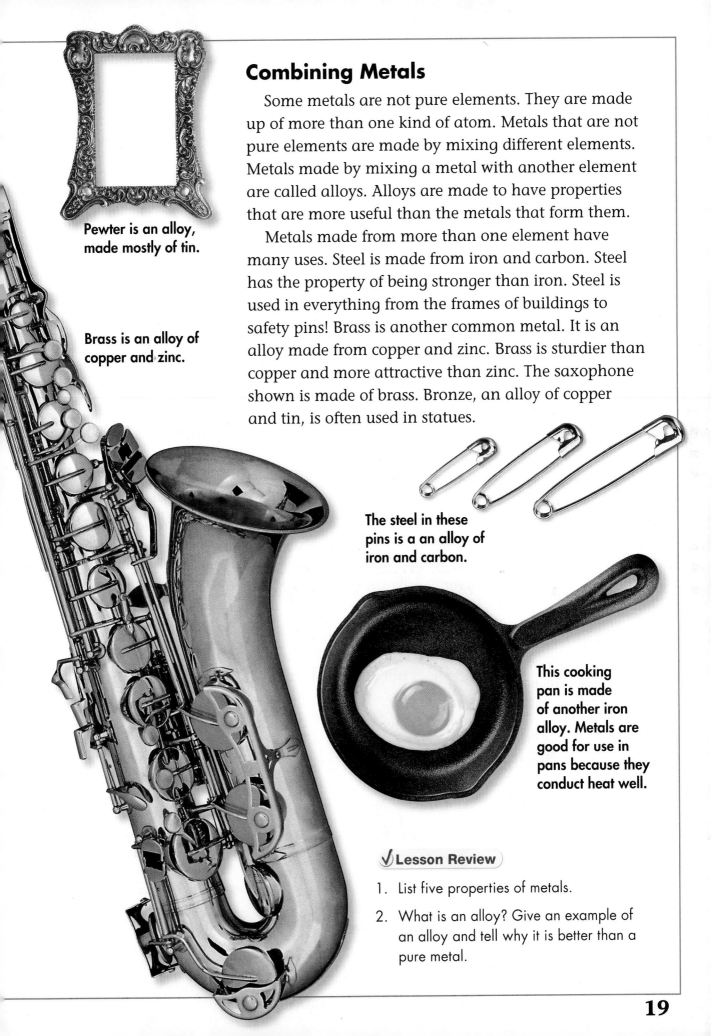

Pewter is an alloy, made mostly of tin.

Brass is an alloy of copper and zinc.

Combining Metals

Some metals are not pure elements. They are made up of more than one kind of atom. Metals that are not pure elements are made by mixing different elements. Metals made by mixing a metal with another element are called alloys. Alloys are made to have properties that are more useful than the metals that form them.

Metals made from more than one element have many uses. Steel is made from iron and carbon. Steel has the property of being stronger than iron. Steel is used in everything from the frames of buildings to safety pins! Brass is another common metal. It is an alloy made from copper and zinc. Brass is sturdier than copper and more attractive than zinc. The saxophone shown is made of brass. Bronze, an alloy of copper and tin, is often used in statues.

The steel in these pins is a an alloy of iron and carbon.

This cooking pan is made of another iron alloy. Metals are good for use in pans because they conduct heat well.

✓ **Lesson Review**

1. List five properties of metals.

2. What is an alloy? Give an example of an alloy and tell why it is better than a pure metal.

19

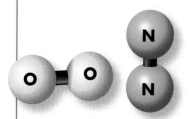

Atoms of oxygen and nitrogen form molecules. They are not compounds because each molecule is made up of only one type of atom.

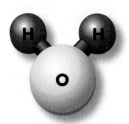

People used to think water was an element. We now know water is a compound made up of hydrogen and oxygen atoms.

In Unit B, you will learn how plants use carbon dioxide to make food.

Lesson 3

What are compounds?

Compounds have molecules made of more than one kind of element. Most things you see around you are compounds.

Properties of Compounds

A **compound** is a kind of matter made of a combination of two or more elements. Properties of compounds are different from the properties of the elements that they contain. For example, sugar is made of atoms of carbon, hydrogen, and oxygen. At room temperature, pure oxygen and hydrogen are invisible gases that have no taste. Black coal is made up mostly of pure carbon atoms. Coal surely does not taste sweet! Yet when these three elements combine in the right way, they form a sweet, white solid.

Every compound has a formula that shows how many atoms of each element are in the compound. For example, water has the formula H_2O. The "2" after the "H" in the formula shows that a molecule of water has two hydrogen atoms. The "O" stands for oxygen. Because there is no number, you know that there is only one atom of oxygen in the molecule.

A carbon dioxide molecule has the formula CO_2. It has one atom of carbon and two atoms of oxygen. Carbon dioxide does not burn. In fact, it can be used to put out fires. When cooled to a temperature of –78°C, carbon dioxide gas becomes a white solid called dry ice.

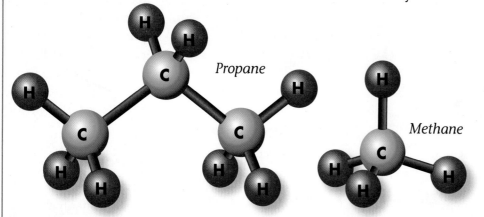

Propane

Methane

Propane and methane both contain the elements carbon and hydrogen. The elements combine in different ways to make different compounds.

Standards Focus 5PS1.0 Elements and their combinations account for all the varied types of matter in the world. As a basis for understanding this concept:
5PS1.b Students know all matter is made of atoms, which may combine to form molecules.
5PS1.i Students know the common properties of salts, such as sodium chloride (NaCl).

The Same Element in Different Compounds

An element can be present in more than one compound. Look at the pictures below. Which element appears in both compounds? Notice that the two compounds that contain sodium are very different.

Compounds are important to your body. For example, water is a compound. It makes up about 60 percent of your body. Other compounds make up much of your skin, bones, tendons, and ligaments.

When sodium combines with chlorine, it forms sodium chloride, common table salt.

Sodium   *Chlorine*   *Sodium chloride (table salt)*

When sodium combines with water, it reacts violently to form hydrogen gas and a compound called sodium hydroxide.

Sodium   *Water*

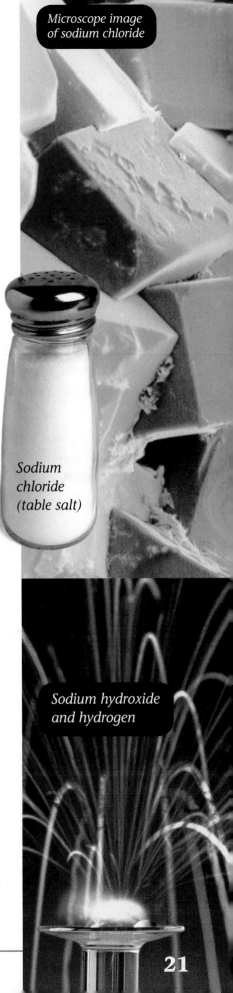

Microscope image of sodium chloride

Sodium hydroxide and hydrogen

1. ✓**Checkpoint** The chemical formula for glucose, a type of sugar, is $C_6H_{12}O_6$. Is glucose an element or a compound? How do you know?

2. Give an example of a molecule that is a compound and one that is not a compound.

Salts

Salts are compounds made of particles held together by opposite charges. The particles may be charged atoms or groups of atoms. Particles with more electrons than protons have a negative charge. Particles with more protons than electrons have a positive charge.

There are many kinds of salts, but most salts have two properties. First, almost every salt is made up of at least one metal element and one nonmetal element. Second, all salts can form crystals. Crystals form when particles arrange themselves in a regular pattern. These crystals are brittle. That means they can break apart easily.

Microscope image of table salt

Table salt

Table salt is made from the metal sodium and the nonmetal chlorine. Its crystals have a cube shape.

Forming Salts

Salts can form when chemicals called acids and bases react. For example, two dangerous chemicals—hydrochloric acid (HCl) and sodium hydroxide (NaOH)—combine to form a salt, sodium chloride (NaCl), and water. The salt that forms is dissolved in the water. If the water evaporates, the sodium chloride is left behind in crystals.

Many acids and bases are dangerous. Both can be poisonous and some can burn your skin. All chemicals must be handled carefully. NEVER taste any material formed in a science experiment. Although sodium chloride is the table salt common in foods, many salts are poisonous.

Poisonous

Corrosive or Destructive

Dangerous to the Environment

Harmful or Irritating

The top two chemical warning labels are used to identify substances that are poisonous and corrosive or destructive. The bottom two labels indicate substances that are dangerous to living things and harmful or irritating.

When an acid and a base are mixed together safely and in the correct amounts, they can form water and a salt.

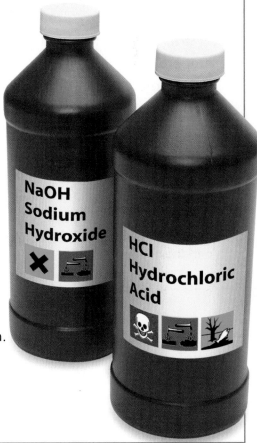

1. ✓ **Checkpoint** What compounds form when an acid reacts with a base?

2. ✎ **Writing in Science**
    Descriptive Suppose that you are writing an article in a science magazine for young children. Write a description of salts and how they form.

Properties of Salts

When you hear the word *salt,* what substance do you think of? What properties does the substance have? You probably think of the solid white crystals you find in a salt shaker. These crystals are sodium chloride, or table salt. Table salt is just one of many salts that share common properties.

You have read that salts are made of metal and nonmetal elements. Many, but not all, salts are formed when an element in the group under sodium or magnesium in the periodic table combines with an element under fluorine. Most salts also form brittle crystals and melt only at very high temperatures.

One important property that most salts share is that they dissolve in water. When these salts are dissolved in water, they conduct electricity well.

Salt can be dissolved in water. If you try this, you will see there is a point at which no more salt will dissolve, no matter how much you stir.

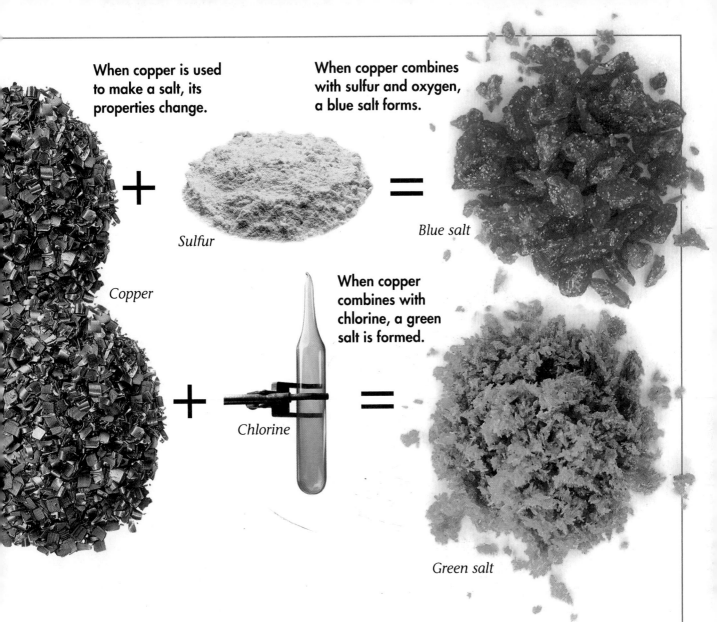

When copper is used to make a salt, its properties change.

Copper

+

Sulfur

When copper combines with sulfur and oxygen, a blue salt forms.

=

Blue salt

When copper combines with chlorine, a green salt is formed.

+

Chlorine

=

Green salt

Properties of salts are different from the properties of the elements that combine to form them. For example, copper can combine with sulfur and oxygen to make a blue salt. None of these elements are blue. When copper is combined with chlorine, it forms a green salt. Unlike copper, neither salt is able to be made into wire. These salts are two examples of poisonous salts.

Copper salts cannot be bent or made into wire as pure copper can.

✔ **Lesson Review**

1. List some properties of salts.

2. **Make Inferences** Suppose your teacher gives you a sample of an unknown chemical. You know the sample will dissolve in water and it has a low melting temperature. Would you infer that the chemical is a salt? Why or why not?

TARGET SKILL

How can we separate mixtures?

The parts of this soup are not chemically combined.

Sometimes elements and compounds are mixed together but are not chemically combined.

Mixtures

In a mixture, different materials are placed together but are not chemically combined to form new compounds. Unlike the elements that form compounds, each material in a mixture keeps its own properties. If salt and pepper are put together to make a mixture, the salt and the pepper do not change their flavors or colors.

Most of the foods you eat are mixtures. For example, the soup in the picture above has chicken, noodles, celery, carrots, and other vegetables. The carrots are separate and can be easily identified. If you really like carrots, you could easily pick them out with a spoon to eat them first. The components of a mixture are not in fixed amounts. One bowl of soup may have more carrots than another bowl.

You can use the different properties of the materials in a mixture, like this mixture of soil and water, to separate the materials.

The water in the cup on the far right may look clear, but you wouldn't want to drink it.

Standards Focus 5PS1.f Students know differences in chemical and physical properties of substances are used to separate mixtures and identify compounds.

Separating Mixtures

You would not want to drink from the cup shown on page 26. It holds a mixture of soil and water. When the mixture is poured through a filter, the water passes through the filter. The soil particles are too large to pass through the filter. You still would not want to drink the filtered water. There may be smaller particles or dissolved substances that you can't see that would make it unfit to drink.

Look at the mixture on the bottom of the page. How could you separate the iron filings from the rest of the sand? You could use the different physical properties of these materials. Separating mixtures requires knowing how the parts of the mixtures are different. Iron is magnetic, but the rest of the sand is not. As a result, you can use a magnet to separate the iron filings from the mixture. The magnet will attract the filings but not the rest of the sand. The picture shows a magnet in a plastic bag attracting iron filings. The plastic bag is used to keep the tiny filings from touching the magnet.

Magnetic force can act through the plastic bag to separate iron filings from the rest of the sand.

1. **✓Checkpoint** List 3 ways you can separate various mixtures.

2. **✎ Writing in Science Descriptive** Most foods, such as salads, soups, and sandwiches, are mixtures. Write a story in which a character makes a mixture of food to eat. Be sure to clearly state the steps required to make the mixture.

Solutions

When soil and water make a mixture, the soil will slowly settle to the bottom. When salt dissolves in a tall glass of water to make a mixture, the salt will not settle to the bottom. Salt and water make a special kind of mixture called a solution. A **solution** is a special mixture in which a substance is dissolved. The substance is spread out evenly and will not settle.

In a solution, the substance that dissolves is called the *solute.* The *solvent* is the substance in which the solute is being dissolved. In the salt and water solution, salt is the solute and water is the solvent. Water can be a solvent in so many solutions that it is called "the universal solvent"!

Solubility is a physical property of a substance. It is the amount of a substance that can be dissolved by a solvent at a certain temperature. Many times, solutions can be separated only by heating or cooling the solution to remove the solute.

A dilute solution has little solute in comparison with how much could dissolve.

A concentrated solution has a large amount of solute in comparison with the amount of solvent.

Chromatography

Differences in solubility can be used to identify and separate substances in a mixture. This paper strip to the left shows the separation of colored substances that are found in rose petals. Liquid mixed with the petals moves up the strip producing bands of different substances. These are called pigments.

Many police departments use this procedure, called chromatography, to separate and identify many kinds of substances.

Reviewing Mixtures, Compounds, and Elements

Mixtures
- Made of two or more substances
- Do not have a symbol or formula
- Can be separated by physical means

Look for Active Art animations at www.pearsonsuccessnet.com

Sand

Sea shells (Calcium carbonate)

Compounds
- Made of two or more elements
- Have a chemical formula
- Can be broken down into simpler substances

Quartz (Silicon dioxide)

Calcium

Carbon

Oxygen (model)

Silicon

Elements
- Made of only one kind of atom
- Have a chemical symbol
- Can't be divided into simpler substances

✓ Lesson Review

1. Is a mixture of pepper and water a solution? Is a mixture of salt and water a solution? Explain your answers.

2. What techniques can be used to separate a mixture?

3. **Writing in Science Descriptive** Observe the pictures on page 28 that show the making of a solution of water and a purple salt. Write a description of the solution's appearance in each photo.

Making and Using a Chart

Scientists use charts to display data. Charts help make data easy to read. Charts help scientists organize and interpret their data.

The **title** tells what the chart shows. Each column and row has a heading. A **column heading** tells what kind of data is in a column. A **row heading** tells what kind of data is in a row.

Title

	Column Heading
Row Heading	
Row Heading	
Row Heading	

The periodic table below shows the state of matter of each element at room temperature.

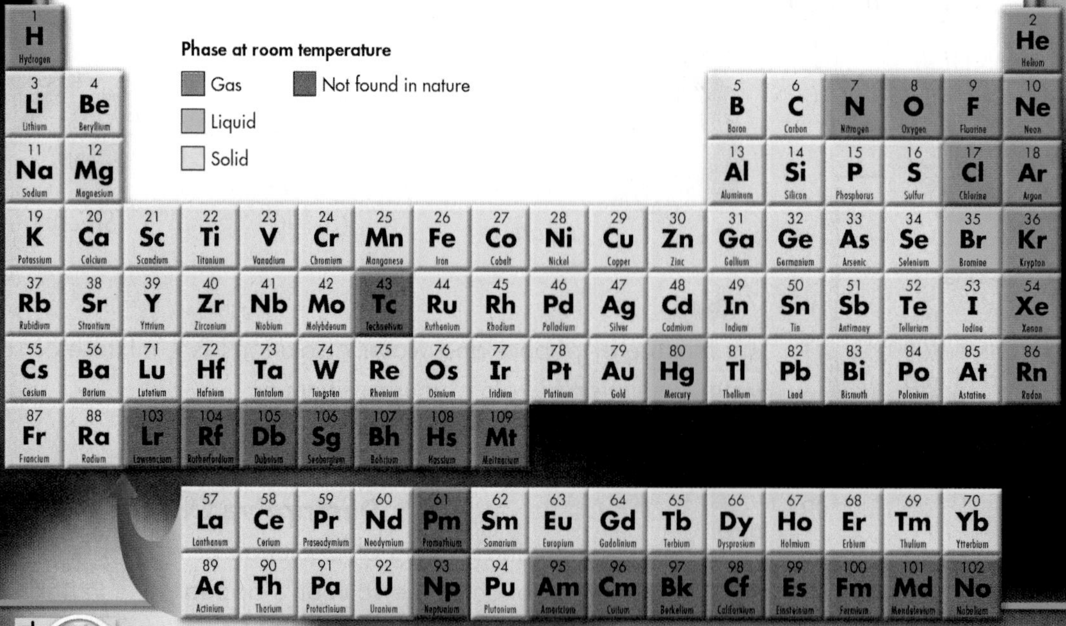

Phase at room temperature
- Gas
- Liquid
- Solid
- Not found in nature

1 H Hydrogen																	2 He Helium
3 Li Lithium	4 Be Beryllium											5 B Boron	6 C Carbon	7 N Nitrogen	8 O Oxygen	9 F Fluorine	10 Ne Neon
11 Na Sodium	12 Mg Magnesium											13 Al Aluminum	14 Si Silicon	15 P Phosphorus	16 S Sulfur	17 Cl Chlorine	18 Ar Argon
19 K Potassium	20 Ca Calcium	21 Sc Scandium	22 Ti Titanium	23 V Vanadium	24 Cr Chromium	25 Mn Manganese	26 Fe Iron	27 Co Cobalt	28 Ni Nickel	29 Cu Copper	30 Zn Zinc	31 Ga Gallium	32 Ge Germanium	33 As Arsenic	34 Se Selenium	35 Br Bromine	36 Kr Krypton
37 Rb Rubidium	38 Sr Strontium	39 Y Yttrium	40 Zr Zirconium	41 Nb Niobium	42 Mo Molybdenum	43 Tc Technetium	44 Ru Ruthenium	45 Rh Rhodium	46 Pd Palladium	47 Ag Silver	48 Cd Cadmium	49 In Indium	50 Sn Tin	51 Sb Antimony	52 Te Tellurium	53 I Iodine	54 Xe Xenon
55 Cs Cesium	56 Ba Barium	71 Lu Lutetium	72 Hf Hafnium	73 Ta Tantalum	74 W Tungsten	75 Re Rhenium	76 Os Osmium	77 Ir Iridium	78 Pt Platinum	79 Au Gold	80 Hg Mercury	81 Tl Thallium	82 Pb Lead	83 Bi Bismuth	84 Po Polonium	85 At Astatine	86 Rn Radon
87 Fr Francium	88 Ra Radium	103 Lr Lawrencium	104 Rf Rutherfordium	105 Db Dubnium	106 Sg Seaborgium	107 Bh Bohrium	108 Hs Hassium	109 Mt Meitnerium									

57 La Lanthanum	58 Ce Cerium	59 Pr Praseodymium	60 Nd Neodymium	61 Pm Promethium	62 Sm Samarium	63 Eu Europium	64 Gd Gadolinium	65 Tb Terbium	66 Dy Dysprosium	67 Ho Holmium	68 Er Erbium	69 Tm Thulium	70 Yb Ytterbium
89 Ac Actinium	90 Th Thorium	91 Pa Protactinium	92 U Uranium	93 Np Neptunium	94 Pu Plutonium	95 Am Americium	96 Cm Curium	97 Bk Berkelium	98 Cf Californium	99 Es Einsteinium	100 Fm Fermium	101 Md Mendelevium	102 No Nobelium

States of Matter of the Elements at Room Temperature

State of Matter at Room Temperature	Number of Elements
Gas	11
Liquid	2
Solid	78
Not found in nature	18

The chart above shows the number of elements that are in each state of matter at room temperature.

There are 2 elements that are liquids at room temperature.

Make a chart showing how many elements are metals, nonmetals, and metalloids. Find the information you need in the periodic table below. Remember to choose a title for your chart.

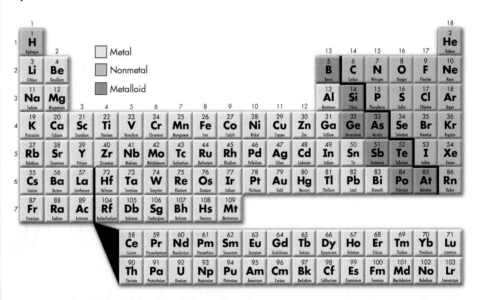

Lab zone Take-Home Activity

Find other groups of things you can list in charts. Practice making charts with two or more columns.

Investigate How can properties help you separate a mixture?

Be careful!

Wear safety goggles.

In this activity you separate a mixture of particles using 2 physical properties—the size of the particles and their ability to dissolve in water.

Materials

safety goggles

4 foam cups and a spoon

salt, sand, 3 marbles

warm water and graduated cylinder

 pencil

coffee filter and rubber band

piece of foil

What to Do

1 Label the 4 cups A, B, C, and D. Put 1 spoonful of salt, 2 spoonfuls of sand, 3 marbles, and 100 mL of water in cup A. Stir the mixture for about 1 minute.

2 Make 4 holes in the bottom of cup B by pushing a pencil through the bottom of the cup from the inside.

3 Hold cup B over cup C. All at once, pour the mixture from cup A into cup B. Move cup B around to clean the marbles. Record the part of the mixture that was removed by straining.

Tap cup A as you pour. Less sand will stick in the cup.

Process Skills

You can use the data you record in a chart to help make an **inference.**

5PS1.f Students know differences in chemical and physical properties of substances are used to separate mixtures and identify compounds. **5IE6.g** Record data by using appropriate graphic representations (including charts, graphs, and labeled diagrams) and make inferences based on those data. (Also **5IE6.c**)

4 Put a coffee filter in cup D. Fasten with a rubber band. Slowly pour the mixture from cup C into cup D. Record the part of the mixture that was removed by filtering.

5 Take off the filter. Dip the spoon in cup D. Let 2 drops of the liquid drip on a piece of foil. Let the liquid evaporate. Record the part of the mixture that was removed by evaporation.

coffee filter

rubber band

D

You may need to leave the foil overnight.

Be careful!

Wipe up any spills right away.

To record your data, use a graphic representation such as the chart below or design one of your own.

Separating Method	Results of Separation	
	Part Removed	**Part that Remains**
Straining		
Filtering		
Evaporating		

Explain Your Results

1. Which physical properties did you use to separate the mixture?

2. Make an **inference** based on the data in your chart. Both sugar and salt dissolve in water. If you used sugar instead of salt, would your results change? Explain.

Go Further

How could you separate a mixture of iron filings, sand, and water? Plan and conduct a simple investigation to answer this question or one of your own.

Chapter 1 Reviewing Key Concepts

Focus on the BIG Idea Everything around us is made of atoms that combine in different ways to form different substances.

Lesson 1

What are properties of matter?

- Most living and nonliving things are made of just a few elements. Elements can combine in many ways to form everything around you.
- Matter has both physical and chemical properties. Physical properties are properties that can be observed or measured without changing the matter. Chemical properties describe how a material changes into different materials.
- Each kind of matter has its own set of properties. These properties are used to identify substances.

Lesson 2

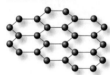

What makes up matter?

- All matter is made of atoms, which may combine to form molecules.
- Elements are organized in the periodic table according to their chemical properties.
- Metals can be pure elements or mixtures. Properties of metals include the ability to conduct heat and electricity, shininess, and the ability to be made into wire, hammered into sheets, and bent without breaking.
- Scientists have developed instruments that can produce images of molecules. These images show that atoms and molecules often appear in well-ordered arrangements.

Lesson 3

What are compounds?

- A compound is made of a combination of more than one element. The properties of a compound are different from the properties of the elements that make it up.
- The smallest part of a compound is a molecule.
- Salts are compounds that are held together by atoms or groups of atoms with opposite charges. Salts can be made when an acid reacts with a base. When salts dissolve in water, they become conductors of electricity.

Lesson 4

How can we separate mixtures?

- In a mixture, different materials are combined, but they do not combine to form new molecules.
- The physical properties of the materials in a mixture can be used to separate the materials.

Cross-Curricular Links

English–Language Arts

Building Vocabulary

Look again at pages 4–5. Identify the picture behind the terms *atom* and *molecule*. Write a paragraph about each term. Tell how each term relates to the picture.

Mathematics

Calculating Numbers of Atoms

There are 24,000 hydrogen atoms in a sample of glucose ($C_6H_{12}O_6$). How many carbon atoms are there in the sample?

History–Social Science

Coronado

Gold was a valuable element to early European explorers of the Americas. Research Francisco Vásquez de Coronado from Spain. Write an expository composition describing his search for gold in what is now the southwestern United States.

Challenge!

English–Language Arts

Everyday Metals

Identify three common things in your home or school that are made mostly of metal. Research to find out more about each object and how it is made. Then write a descriptive composition that describes each object, its use, and what properties of metals make it well suited for its use.

Chapter 1 Review/Test

Use Vocabulary

atom (p. 12)	**element** (p. 9)
atomic number (p. 12)	**molecule** (p. 13)
chemical property (p. 11)	**physical property** (p. 10)
compound (p. 20)	**solution** (p. 28)

Fill in the blanks with the correct vocabulary terms. If you have trouble answering a question, read the listed page again.

1. An element's _____ is the same as the number of protons in its nucleus.

2. A(n) _____ may describe the color, texture, mass, or weight of a material.

3. A(n) _____ is a mixture in which a substance is spread out evenly and will not settle.

4. The smallest particle of an element is a(n) _____.

5. A(n) _____ describes how a material changes into other materials.

6. A(n) _____ is a type of matter made from a combination of two or more elements.

7. The smallest part of a compound that has all the properties of the compound is a(n) _____.

8. A(n) _____ is the basic building block of all matter.

Think About It

9. Identify at least one physical property and one chemical property of water.

10. **Process Skills** **Infer** You make a dressing for a salad by mixing oil and vinegar in a jar. After a few minutes, you observe that the oil and vinegar have separated into two layers. Is the dressing a mixture? Is it a solution? Explain your answer.

11. **Make Inferences** Make a graphic organizer like the one below. Use the facts given to make an inference.

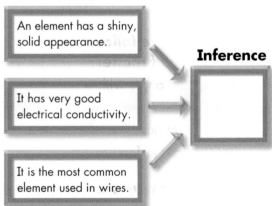

Facts

An element has a shiny, solid appearance.

It has very good electrical conductivity.

It is the most common element used in wires.

Inference

12. **Writing in Science**
Expository Suppose that you are writing an article for your school newspaper titled "What makes up everything around us?" Write a paragraph that could be used in your article. Include the terms *element, compound,* and *mixture.*

California Standards Practice

Write the letter of the correct answer.

13. Which of the following makes up all matter?

   A atoms

   B solutions

   C mixtures

   D compounds

14. Which of the following is an alloy?

   A copper

   B aluminum

   C steel

   D sulfur

15. Which of the following is a physical property of matter?

   A reacts strongly with water

   B color

   C does not burn

   D combines to form a salt

16. A scientist needs an image of a group of atoms. Which of the following would be the best tool for this job?

   A hand lens

   B the periodic table

   C telescope

   D electron microscope

17. Salts can be made by mixing

   A water and a base.

   B water and an acid.

   C a metal and a metal.

   D an acid and a base.

18. Which of the following is a chemical property of matter?

   A color

   B texture

   C mass

   D ability to burn

19. Which of the following is used to separate the parts of mixtures?

   A atomic number

   B physical properties

   C microscopes

   D burning

20. The drawing below shows a water molecule.

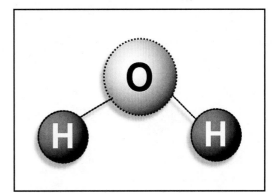

From the drawing, what can you infer about water?

   A Water is an element.

   B Water is a compound.

   C Water is an atom.

   D Water is a metal.

Chemical Technician

You can learn about science in many ways. You can read about it, talk about it, and think about it. You can also investigate it with activities and experiments. If this is your favorite way to learn science, you might like to be a chemical technician.

Chemical technicians work with chemists. For example, a chemist might identify a problem and an experiment to solve it. The chemical technician would help design, set up, and run the experiment. The technician works closely with the chemist to make observations, record data, and help develop conclusions.

Some chemical technicians do basic research in universities and private or government laboratories. Other technicians work for companies to help invent or improve products. They might work on the product itself or the packaging of the product.

Computers are part of many experiments that chemical technicians run. Strong computer skills are a must for this career. It's important to take lots of science and math courses too. Most technicians have at least a two-year college degree. Some of the skills are learned or sharpened during on-the-job training.

Lab zone Take-Home Activity

Look for a product that you think a chemical technician might have helped develop. (Hint: It could be just about anything.) Write a paragraph explaining how you think the technician was involved.

Chapter 2
Changes in Matter

CALIFORNIA Standards Preview

5PS1.0 Elements and their combinations account for all the varied types of matter in the world. As a basis for understanding this concept:

5PS1.a Students know that during chemical reactions the atoms in the reactants rearrange to form products with different properties.

5PS1.c Students know metals have properties in common, such as high electrical and thermal conductivity. Some metals, such as aluminum (Al), iron (Fe), nickel (Ni), copper (Cu), silver (Ag), and gold (Au), are pure elements; others, such as steel and brass, are composed of a combination of elemental metals.

5PS1.f Students know differences in chemical and physical properties of substances are used to separate mixtures and identify compounds.

5PS1.g Students know properties of solid, liquid, and gaseous substances, such as sugar ($C_6H_{12}O_6$), water (H_2O), helium (He), oxygen (O_2), nitrogen (N_2), and carbon dioxide (CO_2)

5IE6.0 Scientific progress is made by asking meaningful questions and conducting careful investigations. As a basis for understanding this concept and addressing the content in the other three strands, students should develop their own questions and perform investigations. (Also **5IE6.c**, **5IE6.d**, **5IE6.e**, **5IE6.f**, **5IE6.g**, **5IE6.h**, **5IE6.i**,)

Standards Focus Questions

- What are physical and chemical changes?

- How does matter change state?

- What are some kinds of chemical reactions?

- How are chemical properties used?

How do you use chemistry every day?

physical change

chemical change

evaporation

condensation

DIGITAL

Chapter 2 Vocabulary

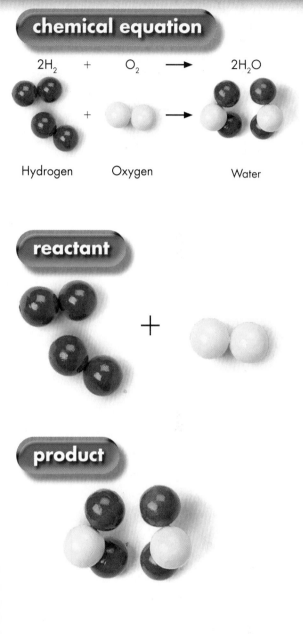

chemical equation

$$2H_2 \quad + \quad O_2 \quad \longrightarrow \quad 2H_2O$$

Hydrogen   Oxygen   Water

reactant

$+$

product

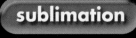

sublimation

41

Explore What can happen during a chemical reaction?

Materials

safety goggles

cup

graduated cylinder
and water

thermometer and
3 fizzy antacid tablets

timer or clock
with a second hand

What to Do

1 Put 50 mL of water and a thermometer in a cup. After 1 minute, **observe** the temperature.

2 Add 3 fizzy antacid tablets. Wait 1 minute. Observe the temperature.

Be careful!

Wear safety goggles. Do not taste the tablets or the liquid.

Process Skills

Careful **observations** help you infer and draw conclusions.

Explain Your Results

Think about your **observations.**

Infer Draw a conclusion about how temperature can change during a chemical reaction.

5PS1.a Students know that during chemical reactions the atoms in the reactants rearrange to form products with different properties. **5IE6.f** Select appropriate tools (e.g., thermometers, metersticks, balances, and graduated cylinders) and make quantitative observations. (Also **5IE6.h**)

How to Read Science

Draw Conclusions

Your science book is full of facts. You can put these facts together with your own knowledge of the world to draw conclusions. Drawing conclusions helps you sharpen your understanding of science.

- Read the facts presented in this article.

- Think about what you already know about the topic to **make an inference** about it.

- Use the science facts and your own knowledge to draw a conclusion.

Cooking Article

Baking Bread

Bakers use yeast to bake bread. They mix the yeast with warm water and sugar. Then they add flour. The yeast digests the sugar and gives off bubbles of carbon dioxide. This makes the bread dough rise. The heat of baking kills the yeast. Look at the holes in a slice of bread. What conclusion can you draw about it that relates to the yeast and its activity?

Apply It!

Make a graphic organizer like the one shown here. List facts from the cooking article, and **draw a conclusion.**

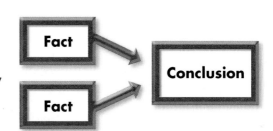

You Are There!

The smell of the ocean fills the air. You feel the warmth of the Sun and hear the crashing of the surf. As you look into the ocean, you notice a large, abandoned ship. The ship has been abandoned in the sea for over six decades. It has changed a great deal since it was abandoned. The once-sturdy wood is soft with rot. The metal no longer gleams, but flakes with rust. The ocean has slowly changed the materials of the ship. What will the ship look like in another sixty years?

DIGITAL

Standards Focus 5PS1.a Students know that during chemical reactions the atoms in the reactants rearrange to form products with different properties.

What are physical and chemical changes?

Matter changes all the time. Some changes are physical changes. Others are chemical changes.

Changes in Matter

Matter can go through physical changes and chemical changes. When a **physical change** occurs, matter keeps the same chemical properties. A **chemical change** occurs when one kind of matter changes into a different kind of matter with different properties.

Physical Changes

Changes in size, shape, volume, and state of matter are physical changes. For example, falling raindrops can freeze to form sleet. Although the raindrops and the sleet differ in size, shape, volume, and state of matter, both are the same substance—water.

Sawing wood, shredding paper, and melting wax are all physical changes. Grating a potato is also a physical change. Copper can be hammered into sheets, and gemstones can be carved into beautiful shapes as a result of physical changes. In each case, the substance does not change into something else.

Some substances may look different after a physical change. Salt crystals seem to disappear when you dissolve them in water, but the salt is still there. If you allow the water to evaporate, the salt crystals will appear again.

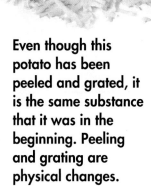

Even though this potato has been peeled and grated, it is the same substance that it was in the beginning. Peeling and grating are physical changes.

1. ✓**Checkpoint** What is a physical change?

2. ✎**Writing in Science** **Descriptive** Think of a time when you have caused a physical change in a substance. Describe what happened.

keyword:
physical/chemical changes
code:
gr5p45

45

Chemical Changes

A chemical change occurs when one kind of matter changes into a different kind of matter with different properties. For example, when you cook foods, they go through chemical changes. Unlike the raw potato on page 45, the potato in the picture on the left is starting to turn brown and crispy. A cooked potato tastes and smells different from a raw potato. The potato's chemical properties have changed.

When a chemical change occurs, atoms rearrange themselves to form different kinds of matter. It is not always easy to tell when chemical changes occur, but there are often clues that they are taking place. Iron is usually gray in color, but rust is red-orange. The color change is a sign of a chemical change. The rust that forms is a new material with different properties. Chemical changes can also cause heat, light, sound, and fizzing. You will learn more about chemical changes in Lesson 3.

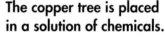

Cooking the potato causes chemical changes to occur. The raw potato becomes a different substance with different properties.

These copper wires have been bent into the shape of a leafless evergreen tree.

The copper tree is placed in a solution of chemicals.

Evidence of Chemical Changes

Chemical changes often produce a gas or a solid. The pictures at the bottom show an experiment in which a tree shape made of copper wire is placed in a solution. Note how the tree changes. Crystals form on the wire branches. These solid crystals are evidence that a chemical change has taken place.

Burning is another chemical change. The candles in the picture and the oxygen in the air all go through this chemical change. Burning produces three new substances: ash, carbon dioxide gas, and water vapor. These substances have different properties from the candles and the oxygen.

✓ **Lesson Review**

1. List three types of evidence of chemical change.

2. Contrast the second and third pictures of the copper tree experiment. Other than the crystals, what evidence of chemical change do you see?

3. **Draw Conclusions** When you cook an egg, does a chemical change occur? Explain your answer.

When candle wax melts, it goes through a physical change. When the wick and wax burn, they go through chemical changes.

A chemical change causes solid crystals to form on the copper tree. The crystals are made by a chemical reaction between the copper and a chemical in the solution. Look at the top of the tree. Why hasn't it changed?

47

Lesson 2

How does matter change state?

An object is a solid, liquid, or gas because of the motions and positions of its atoms or molecules.

States of Matter: Solids and Liquids

When you think of water, you probably think of a liquid. But water has three forms. Water is a solid when it is frozen as ice. It is a liquid in the oceans. In the air, water is a gas. These three forms are called phases, or states, of matter. The phase of water or of any material is the result of motions and positions of its molecules or atoms. The state of a material as a solid, a liquid, or a gas at room temperature is a physical property.

Solids have their own shape and a solid's volume does not change. The particles of a solid vibrate in place. Forces between the particles keep them from moving to a new place. In most solids, the particles are very close together.

A solid melts into a liquid as it warms up. The particles no longer vibrate in one place. Forces between particles hold the particles close together, but the particles can move and flow past one another. Liquids do not have their own shape. They take the shape of their container. Because the forces keep the particles close together, a liquid's volume does not change.

Standards Focus 5PS1.c Students know metals have properties in common, such as high electrical and thermal conductivity. Some metals, such as aluminum (Al), iron (Fe), nickel (Ni), copper (Cu), silver (Ag), and gold (Au), are pure elements; others, such as steel and brass, are composed of a combination of elemental metals.
5PS1.g Students know properties of solid, liquid, and gaseous substances, such as sugar ($C_6H_{12}O_6$), water (H_2O), helium (He), oxygen (O_2), nitrogen (N_2) and carbon dioxide (CO_2).

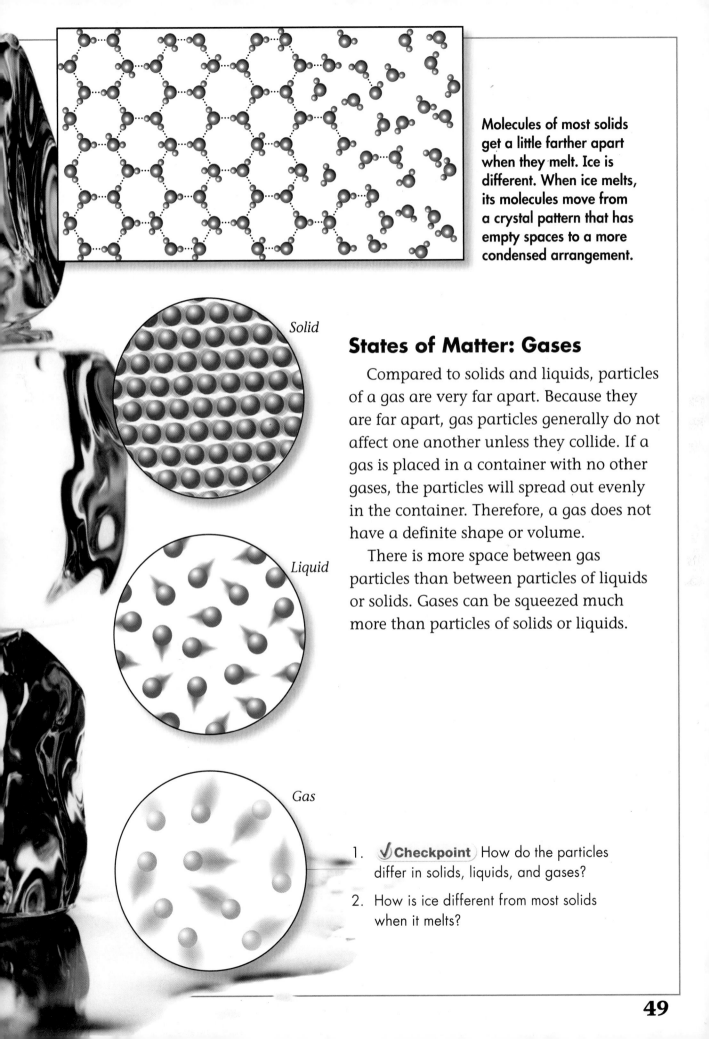

Molecules of most solids get a little farther apart when they melt. Ice is different. When ice melts, its molecules move from a crystal pattern that has empty spaces to a more condensed arrangement.

Solid

Liquid

Gas

States of Matter: Gases

Compared to solids and liquids, particles of a gas are very far apart. Because they are far apart, gas particles generally do not affect one another unless they collide. If a gas is placed in a container with no other gases, the particles will spread out evenly in the container. Therefore, a gas does not have a definite shape or volume.

There is more space between gas particles than between particles of liquids or solids. Gases can be squeezed much more than particles of solids or liquids.

1. ✔**Checkpoint** How do the particles differ in solids, liquids, and gases?

2. How is ice different from most solids when it melts?

Freezing and Melting

As liquids get colder and freeze, their particles slow down and vibrate in place. The temperature at which a material changes between solid and liquid states has two names. This temperature is called the freezing point when a liquid turns into a solid. It is called the melting point when a solid turns into a liquid. Even though this temperature is where both freezing and melting occur, we often just refer to it as the melting point, or melting temperature.

Each material has its own melting temperature. Therefore, melting temperature is a physical property that can be used to help identify a material. The table on page 51 lists some melting temperatures of several materials. Notice the big difference in the melting temperatures of mercury, at −39°C, and tungsten, at 3410°C! A material's melting temperature does not change with the amount of material. The melting temperature of a solid may change when things are added to the solid. For example, adding salt to ice lowers its melting point. This also means the freezing point of salt water is lower than the freezing point of fresh water.

Particles in Motion

Materials change size when they change temperature. This change does not occur because material is made or destroyed. You have read that particles are always moving. Particles of a material move faster as the material gets hotter. These fast-moving particles usually have more space between them. This extra space causes the material to get a little larger. You can see this in a thermometer. The liquid inside the glass tube expands as it gets warmer.

When materials cool, they may get a little smaller. This happens as particles move more slowly and the amount of space between them decreases. Particles never get cold enough to stop vibrating, though.

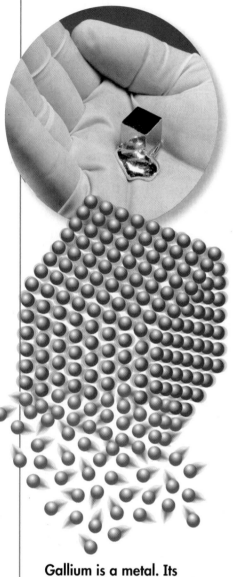

Gallium is a metal. Its melting temperature is so near normal human body temperature that gallium will melt in your hand! Solids melt as their particles gain energy.

Material	Melting Temperature
Oxygen	–218°C
Nitrogen	–210°C
Mercury	–39°C
Fresh water	0°C
Sugar (Glucose)	146°C
Table sugar (Sucrose)	185°C
Aluminum	660°C
Gold	1063°C
Nickel	1453°C
Iron	1535°C
Tungsten	3410°C

1. **Checkpoint** Why do materials change size when they change temperature?

2. **Draw Conclusions** Why might you want to consider the melting point of a substance before choosing materials for frying pans or engine parts?

Evaporation

Evaporation takes place when particles leave a liquid and become a gas. Particles evaporate from a liquid when they are at the surface of the liquid and are moving upward with enough speed. This is how water puddles evaporate.

If the temperature of a liquid is high enough, particles will change to a gas not only at the surface, but throughout the liquid. As gas particles move quickly upward through a liquid, bubbles of gas form under the liquid's surface. The boiling point of a liquid is the temperature at which the liquid turns into gas throughout the liquid.

The boiling point is a physical property of a liquid. The boiling point is the same for a liquid no matter how much liquid is being heated. Each liquid has its own boiling point. For this reason, boiling point can be used to help identify a liquid.

When a liquid turns into a gas, the gas takes up more space. This does not mean that gases have more matter than liquids. The particles of a gas move faster and take up more space than than the particles of a liquid.

Condensation

Condensation occurs when a gas turns into a liquid. This process often occurs when gas particles touch a cold surface and their temperature drops. The particles slow down and get trapped by the attractive forces of the cold surface. As more and more gas particles are trapped, they form a liquid drop. Clouds in the sky and dew on the ground form by condensation.

Particles of liquids can change to a gas even if the temperature of the liquid does not reach the boiling point. This is why wet clothes get dry.

At the boiling point, liquid under the surface turns into gas. The gas forms bubbles that rise to the surface. Liquid also turns to a gas at the surface. You can see that as water vapor hits the cooler glass of the pot, some of it condenses back into liquid.

Water vapor is invisible. When you see steam, you are actually seeing tiny water droplets formed by condensation.

Material	Boiling Point
Helium	–268.9°C
Nitrogen	–195.8°C
Oxygen	–183°C
Chlorine	–34°C
Fresh water	100°C
Mercury	357°C
Aluminum	2467°C

Dry ice

Sublimation

Some solids change directly to gases without first becoming liquids in a process called **sublimation.** In its solid form, carbon dioxide is known as dry ice. Dry ice exists only when temperatures are below –78.5°C. At –78.5°C, the particles in dry ice begin moving so fast that they escape from the surface of the solid as a gas.

✓ Lesson Review

1. Compare the motion and spacing of particles as a material cools from a gas to a liquid and then to a solid phase. Do particles ever stop moving?

2. Define and compare boiling point, melting point, and freezing point.

3. **Writing in Science** **Narrative** Suppose that you are a solid substance, such as ice. Write a story telling what happens to you as you are heated to your melting and boiling points.

53

What are some kinds of chemical reactions?

Chemical changes occur during chemical reactions.
There are several kinds of chemical reactions.

Chemical Equations

During a chemical reaction, substances change into other substances. A substance used in the reaction is called a **reactant.** A substance made by the reaction is called a **product.** Atoms of the reactants rearrange to form the products. The physical and chemical properties of these products differ from those of the reactants.

A **chemical equation** shows what happens during a chemical reaction. The reactants are listed on the left side of the chemical equation. The products are listed on the right side. An arrow between the reactants and products is sometimes read as "makes." It is like the equal sign in a mathematics equation.

In the picture, electricity is flowing through the water. This causes the atoms in the water molecules to rearrange and form hydrogen and oxygen gases. Water is the reactant. Hydrogen and oxygen gases are the products. The equation for this reaction looks like this:

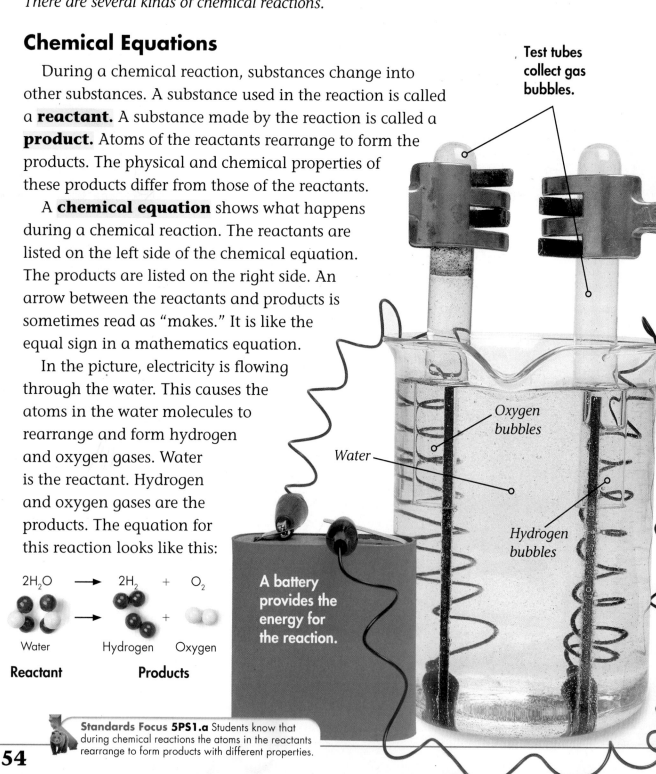

Test tubes collect gas bubbles.

Oxygen bubbles

Water

Hydrogen bubbles

$$2H_2O \longrightarrow 2H_2 + O_2$$

Water → Hydrogen + Oxygen

Reactant   **Products**

A battery provides the energy for the reaction.

Standards Focus 5PS1.a Students know that during chemical reactions the atoms in the reactants rearrange to form products with different properties.

Chemical Reactions

Magnesium is a silvery metal. At a high temperature, it reacts with oxygen in the air and burns with a bright, white glow. Because of this, magnesium is often used in fireworks. A white powder forms during this chemical reaction. This powder, magnesium oxide, is the product of the reaction.

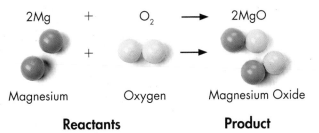

2Mg	+	O₂	→	2MgO
Magnesium		Oxygen		Magnesium Oxide
Reactants				**Product**

$$2Mg + O_2 \rightarrow 2MgO$$

Magnesium is a silvery metal.

Matter Is Always Conserved

Matter cannot be created or destroyed during a chemical reaction. This statement is called the Law of Conservation of Mass. This law explains that the total mass of the reactants equals the total mass of the products. Suppose that you bake a cake. The mass of the ingredients equals the mass of the cake plus the mass of the water vapor, carbon dioxide, and other gases that waft from the oven, making the cake smell so good.

Magnesium can combine with oxygen. These elements are reactants. Bright light and heat are evidence of a chemical reaction.

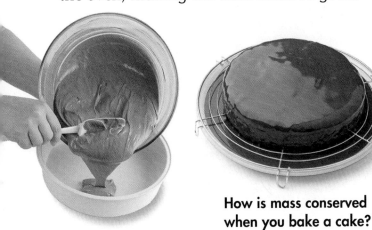

How is mass conserved when you bake a cake?

1. ✓Checkpoint What do chemical equations show?

2. Identify the products and reactants in the equation below.

   HCl + NaOH → NaCl + H₂O

   $$HCl + NaOH \rightarrow NaCl + H_2O$$

The products are molecules of magnesium oxide. This product has properties that differ from those of the reactants.

Types of Chemical Reactions

You can use a model to help you learn about chemical reactions. A model is something that is different from the real thing but can still be used to learn something about the real thing. You can use trucks and trailers as models of atoms in reactions. There are many kinds of chemical reactions. Three important kinds are described here.

In one kind of reaction, compounds split apart to form smaller compounds or elements. This is called a *decomposition reaction*. To picture a decomposition reaction, think of a truck being unhitched from a trailer. This kind of reaction occurs in the experiment shown on page 54. In this experiment, electricity causes water to break apart, forming hydrogen and oxygen gases.

In another kind of reaction, elements or compounds come together to form new compounds. This is called a *combination reaction*. To picture a combination reaction, think of a truck being connected to a trailer. A combination reaction occurs when iron and sulfur join to form a compound called iron sulfide. This combination reaction is shown in the pictures on these pages.

Before the reaction, iron is a dark magnetic material.

Sulfur is a yellow powder that is not magnetic.

More Chemical Reactions

In a third kind of reaction, two or more compounds split apart. The parts then switch places, just as two trucks can switch trailers. This kind of reaction is known as a *replacement reaction*. One example of a replacement reaction is the burning of a candle. Some candle waxes are long molecules of carbon and hydrogen atoms. You have read that oxygen gas is a molecule made of two oxygen atoms. When wax burns, the long molecules and oxygen molecules break apart. They rejoin in new compounds, such as carbon dioxide and water.

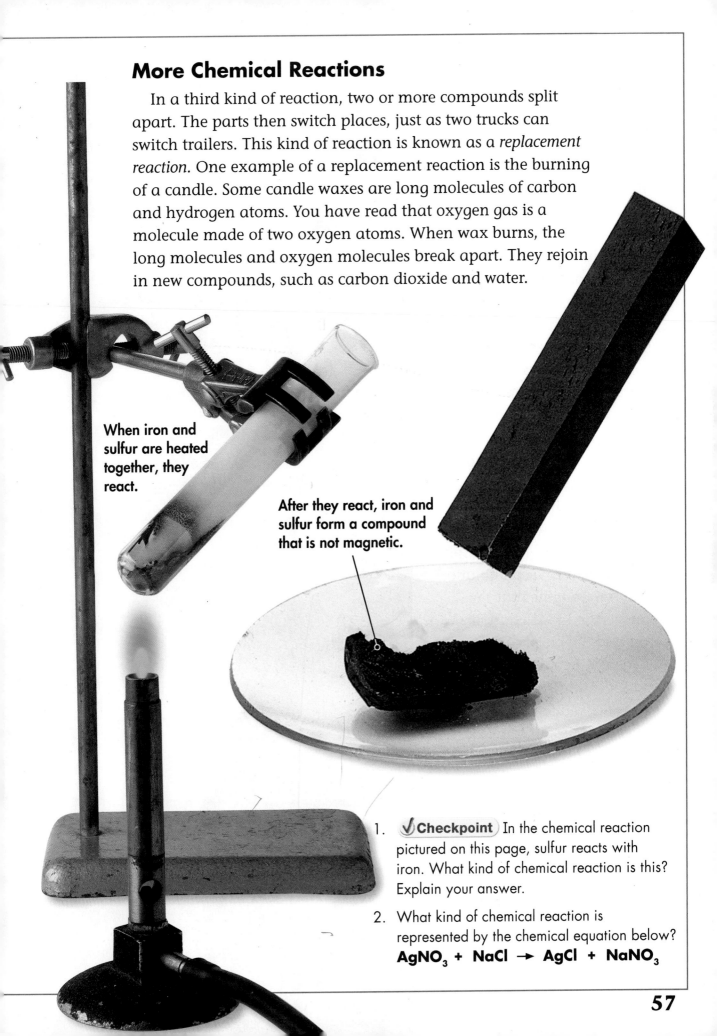

When iron and sulfur are heated together, they react.

After they react, iron and sulfur form a compound that is not magnetic.

1. ✓Checkpoint In the chemical reaction pictured on this page, sulfur reacts with iron. What kind of chemical reaction is this? Explain your answer.

2. What kind of chemical reaction is represented by the chemical equation below?
$AgNO_3 + NaCl \rightarrow AgCl + NaNO_3$

Examples of Chemical Reactions

You have read that a chemical change occurs when one substance changes into a different substance with different properties. All chemical changes take place during chemical reactions.

During a chemical reaction, atoms in the reactants rearrange to form products that have different properties. Remember that no original atoms are lost, and no new atoms are added in this process. The atoms simply combine in new ways to form new substances.

The chart shows how three types of chemical reactions rearrange atoms. For example, rust forms from a combination reaction. Imagine that the green circle in the chart is iron and the purple circle is oxygen. When these substances combine, they form a new substance made up of both kinds of circles. In this case, the new substance is iron oxide, or rust.

The rust on these chains formed through a combination reaction between iron and oxygen.

Type of Reaction	Model
Decomposition	●● → ● + ●
Combination	● + ● → ●●
Replacement	●● + ● → ● + ●●

The forming of the yellow substance indicates a chemical change.

Hydrogen peroxide (H_2O_2) is a compound formed from oxygen and hydrogen.

More Examples of Chemical Reactions

The photo shows the chemical change that occurred when two colorless liquids were mixed together. One of the new substances formed in this reaction is the yellow substance that you see. The other new substance dissolves in the water, so you cannot see it. What type of reaction do you think has occurred?

As it turns out, this is a replacement reaction. Find the model of the replacement reaction in the chart on page 58. This model shows that during a replacement reaction, the particles that make up the different substances switch places to make new substances.

Have you ever seen an adult put hydrogen peroxide on a cut? Hydrogen peroxide can break down in a decomposition reaction. Hydrogen peroxide is made up of hydrogen and oxygen particles. It can break down into water and oxygen gas. This reaction is a decomposition reaction because one substance breaks apart to form new substances.

✓ Lesson Review

1. Describe three kinds of chemical reactions.

2. How are chemical changes and chemical reactions related?

3. **Draw Conclusions** During a combination reaction, two hydrogen atoms combine with two oxygen atoms. How many hydrogen and oxygen atoms will be present in the product? Explain your answer.

TARGET SKILL

How are chemical properties used?

Chemical and physical properties are helpful in many ways. They can be used to separate mixtures and to help identify materials.

Separating Mixtures

You read in Chapter 1 that substances in some mixtures can be separated by physical means. For example, you can separate salt and pepper because they have different physical properties. But some mixtures cannot be easily separated by physical means. How could you separate these mixtures?

Chemical properties may be used to separate some mixtures. For example, scientists who study fossils use chemical properties to separate fossils from the rock in which they are found. Fossils are often scattered throughout limestone. It can be hard to chip limestone from a fossil without damaging the fossil. But vinegar can break down limestone. Fossils made from rock other than limestone do not react with the vinegar. So, scientists sometimes use vinegar to separate fossils from rock.

Separating Metals from Ores

Ores are rocks that include metals combined with other substances. People may use chemical properties to separate metals from their ores. For example, iron ore contains iron oxide. Heating iron ore in a hot furnace with solid carbon allows the iron to separate from the oxygen in the ore. The result is pure iron and carbon dioxide. This process works because of chemical properties.

The fossil does not react quickly with vinegar, but the limestone around the fossil does. What evidence of this reaction can you detect?

Iron is separated from iron ore in a blast furnace. The process relies on the different chemical properties of the substances being heated.

Standards Focus 5PS1.f Students know differences in chemical and physical properties of substances are used to separate mixtures and identify compounds.

60

Separating Solutions

Sometimes chemical properties can be used to separate elements from solutions. For example, lead can be removed from a solution that contains water and a compound containing lead. The solution is poured into a container with a second solution that contains a compound of iodine. Both solutions are clear liquids. When the solutions mix, the lead reacts with the iodine. These two elements form a compound called lead iodide, a yellow solid. The lead iodide can be filtered from the liquid to remove the lead from the solution.

This solution contains a lead compound. Chemical properties can be used to remove the lead from this solution.

The solution is poured into a second solution that contains a compound of iodine.

The lead combines with the iodine and forms a yellow solid. This solid can be filtered to remove the lead from the solution.

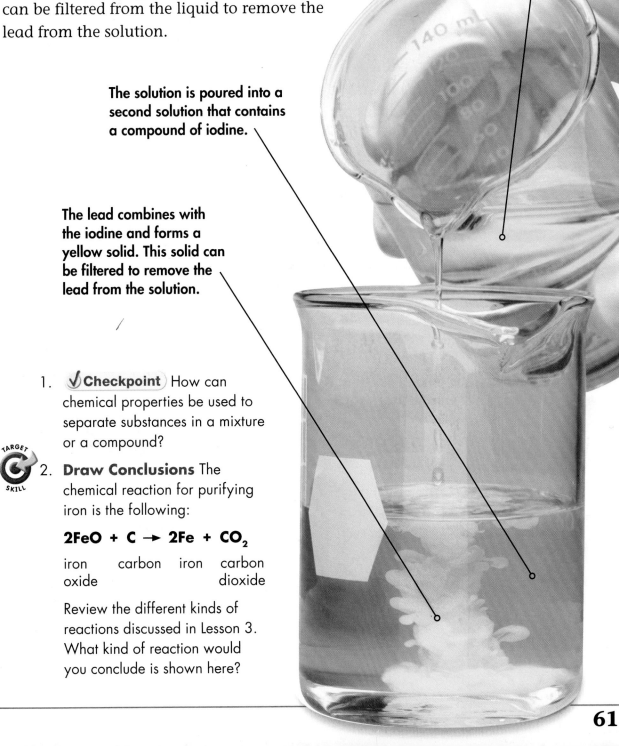

1. **✓ Checkpoint** How can chemical properties be used to separate substances in a mixture or a compound?

2. **Draw Conclusions** The chemical reaction for purifying iron is the following:

2FeO + C → 2Fe + CO$_2$

iron   carbon   iron   carbon
oxide   dioxide

Review the different kinds of reactions discussed in Lesson 3. What kind of reaction would you conclude is shown here?

Fruits such as oranges and lemons contain acid.

Soaps may contain bases.

Bases cause universal indicator paper to turn shades of green, blue, and purple. Acids make the paper turn orange or red.

Identifying Substances

Scientists use physical properties to identify substances. They can use chemical properties in the same way.

As you read in Chapter 1, acids and bases are two types of substances. Lemon juice and vinegar are acids. Household cleaners may contain bases. Strong acids or bases react more easily with materials than do weak acids or bases.

Chemical properties can be used to identify acids and bases. Acids and bases react with chemicals in special paper called universal indicator paper. The reactions cause color changes in the paper. Very acidic liquids will turn the paper red. Very basic liquids will turn the paper purple. Weaker acids or bases will make different colors. Other kinds of papers and liquids will change colors because of acids or bases.

Universal indicator paper and similar products cannot be used alone to identify a substance. Many different acids will turn indicator paper red. Many bases will turn it purple. Indicator paper is helpful, though, in providing clues to the identity of a substance.

DIGITAL Look for Active Art animations at www.pearsonsuccessnet.com

Universal Indicator Paper

Lemon juice

Tomato juice

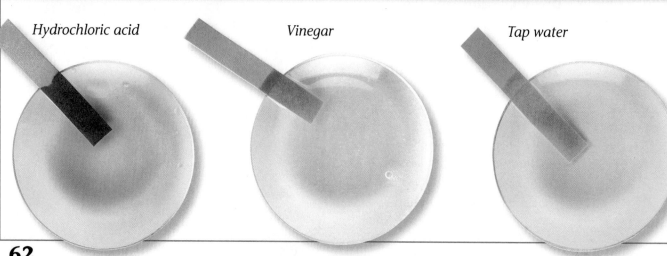

Hydrochloric acid

Vinegar

Tap water

Strontium chloride *Barium chloride* *Calcium chloride* *Potassium chloride*

Scientists may use flame tests to identify a substance. In a flame test, a material is heated to a high temperature in a flame. Different substances cause the flame to have different colors. When these flames are studied closely with laboratory equipment, the substances can be identified. In the photo, what color flame is made by calcium chloride?

These wires were dipped in different metal salts. When the metal is heated to a high temperature, the color of the flame can be used to identify the salt.

✓**Lesson Review**

1. How might a scientist distinguish between strontium chloride and potassium chloride?

2. What color do you think indicator paper would turn if it were dipped in shampoo? Explain your answer.

3. **Writing in Science Expository** Use what you have learned about flame tests to explain how compounds that contain strontium and barium could be used in fireworks.

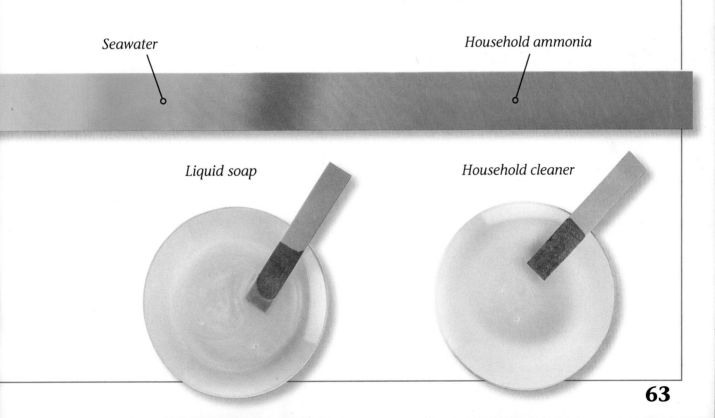

Seawater

Household ammonia

Liquid soap

Household cleaner

63

Math in Science

Solving Equations About Mass

You have learned about the Law of Conservation of Mass. It says that, in a chemical reaction, the total mass of the reactants equals the total mass of the products.

If 6 grams of hydrogen are combined with oxygen to form 54 grams of water, how much oxygen was used?

You can find the answer by writing and solving an equation. Remember, when you solve an equation, you are finding a number that will replace a symbol and make the equation true.

Let x represent the number of grams of oxygen.

grams of hydrogen		grams of oxygen		grams of water
6	+	x	=	54

The equation $6 + x = 54$ is true only if the symbol x is replaced by a certain number.

Try 45. Does $6 + 45$ equal 54? No. 45 is too small.
Try 48. Does $6 + 48$ equal 54? Yes.

$$x = 48$$

The number 48 can replace x to make $6 + x = 54$ true.

The amount of oxygen used was 48 grams.

DIGITAL

Solve each equation.

1 $x + 25 = 78$ **2** $425 + n = 600$

3 $187 - x = 97$ **4** $n + 725 = 800$

Write and solve an equation to find each answer.

5 If 200 grams of sodium are combined with chlorine to give 508 grams of sodium chloride, how much chlorine was used?

6 If 360 grams of water are decomposed to give 40 grams of hydrogen gas, how much oxygen gas will be made?

Lab zone Take-Home Activity

Find some household products that are chemical compounds. Examples include table salt, baking soda, vinegar, and detergent. Research to find the chemical elements that make up each compound. For example, water is made up of hydrogen and oxygen. Make a table showing what you found.

Investigate What is one clue that a chemical reaction has occurred?

In this investigation the reactants both dissolve in water. The product will not stay dissolved in water. It forms a solid.

Be careful!

Wear safety goggles.

Do not smell or taste the powders or liquids.

Materials

safety goggles

water and a graduated cylinder

magnesium sulfate

calcium chloride

2 plastic cups and 2 spoons

balance and gram cubes

Process Skills

Recording data on a chart, can help you make **inferences** based on the data.

What to Do

1 Put 50 mL of water in a cup. Add $\frac{1}{3}$ spoonful of magnesium sulfate. Put 50 mL of water in another cup. Add $\frac{1}{3}$ spoonful of calcium chloride.

2 Stir the liquids with the spoons until the chemicals dissolve.

Measure and record the mass of the powders prior to starting the activity.

5PS1.a Students know that during chemical reactions the atoms in the reactants rearrange to form products with different properties. **5IE6.0** Scientific progress is made by asking meaningful questions and conducting careful investigations. As a basis for understanding this concept and addressing the content in the other three stands, students should develop their own questions and perform investigations. **5IE6.g** Record data by using appropriate graphic representations (including charts, graphs, and labeled diagrams) and make inferences based on those data. (Also **5IE6.f**)

3 Pour the liquid from one cup into the other. **Observe** carefully for 10 minutes. Record what you see.

To help collect and record your data, use a chart like this one or make your own table, chart, or diagram.

Time (minutes)	Changes Observed
2	
4	
6	
8	
10	

Explain Your Results

Infer Did a chemical reaction occur? Look at the data you recorded. Explain how your data helped you make your inference.

Go Further

Could temperature affect your results? Plan and conduct an experiment to find out. Write a report explaining your results.

Chapter 2 Reviewing Key Concepts

Chemistry is used every day to cook foods, make products, and identify substances.

Lesson 1

What are physical and chemical changes?
- Physical changes do not change the chemical properties of a substance.
- Chemical changes occur when one substance is chemically changed into a new substance with different properties.

Lesson 2

How does matter change state?
- When matter changes state, a physical change occurs.
- A substance's melting temperature is a physical property that can be used to help identify the substance.
- Metals have a wide range of melting temperatures.

Lesson 3

What are some kinds of chemical reactions?
- A chemical equation shows what happens during a chemical reaction. It includes both reactants and products.
- Three types of chemical reactions are combination, decomposition, and replacement reactions.

Lesson 4

How are chemical properties used?
- Chemical properties of substances can be used for many practical purposes.
- Chemical properties can help identify substances and separate mixtures.

Cross-Curricular Links

English–Language Arts

Building Vocabulary

Look again at pages 40–41. Identify the pictures behind the terms *evaporation*, *chemical equation*, and *sublimation*. Write a paragraph about each term. Tell how each term relates to the picture and to the other terms.

Mathematics

Chemical Equations

Look at the chemical equation below.

$$2Mg + O_2 \rightarrow 2MgO$$

Suppose that you start with 100 atoms of magnesium. How many molecules of oxygen are needed to react with all of the magnesium? Explain your answer.

Visual and Performing Arts

Picturing Reactions

Think of a model you could use to represent chemical reactions. Draw pictures to show how your model works for two different kinds of chemical reactions.

Challenge!

English–Language Arts

Changing Forms of Water

Use resources from the library-media center to write a report on how water changes state in the environment. Use the words *evaporation*, *condensation*, and *sublimation* in your report.

Chapter 2 Review/Test

Use Vocabulary

chemical change (p. 45)	**physical change** (p. 45)
chemical equation (p. 54)	**product** (p. 54)
condensation (p. 52)	**reactant** (p. 54)
evaporation (p. 52)	**sublimation** (p. 53)

Fill in the blanks with the correct vocabulary terms. If you have trouble answering a question, read the listed page again.

1. A change in phase from a solid directly to a gas is called ____.

2. A(n) ____ happens when one substance changes into another substance.

3. During a(n) ___, such as tearing or crushing, a substance keeps its identity.

4. A sentence that describes a chemical reaction using symbols is called a(n) ____.

5. A substance formed by a chemical reaction is called a(n) ____.

6. The change of phase from a gas to a liquid is called ____.

7. A substance that is used in a chemical reaction is called a(n) ____.

Think About It

8. Explain the differences between physical changes and chemical changes.

9. How is knowing the chemical properties of a substance useful to scientists? Give an example.

10. **Process Skills** **Classify** Decide whether each change below is a physical change or a chemical change. Explain your answers.
- ice melting
- paper being torn
- an iron gate rusting
- a salt forming

11. **Infer** Refer to the pictures of the flame test on page 63. How do you know that the chlorine in the compounds gives off no strong color in this test?

12. **Draw Conclusions** Read the passage. What can you conclude from the facts presented?

> José buys vinegar and ammonia in large bottles. He then pours the liquids into two smaller containers, but he forgets to label the bottles. José knows that vinegar is an acid and that ammonia is a base. He also knows that a base causes indicator paper to turn purple. He dips a strip of indicator paper into the first bottle. The paper turns a red-orange color.

Make a graphic organizer like this one. Put the facts and conclusion into your graphic organizer.

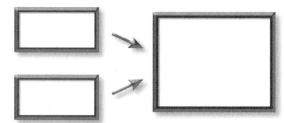

13. **Writing in Science**
Narrative Physical and chemical changes are part of your daily life. Write a journal entry describing at least four ways that you have used chemistry today.

California Standards Practice

Write the letter of the correct answer.

14. Which of the following indicates that a physical change has occurred?

A A material fizzes when it interacts with another material.

B A substance changes color.

C A substance changes state from solid to liquid.

D A metal is no longer magnetic after it is combined with another substance.

15. Which of the following is a property of a liquid?

A It has a definite shape.

B It has a definite volume.

C The particles are very far apart.

D Its particles vibrate in place.

16. Which of the following is a way in which chemical properties are used?

A Separating metals using magnets

B Filtering sand from water

C Breaking down materials around fossils

D Removing carrots from soup

17. What kind of reaction takes place when iron and oxygen form rust (iron oxide)?

A a decomposition reaction

B a replacement reaction

C a combination reaction

D an acid-base reaction

18. Which of the following occurs when a liquid changes to a gas?

A evaporation

B sublimation

C melting

D freezing

19. Which of the following indicates that a chemical change has occurred?

A A substance changes shape.

B A new substance forms.

C A substance changes phase.

D The mass of a substance changes.

20. Iron is purified in a blast furnace. The chemical equation for this reaction is shown below. Which substance or substances are the reactants?

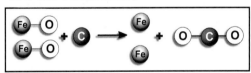

$$2FeO + C \rightarrow 2Fe + CO_2$$

iron   carbon   iron   carbon
oxide   dioxide

A iron

B iron and carbon dioxide

C carbon

D iron oxide and carbon

the DIME Challenge

What do you think it would be like to conduct an experiment in a NASA test facility, just like NASA scientists do? In April every year, four teams of high school students get to find out.

Each year, NASA invites teams of high school students to design and build a science experiment using microgravity—the near weightlessness that astronauts experience in outer space. The competition is called DIME, which stands for Dropping in a Microgravity Environment.

Each team designs an experiment that will use a NASA "microgravity drop tower" at the Glenn Research Center in Cleveland, Ohio. A drop tower is a facility that creates a microgravity environment. The only way microgravity can be achieved on Earth is to put an object in free fall. In other words, you drop it from a high place.

Student-designed apparatus

Microgravity Drop Tower

The Glenn drop tower is eight stories tall. When an object drops that distance, it experiences microgravity for just 2.2 seconds. Each experiment must be designed to find results in that short time. Most of the experiments that teams have conducted have involved burning, because flames can spread quickly.

Teams that enter the competition consist of four high school students and an adult advisor. Although teams enter from all across the United States and Puerto Rico, only four experiments are chosen. NASA then pays to bring the four teams to Cleveland to conduct their experiments.

For the winning teams, conducting the experiment is a dream come true. They use the same facility and measuring tools, such as high-speed video cameras, that NASA and university scientists use.

Lab zone Take-Home Activity

Think of an experiment that you would like to conduct at the Glenn Research Center's drop tower. Outline the experiment and the question you would hope the experiment could answer. DIME rules do not allow the use of a living organism in the experiment. Otherwise, let your imagination be your guide!

Analytical Chemist

Dionne Broxton Jackson is an analytical chemist at NASA. She works with metals.

What if your pencil bent every time you tried to write with it? What if your pillow were made of metal? All of the properties of matter are important in deciding how it is used. Matter can be hard or soft, rough or smooth. It can be sticky, stretchy, spongy, or slick. Some chemists who work for NASA make matter that can be used on space vehicles.

Metals used for space shuttles must not be damaged by a lot of heat. Some metals are better than others at handling heat. Chemists can also mix metals to make a material that can stand more heat than either metal could on its own. The Kennedy Space Center is close to the ocean. There is so much salty water nearby that metals often rust. The metals NASA uses cannot rust easily.

Plastics are also important materials used in space. They may need to be hard and slick, or soft and rubbery. Chemists can make plastics that have many different properties.

Analytical chemists need to understand math and science well. They must graduate from a college or university. They can work in many different places.

Lab zone Take-Home Activity

Gather different materials in your home, such as kitchen utensils, toothbrushes, and food containers. Make a list of which products you think might be useful in space.

Unit A Summary

Chapter 1

What makes up everything around us?
- All matter is made of atoms, which may combine to form molecules.
- Slightly more than 100 different elements combine to form all the living and nonliving matter on Earth. An element is made up of only one type of atom.
- Elements on the periodic table are organized by atomic numbers. Groups and periods of elements share similar properties.
- Metals, one kind of matter, share properties such as being good conductors of heat and electricity.
- Scientists have developed technology that allows them to make images of atoms and molecules.
- A compound is a substance whose molecules are made up of two or more different elements.
- Salts are typically made of a metal and a nonmetal, and are brittle and soluble in water.
- A solution is a special type of mixture.

Chapter 2

How do you use chemistry every day?
- Matter can undergo physical changes and chemical changes.
- Matter is solid, liquid, or gas depending on the arrangement and movement of the atoms or molecules. Matter can change between these states by heating or cooling.
- Chemical reactions take place when matter changes its chemical properties. Reactants form products. These reactions can be represented by a chemical equation.
- People can use chemical and physical properties to separate mixtures and to identify materials.

Experiment What materials can conduct electricity?

Materials

safety goggles

battery and battery holder

light bulb and bulb holder

insulated wires

meterstick

items to test (short insulated wire, long insulated wire, and other items)

Process Skills

In a scientific investigation you first make sure to **identify and control variables.** Then you **collect data.** When finished, you can use this information to answer questions about the results of your **experiment.**

Ask a question.

What materials—metals or nonmetals—will conduct electricity?

State a hypothesis.

If metals and nonmetals are tested, then will the results show that only metals conduct electricity, that only nonmetals conduct electricity, or that both conduct electricity? Write your hypothesis.

Identify and control variables.

In this **experiment,** you will test which materials can conduct electricity. The **variable** that you change is the material you test. The variable that you observe is whether the material conducts electricity. Everything else must be **controlled,** or kept the same. Test each material in the same way.

5PS1.c Students know metals have properties in common, such as high electrical and thermal conductivity. **5IE6.c** Plan and conduct a simple investigation based on a student-developed question and write instructions others can follow to carry out the procedure. **5IE6.d** Identify the dependent and controlled variables in an investigation **5IE6.e** Identify a single independent variable in a scientific investigation and explain how this variable can be used to collect information to answer a question about the results of the experiment. **5IE6.f** Select appropriate tools (eg., thermometers, metersticks, balances and graduated cylinders) and make quantitative observations. **5IE6.h** Draw conclusions from scientific evidence and indicate whether further information is needed to support a specific conclusion. **5IE6.i** Write a report of an investigation that includes conducting tests, collecting data or examining evidence, and drawing conclusions. (Also **5IE6.g**)

Variables

An *independent variable* is what you change in an experiment.

A *dependent variable* is what you measure or observe.

A *controlled variable* is what could be changed but must not be changed for the experiment to be a fair test.

Identify the variables in this experiment. What is the independent variable? What is the dependent variable? What are some controlled variables?

Test your hypothesis.

1 Make the circuit shown.

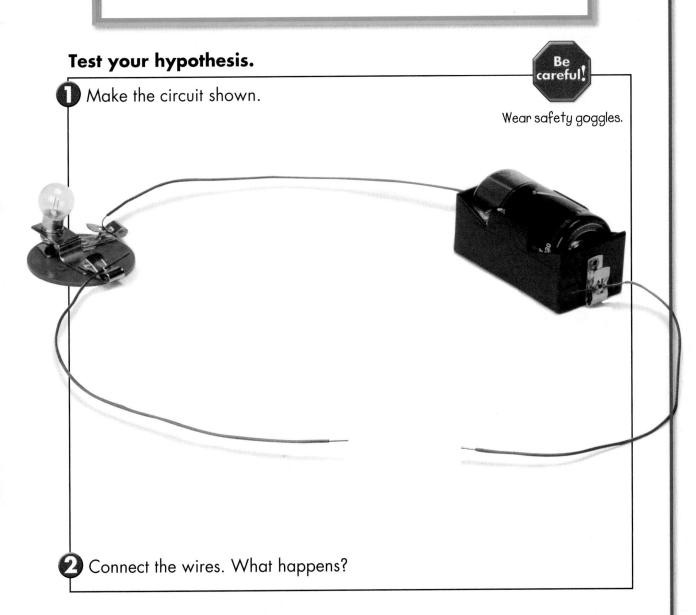

Be careful!

Wear safety goggles.

2 Connect the wires. What happens?

3 Develop a test to determine if a material conducts electricity. Identify your variables. Write instructions for your procedure. The instructions should be clear enough that others could follow them.

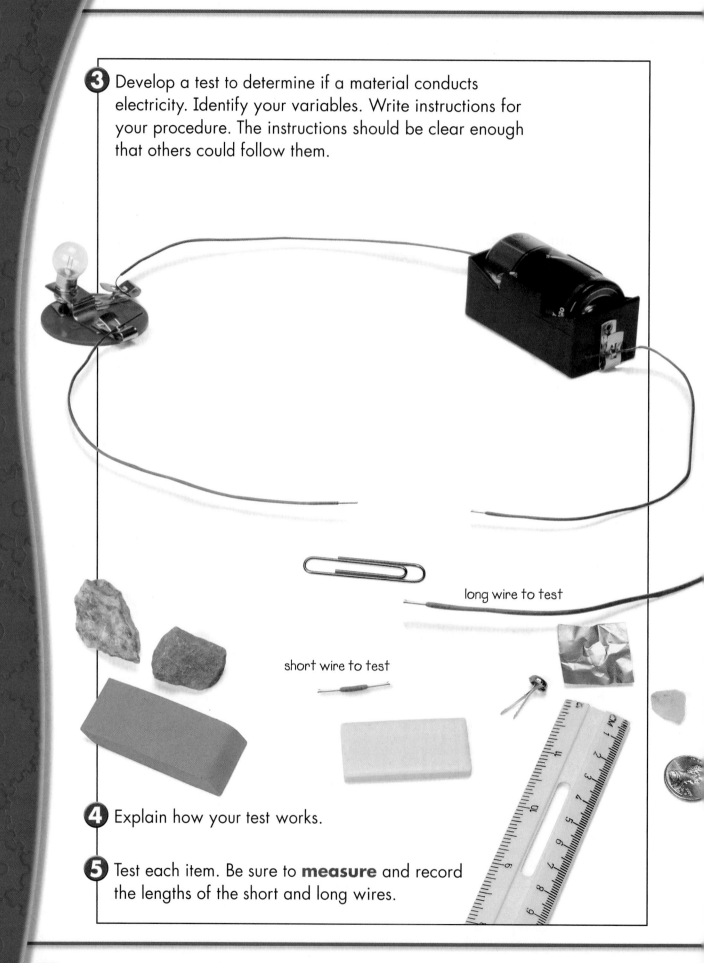

long wire to test

short wire to test

4 Explain how your test works.

5 Test each item. Be sure to **measure** and record the lengths of the short and long wires.

Collect and record your data.

Record your data on a chart.

Item	Conducts Electricity	Does Not Conduct Electricity
Paper clip		
Eraser		
Short wire (____ cm)		
Long wire (____ meters)		

Interpret your data

Examine the data in your chart. Which materials conducted electricity? How were they alike? Which did not conduct electricity? How were they alike?

State your conclusion.

Use your data to help make **inferences.** Then, **draw a conclusion** based on your evidence. **Communicate** your conclusion. Does it agree with your hypothesis? Is further information needed to support your conclusion? Explain.

Your teacher may ask you to write a report on your experiment. Make sure to include the tests you conducted and the data you collected or the evidence you examined. State your conclusion clearly.

Go Further

Which conducts heat best—metals or nonmetals? Develop a test to find out. Write a laboratory report. Include your tests, data, evidence, and conclusions.

Show What You Know

Collect and Classify Objects

Everything around you is made up of elements and compounds. Research what elements and compounds make up familiar objects. Then create a display of objects and pictures of objects that you researched. Group objects made up of similar elements or compounds together in your display. Use labels to identify the elements and compounds that make up each object.

Plan an Investigation

Suppose that you are given a sample of an unknown solid by your teacher. How can you identify the material? Think about what you have learned about chemical properties. Use this information to plan an investigation that could be used to identify the unknown substance. Your investigation should include the following:

- A testable question
- Written instructions to identify an unknown substance
- A list of materials and tools to carry out the investigation

MATERIALS
- Saftey goggles
- 2 clear plastic cups
- 2 sheets of paper
- plastic spoon and vinegar
- Compound A and Compound B

Write a Biography

Some scientists who were involved in the development of the atomic model include Democritus, John Dalton, Joseph John Thomson, Ernest Rutherford, Niels Bohr, and Erwin Schrödinger. Choose one scientist from this list about whom you would like to know more. Research the life and work of this scientist. Then use what you learn to write a biography of the scientist. Remember that a biography is a work of nonfiction that tells about a person's life. The biography should include the following:

- Factual information about the life of the person you research
- Information about the scientist's work and why it has been important over time

Read More About Physical Sciences

Look for other books about Physical Sciences in the library. Here is one you may want to read.

Iron
by Giles Sparrow

One of the most common metals in the world, iron has played an important role in history. Humans learned that iron could be separated from ore to make tools and structures that are very strong. In this book, Giles Sparrow illustrates the many uses of iron, and the many forms iron takes. This element is used to make steel, a very strong metal construction material. It also makes rust when it reacts with oxygen in water or air. Iron has been found in meteorites, magnets, and even the human body!

Science Fair Projects

Using Scientific Methods

1. Ask a question.
2. State a hypothesis.
3. Identify and control variables.
4. Test your hypothesis.
5. Collect and record your data.
6. Interpret your data.
7. State your conclusion.
8. Go further.

What is the best way to remove salt from sea water?

Salt can be removed from sea water in several ways, such as by freezing or by evaporation and condensation. Compare methods for removing salt from sea water.

Idea: Choose two or more methods to compare. Write a hypothesis predicting which method will be best for producing fresh water. Decide on a way to measure the amount of fresh water produced by each method.

Which substance has the highest solubility?

Solubility is one physical property of matter. Compare the solubility of materials to determine which material has the highest solubility in water.

Idea: Choose several substances to compare. Predict which substance will have the highest solubility. Develop a procedure to test your prediction.

How does temperature affect condensation?

The air around you contains water vapor, which is water in the gas phase. When this water vapor condenses, it becomes liquid. Plan an experiment to find out how temperature affects condensation.

Idea: Develop a way to measure and record the amount of water that condenses at different temperatures.

Unit A California Standards Practice

Write the letter of the correct answer.

1. **Which of the following describes what happens during a chemical reaction between two compounds?**

   A Some atoms are lost during the reaction.

   B Atoms in the reactants rearrange to form products with different properties.

   C A solid dissolves in a liquid.

   D New atoms form during the reaction.

2. **Which of the following makes up all matter?**

   A atoms

   B metals

   C minerals

   D mixtures

3. **During a chemical reaction, magnesium (Mg) combines with oxygen (O_2) to form magnesium oxide (MgO). An equation for this reaction is shown below.**

   $$4Mg + 2O_2 \longrightarrow 4MgO$$

   Which of the following best describes the *product* of this reaction?

   A It is an element.

   B It is an atom.

   C It is a compound.

   D It is a mixture.

4. **What is the smallest part of a compound that has the properties of the compound?**

   A atom

   B element

   C molecule

   D solution

5. **Brass is a combination of copper and zinc. Which of the following is also a combination of two or more metals?**

   A gold

   B sulfur

   C nickel

   D bronze

6. **The picture shows one common use for copper.**

   copper

   What properties of metals make the copper useful for the purpose shown in the picture?

   A Most metals are poor conductors of heat and electricity.

   B Most metals can be made into wire and are good conductors of electricity.

   C Most metals bend easily and are good conductors of heat.

   D Most metals are shiny and bendable.

83

Unit A California Standards Practice

7. For the following question, refer to the periodic table on page 86. Which of the following elements has the highest atomic number?

   A carbon

   B helium

   C titanium

   D iodine

8. Which of the following is true of an element?

   A It is made of only one kind of atom.

   B It is made of two or more kinds of atoms that are joined together.

   C It is made of a metal and a nonmetal that are joined together.

   D It can be broken down into simpler substances.

9. Which of the following is used to organize elements in the periodic table?

   A chemical properties

   B color

   C date of discovery

   D state of matter at room temperature

10. Which of the following determines where in the periodic table an element is found?

   A melting point

   B name

   C number of protons

   D color

11. Scientists use computers and other technology to make images of atoms and molecules. How are atoms and molecules usually arranged in these images?

   A in a random pattern

   B according to atomic weight

   C in a well-ordered array

   D according to atomic number

12. Which of the following is *most* helpful for identifying a compound?

   A the number of atoms in the compound

   B physical and chemical properties of the compound

   C the properties of the elements in the compound

   D determining whether the compound conducts electricity

13. A student uses the technique shown to separate one substance from a mixture.

Which of the following is *most* likely to be separated from the mixture in this way?

   A iron filings

   B pepper

   C salt

   D sugar

Unit A California Standards Practice

14. Which of the following can be used to separate the parts of a mixture?

   A ability to conduct heat

   B flammability

   C physical properties

   D ability to conduct electricity

15. Which of the following substances is normally a solid at room temperature?

   A oxygen (O_2)

   B nitrogen (N_2)

   C glucose ($C_6H_{12}O_6$)

   D water (H_2O)

16. What physical property is shared by oxygen (O_2), helium (He), and carbon dioxide (CO_2)?

   A They have the same freezing point.

   B They are gases at room temperature.

   C They are found in the same column of the periodic table.

   D They react easily with other substances.

17. The graph shows the main elements that make up the human body.

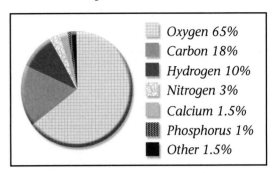

Oxygen 65%
Carbon 18%
Hydrogen 10%
Nitrogen 3%
Calcium 1.5%
Phosphorus 1%
Other 1.5%

What element makes up the largest part of the human body?

   A carbon

   B hydrogen

   C oxygen

   D water

18. What two types of elements combine to form most salts?

   A water and an acid

   B water and a base

   C a metal and a nonmetal

   D a nonmetal and water

CALIFORNIA

19. Salts have which of the following properties?

A They are not soluble in water.

B They conduct electricity poorly when dissolved in water.

C They are solids with high melting temperatures.

D They are usually liquids.

20. What type of compound usually forms when a strong acid reacts with a strong base?

A a gas

B a metal

C a nonmetal

D a salt

Periodic Table of the Elements

Key

11 — Atomic number
Na — Element symbol
Sodium — Element name

☐ Metals
▨ Metalloids (semimetals)
▨ Nonmetals

1																	18
1 **H** Hydrogen	2											13	14	15	16	17	2 **He** Helium
3 **Li** Lithium	4 **Be** Beryllium											5 **B** Boron	6 **C** Carbon	7 **N** Nitrogen	8 **O** Oxygen	9 **F** Fluorine	10 **Ne** Neon
11 **Na** Sodium	12 **Mg** Magnesium	3	4	5	6	7	8	9	10	11	12	13 **Al** Aluminum	14 **Si** Silicon	15 **P** Phosphorus	16 **S** Sulfur	17 **Cl** Chlorine	18 **Ar** Argon
19 **K** Potassium	20 **Ca** Calcium	21 **Sc** Scandium	22 **Ti** Titanium	23 **V** Vanadium	24 **Cr** Chromium	25 **Mn** Manganese	26 **Fe** Iron	27 **Co** Cobalt	28 **Ni** Nickel	29 **Cu** Copper	30 **Zn** Zinc	31 **Ga** Gallium	32 **Ge** Germanium	33 **As** Arsenic	34 **Se** Selenium	35 **Br** Bromine	36 **Kr** Krypton
37 **Rb** Rubidium	38 **Sr** Strontium	39 **Y** Yttrium	40 **Zr** Zirconium	41 **Nb** Niobium	42 **Mo** Molybdenum	43 **Tc** Technetium	44 **Ru** Ruthenium	45 **Rh** Rhodium	46 **Pd** Palladium	47 **Ag** Silver	48 **Cd** Cadmium	49 **In** Indium	50 **Sn** Tin	51 **Sb** Antimony	52 **Te** Tellurium	53 **I** Iodine	54 **Xe** Xenon
55 **Cs** Cesium	56 **Ba** Barium	57 **La** Lanthanum	72 **Hf** Hafnium	73 **Ta** Tantalum	74 **W** Tungsten	75 **Re** Rhenium	76 **Os** Osmium	77 **Ir** Iridium	78 **Pt** Platinum	79 **Au** Gold	80 **Hg** Mercury	81 **Tl** Thallium	82 **Pb** Lead	83 **Bi** Bismuth	84 **Po** Polonium	85 **At** Astatine	86 **Rn** Radon
87 **Fr** Francium	88 **Ra** Radium	89 **Ac** Actinium	104 **Rf** Rutherfordium	105 **Db** Dubnium	106 **Sg** Seaborgium	107 **Bh** Bohrium	108 **Hs** Hassium	109 **Mt** Meitnerium									

58 **Ce** Cerium	59 **Pr** Praseodymium	60 **Nd** Neodymium	61 **Pm** Promethium	62 **Sm** Samarium	63 **Eu** Europium	64 **Gd** Gadolinium	65 **Tb** Terbium	66 **Dy** Dysprosium	67 **Ho** Holmium	68 **Er** Erbium	69 **Tm** Thulium	70 **Yb** Ytterbium	71 **Lu** Lutetium
90 **Th** Thorium	91 **Pa** Protactinium	92 **U** Uranium	93 **Np** Neptunium	94 **Pu** Plutonium	95 **Am** Americium	96 **Cm** Curium	97 **Bk** Berkelium	98 **Cf** Californium	99 **Es** Einsteinium	100 **Fm** Fermium	101 **Md** Mendelevium	102 **No** Nobelium	103 **Lr** Lawrencium

CALIFORNIA

Life Sciences

South Coast
BOTANIC GARDEN

Palos Verdes Peninsula

Do you enjoy a walk in the woods on a warm, spring day? Do bright colors and sweet smells make you happy? If so, you may enjoy a visit to the South Coast Botanic Garden, located on the Palos Verdes Peninsula.

The South Coast Botanic Garden has more than 150,000 plants on display. In the Garden for the Senses, you are encouraged not only to stop and smell the flowers, but also to touch them. The main attraction of the woodland walk is trees, especially pines. The garden also has a lake, where you can observe a variety of birds, fishes, and insects. Other special displays include a garden of cacti, a garden of herbs, and a water garden. Each area provides you an opportunity to learn more about the different needs of plants and animals.

Find Out More

Research to find out more about botanic gardens and plants that live in your region.

South Coast Botanic Garden

- Use library-media center resources to find out about other botanic gardens located in California. Draw a map to show the locations of these gardens.

- Contact a local college or university to find out what plants are unique to the area in which you live. Research to learn more about these plants. Share your findings with the class in an oral report.

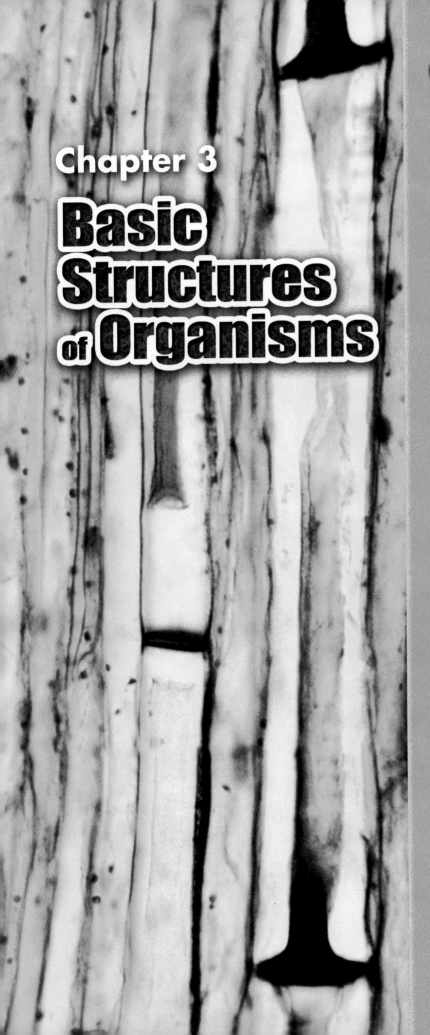

Chapter 3

Basic Structures of Organisms

CALIFORNIA Standards Preview

5LS2.0 Plants and animals have structures for respiration, digestion, waste disposal, and transport of materials. As a basis for understanding this concept:

5LS2.a Students know many multicellular organisms have specialized structures to support the transport of materials.

5LS2.e Students know how sugar, water, and minerals are transported in a vascular plant.

5LS2.f Students know plants use carbon dioxide (CO_2) and energy from sunlight to build molecules of sugar and release oxygen.

5LS2.g Students know plant and animal cells break down sugar to obtain energy, a process resulting in carbon dioxide (CO_2) and water (respiration).

5IE6.0 Scientific progress is made by asking meaningful questions and conducting careful investigations. As a basis for understanding this concept and addressing the content in the other three strands, students should develop their own questions and perform investigations. (Also **5IE6.a**, **5IE6.f**, **5IE6.g**)

Standards Focus Questions

- What makes up multicellular organisms?

- How do materials move through plants?

- How do cells get and use energy?

How do cells help an organism?

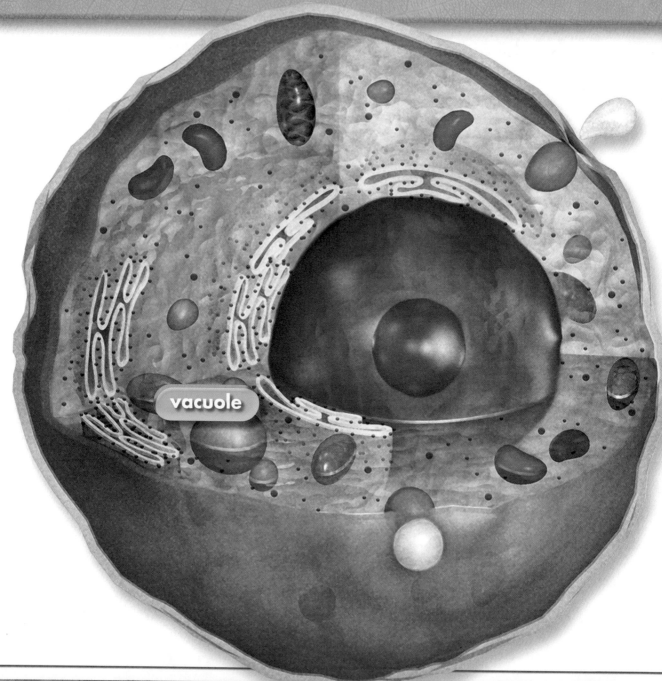

vacuole

tissue

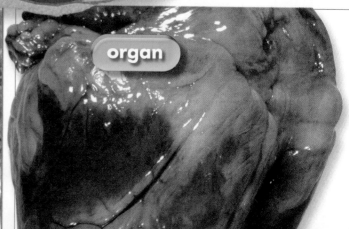

organ

DIGITAL 9

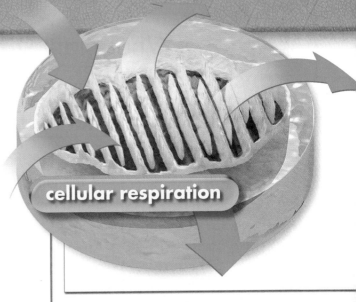

cellular respiration

photosynthesis

chloroplast

chlorophyll

vascular

xylem

phloem

Explore What plant structures transport water?

Materials

plastic jar
with colored water

stalk of celery

scissors

metric ruler

magnifier

microscope (optional)

What to Do

1 **Observe** the base of the celery stalk. Stand the stalk in the jar.

2 After 1 day, cut off the bottom 2 cm of the stalk. Then cut a thin slice from the new bottom.

3 Observe the thin slice with a magnifier or microscope.

4 Observe the whole stalk. Make a labeled diagram to record your observations (data). Draw any structures you see.

Process Skills

Recording data by using a labeled diagram or other graphic representation, can help you **make inferences** based on your **data.**

Explain Your Results

1. How did the bottom of the stalk change?

2. Use your labeled diagram to make an **inference** based on your **data.** What happened to the stalk while it was in the food coloring?

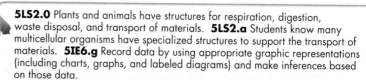

5LS2.0 Plants and animals have structures for respiration, digestion, waste disposal, and transport of materials. **5LS2.a** Students know many multicellular organisms have specialized structures to support the transport of materials. **5IE6.g** Record data by using appropriate graphic representations (including charts, graphs, and labeled diagrams) and make inferences based on those data.

DIGITAL Lab zone

How to Read Science

Make Generalizations

- A generalization can be made after you think about how facts relate to each other.

- Sometimes writers present facts and details and then **make generalizations** for the reader. Sometimes readers must **infer** or make their own generalizations based on the facts.

- Read the science article. Some facts and details are highlighted in yellow. The generalization is highlighted in blue.

Science Article

Types of Blood Cells

Blood contains both red and white blood cells. Both types are produced inside the long bones. Red blood cells carry oxygen from the lungs to all parts of the body. White blood cells protect the body by "eating" germs or by making chemicals that kill germs. Red and white blood cells are important parts of the circulatory system.

Apply It!

Make a graphic organizer like the one shown. Write the facts and the **generalization** from the article in the correct boxes. See what else you can **infer.** Add it to the graphic organizer.

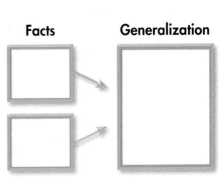

Facts   Generalization

You Are There!

At this very moment, up to 100 trillion living things are forming, doing jobs, and being replaced inside you. Hey, it's a busy place in there! What exactly are these things, and more important, what are they doing inside you?

Standards Focus 5LS2.0 Plants and animals have structures for respiration, digestion, waste disposal, and transport of materials. As a basis for understanding this concept:
5LS2.a Students know many multicellular organisms have specialized structures to support the transport of materials.

DIGITAL

What makes up multicellular organisms?

Cells are the smallest living parts of plants and animals. Cells have the same needs as any organism. They also carry out many of the same activities. Cells are made of smaller parts, each having a specialized job.

Cells and Their Functions

Cells are the basic units of all living things. In fact, the smallest part of your body that is alive is a cell. The tiniest organisms are made of only single cells. By contrast, multicellular organisms are made of many cells, maybe trillions of them.

Most cells are too small to be seen by the eye alone. A single drop of blood holds millions of red blood cells like those shown here. You definitely need a microscope to see these cells.

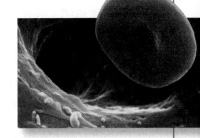

This red blood cell is magnified about 3,000 times.

Most cells have the same needs for survival that you do. Cells do many of the same things you do each day to stay alive. They take in food and get rid of wastes. Cells use materials in food to grow and repair wounds. Although few cells move, all cells have parts inside of them that do move. Cells sense and respond to changes in their surroundings. They often communicate and work with other cells.

All cells need energy. Most cells get energy through cellular respiration. Cellular respiration is the combining of oxygen and food, such as sugar, to get energy. The energy is used for all of the things that cells must do to survive, including growing, moving, and dividing to make new cells. You will learn more about cellular respiration in Lesson 4.

1. **✓ Checkpoint** What is the most basic unit of all living things?

2. **Make Generalizations** Suppose that you saw a small organism move across your desk. Would you infer that this organism is multicellular or a single cell?

95

The Parts of Cells

All cells have some of the same parts, and many cells have similar jobs. You can compare some cell parts to larger structures of your body. For example, your body needs an outside covering of skin. It also needs a control system of nerves, a support system of bones, and places to store food and wastes in the digestive system. Cells have the same needs.

A few of the parts of an animal cell are shown here. The cell membrane surrounds the cell and holds the parts of the cell together. It lets certain materials, such as sugar, water, and oxygen, enter the cell. It allows certain other materials, such as carbon dioxide and other wastes, to exit the cell. Inside the cell are structures called organelles that perform specific functions.

Look for Active Art animations at www.pearsonsuccessnet.com

Mitochondria
Mitochondria are organelles that change the chemical energy of food into a form that the cell can use.

Animal Cell

Cell membrane

Cytoplasm
Cytoplasm is a gel-like fluid that contains the cell's parts. It lies between the nucleus and the cell membrane.

Ribosomes
Ribosomes are organelles that begin the process of making proteins.

Vacuole
A **vacuole** is surrounded by a membrane and contains fluid. It stores water and nutrients. It may also help the cell digest food.

Nucleus
The nucleus directs the cell's activities. It also stores information that will be passed on to new cells.

Plant Cell

Plant cells have all of the parts shown in the animal cell. They also have some parts not found in animal cells.

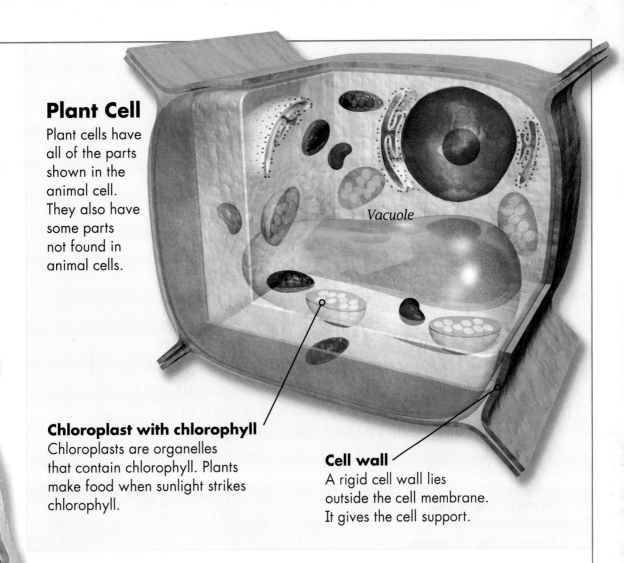

Vacuole

Chloroplast with chlorophyll
Chloroplasts are organelles that contain chlorophyll. Plants make food when sunlight strikes chlorophyll.

Cell wall
A rigid cell wall lies outside the cell membrane. It gives the cell support.

The Size and Shape of Cells

A cell's size must be within certain limits. If a cell is too small, there would not be enough room for all of its parts. If a cell is too large, oxygen and other materials could not travel to all parts of the cell fast enough to keep the cell alive.

A cell's shape is also important. Many cells have a special shape that fits the job the cells do. Many cells also have special structures to help them do their work.

1.   ✔**Checkpoint** List five parts of all cells.
2.   List three important characteristics of cells.

Cells Form Tissues

Have you ever noticed that teamwork is a great way to get work done? Cells rarely work alone. Instead, they often work together in tissues. A **tissue** is a group of the same kind of cells that work together to do the same job. Muscle cells group in bundles to make up muscle tissue. Nerve cells make up nerve tissue.

Tissues Form Organs

Tissues join with other types of tissue to form organs. An **organ** is a group of different tissues that join together into one structure. These tissues work together to do a main job in the body. Your heart, eyes, ears, and stomach are all organs. Many animals have similar tissues and organs. Plants have tissues and organs too. Stems, roots, leaves, and flowers are plant organs.

In plants and animals, cells make up tissues, tissues make up organs, and organs make up organ systems. Here we can see a heart muscle cell, heart muscle tissue, the heart organ, and the circulatory system.

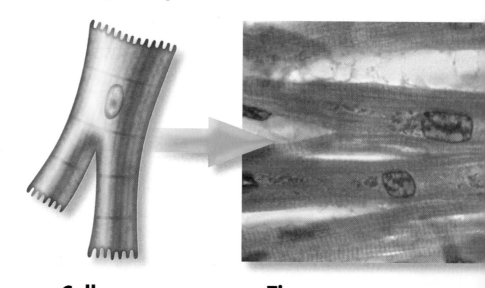

Cell   **Tissue**

In this group of pictures, we see the cells, tissues, leaves, and the entire California oak tree. The tubes inside the tree that go from the roots to the leaves make up the organ system.

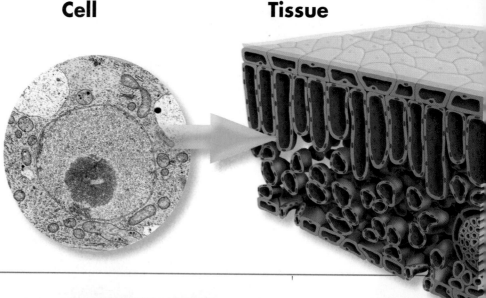

Organ Systems

You have read that cells work together in tissues and that tissues work together in organs. Organs work together too. An organ system is a group of organs that work together to carry out a life process. For example, blood cells, blood vessels, and the heart work together to move materials through the body. The mouth, stomach, intestines, and other organs work together to digest food. You will learn more about the systems in the body in Chapter 4.

1. **√Checkpoint** How is a tissue like a team?

2. List the terms *organ system, tissue, cell,* and *organ* in order from largest and most complex to smallest and simplest.

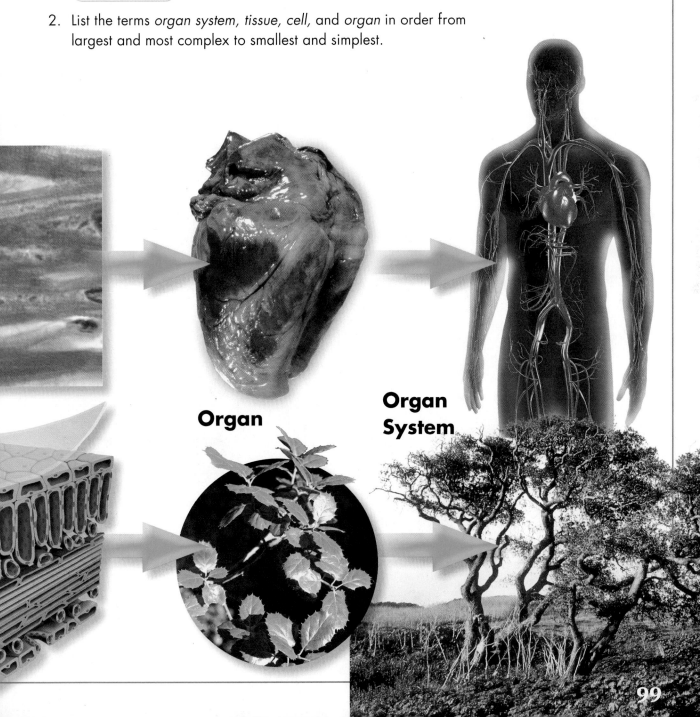

Organ

Organ System

Receiving Food and Oxygen

Every cell needs a supply of food and oxygen and a way to get rid of wastes. In multicellular organisms, organ systems may work together to help the cells meet these needs.

The picture shows the digestive system of a turtle. The digestive system takes in food needed by the body. It then breaks down the food into a form the body cells can use. The substances in food needed by the cells are called nutrients.

Liver

Lung

Small intestine

Stomach

Large intestine

Some organs shown are part of the turtle's digestive system. The lungs are part of the respiratory system. They take in oxygen.

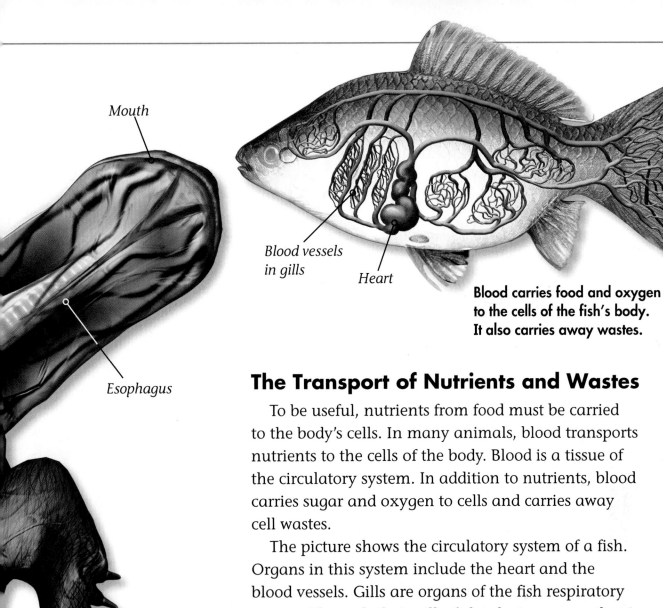

Mouth

Blood vessels
in gills

Heart

Esophagus

**Blood carries food and oxygen
to the cells of the fish's body.
It also carries away wastes.**

The Transport of Nutrients and Wastes

To be useful, nutrients from food must be carried
to the body's cells. In many animals, blood transports
nutrients to the cells of the body. Blood is a tissue of
the circulatory system. In addition to nutrients, blood
carries sugar and oxygen to cells and carries away
cell wastes.

The picture shows the circulatory system of a fish.
Organs in this system include the heart and the
blood vessels. Gills are organs of the fish respiratory
system. Through their gills, fish take in oxygen that is
dissolved in water. This oxygen is then carried by blood
cells to the other cells in the fish's body. At the same
time, wastes made by cells are picked up by the blood.
Some of these wastes, such as carbon dioxide, are
carried back to the gills for removal from the body.
The removal of wastes is the main job of the
excretory system.

✓ Lesson Review

1. List some organ systems and describe their jobs.

2. What kinds of structures make up multicellular organisms?
   Explain how these structures are related.

3. **Writing in Science** **Descriptive** Write a
   summary that describes how structures in different organ
   systems work together.

How do materials move through plants?

Stems and roots are major plant organs. They have special structures and jobs to perform.

Stems and Leaves

Leaves are plant organs. Leaves are attached to stems. Many stems hold leaves high. Why do you think this is helpful? Plants need light to make food. Higher leaves are less likely to be shaded by their neighbors than are lower leaves. Stems also hold fruit and flowers on plants.

Xylem and Phloem

Many plants use a system of tubes to transport materials such as water and minerals. This tube system is called a **vascular** system. The vascular system of plants is made up of two kinds of tissues called xylem and phloem. These tissues are found in roots, stems, and leaves. Not all plants have xylem and phloem, but those that do are called vascular plants.

Xylem tubes carry materials from the plant's roots to its leaves. The roots of a plant soak up water from the soil. This water carries minerals. Plant cells need minerals for some of their activities, including photosynthesis. You will read more about photosynthesis in Lesson 3.

California poppy

Xylem
Xylem tissue carries water and minerals from the roots to the rest of the plant.

Phloem
Phloem tissue carries sugar from the leaves to other plant parts.

Standards Focus 5LS2.0 Plants and animals have structures for respiration, digestion, waste disposal, and transport of materials. As a basis for understanding this concept:
5LS2.a Students know many multicellular organisms have specialized structures to support the transport of materials.
5LS2.e Students know how sugar, water and minerals are transported in a vascular plant.

Kinds of Stems

There are different kinds of stems. Some are woody and some non-woody. Woody stems have lots of xylem tissue. Trees and shrubs have woody stems. Poppies and dandelions are examples of plants that have non-woody stems. Their stems have much less xylem tissue.

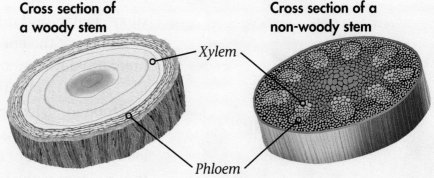

Cross section of a woody stem

Cross section of a non-woody stem

Xylem

Phloem

Phloem tubes carry sugar away from the leaves. The sugar is dissolved in water. Phloem carries this mixture of sugar and water from the leaves throughout the plant.

In trees, phloem is made just beneath the bark. When new phloem cells form and grow, they push old, dead phloem outward. This dead phloem, along with other materials, makes up the bark. Bark protects the phloem beneath it.

Tree stems are hard, woody, and covered by bark. You probably would not want to chew on a tree's stem. However, you have probably eaten other plant stems. Did you know that the parts of asparagus you eat are stems?

1. ✓**Checkpoint** What are the functions of a plant's stem?

TARGET SKILL

2. **Make Generalizations** The California poppy does not have a woody stem. What can you infer about the amount of xylem in this stem compared to that of a very large tree, such as a giant sequoia?

103

More About Stems and Vascular Plants

You have read that vascular plants have a system of tubes that transports materials through the plant. Materials carried by the vascular system include sugar, water, and minerals.

Plants get the energy they need by breaking down sugar. This sugar is the food source of plants. The plant makes this food in its leaves. Once made, much of this sugar is transported from the leaves to the rest of the plant. Recall that phloem is the vascular tissue that transports sugar from the leaves to the roots.

To make food, plants need water. The roots of the plant absorb water from the soil. Xylem transports this water and any minerals it contains from the roots upward to all other parts of the plant.

Celery is a leaf stem that you may have eaten. A leaf stem attaches a plant's leaves to its stem. You can use a stalk of celery to observe the transport of water and minerals upward through a plant stem. The liquid in the jar on this page is water that contains food coloring. The food coloring represents minerals dissolved in the water.

A celery stalk placed in colored water shows that xylem carries water and minerals up through the leaf stem.

A stalk of celery is placed in the water that contains food coloring. As the celery stays in the container, water evaporates from its leaves. Colored water from the container begins moving up the plant stem to replace water that has evaporated from the leaves.

Look at the stalk of celery that is beside the cup. The red areas show where the xylem of the celery leaf stem is located. You can see these areas more clearly in the picture showing a cross section of the celery stem under a microscope.

This magnified cross section of the celery stem clearly shows the colored water in the xylem.

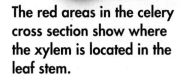

The red areas in the celery cross section show where the xylem is located in the leaf stem.

1. ✓Checkpoint What vascular tissue in plants transports water and dissolved nutrients?

2. Why do you suppose you cannot see the phloem of the celery on this page?

Roots

The cluster shown to the right is another type of plant organ. These long roots spread underground as they grow. Don't let their scrawny looks fool you! Roots are strong. They anchor the plant in the ground and hold it in place as it grows.

There are different kinds of root systems. Each has different structures. One kind of root system is a fibrous root system. In this system, many roots grow out in all directions. The roots divide many times, forming smaller and smaller roots. The fibrous roots of a tree sometimes look like an upside-down version of the above-ground branches.

Another root system is a taproot. Carrots are taproots. A taproot is a large root that grows straight down. It remains the largest root structure as the plant grows. Taproots may store food for the plant. Small roots may grow sideways out of the main taproot.

Roots grow longer because of a special tissue near the root tips. Here, cells divide quickly to form new cells. As the new cells grow longer, they push the root tip further into the ground.

Next time you chomp down on a carrot, remember that you're eating a taproot. Beets, turnips, and radishes are also taproots.

This is a fibrous root system of a sweet pea.

If you were to look at the center of a buttercup root through a microscope, you could see that the xylem tissues are larger than the phloem tissues.

Phloem tissue

Xylem tissue

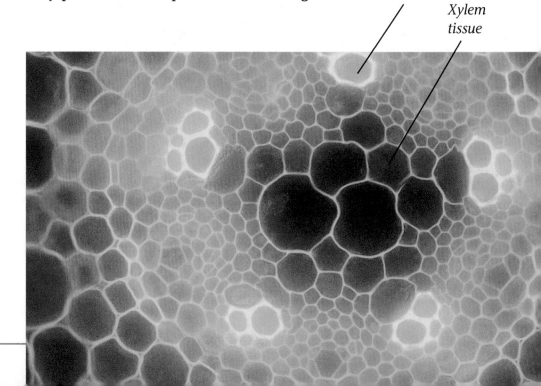

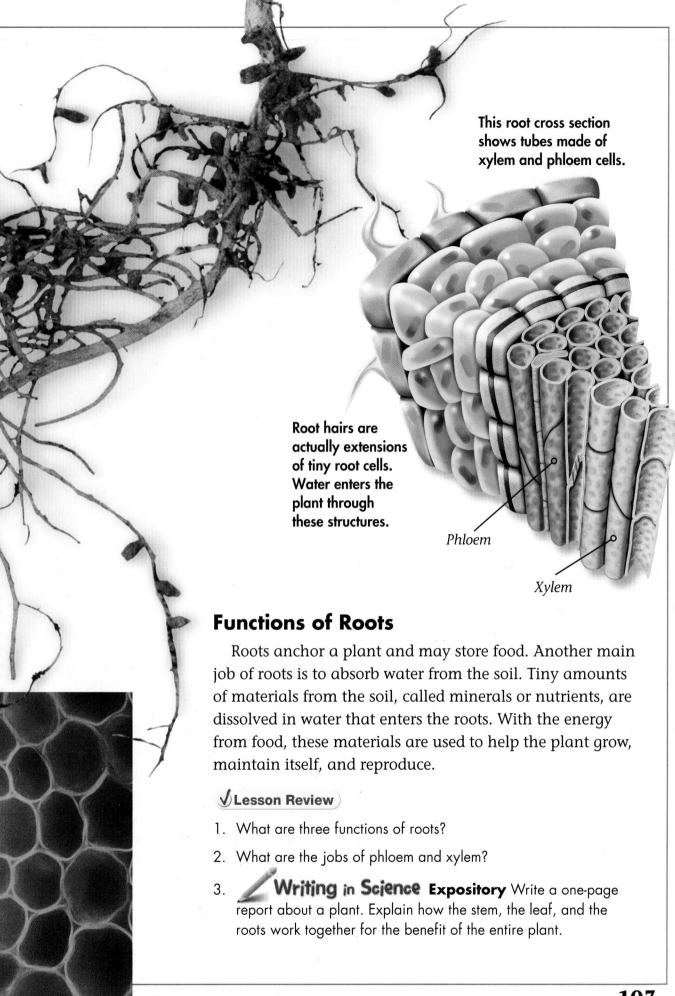

This root cross section shows tubes made of xylem and phloem cells.

Root hairs are actually extensions of tiny root cells. Water enters the plant through these structures.

Phloem

Xylem

Functions of Roots

Roots anchor a plant and may store food. Another main job of roots is to absorb water from the soil. Tiny amounts of materials from the soil, called minerals or nutrients, are dissolved in water that enters the roots. With the energy from food, these materials are used to help the plant grow, maintain itself, and reproduce.

✓ Lesson Review

1. What are three functions of roots?

2. What are the jobs of phloem and xylem?

3. **Writing in Science Expository** Write a one-page report about a plant. Explain how the stem, the leaf, and the roots work together for the benefit of the entire plant.

How do cells get and use energy?

The leaves of a plant make sugar. This sugar contains energy the plant can use for life functions. Cells break down the sugar to release its energy.

Photosynthesis

Leaves and other plant parts are green because of chlorophyll. **Chlorophyll** is a green substance that traps energy from the Sun and allows plants to make their own food—sugar.

Plant cells have structures called chloroplasts. **Chloroplasts** store chlorophyll. Animal cells do not have chloroplasts or chlorophyll. Animals cannot make their own food.

Plants make a sugar, glucose, in a process called **photosynthesis.** During photosynthesis, plants use light energy from sunlight, carbon dioxide from the air, and water to make sugar and oxygen. Energy is stored in the sugar. Plants and organisms that eat plants can use the sugar as a source of energy.

Photosynthesis can happen only when chlorophyll is present. The process can be summarized in this equation:

$$6CO_2 + 6H_2O \longrightarrow C_6H_{12}O_6 + 6O_2$$

$$\text{carbon dioxide} + \text{water} \xrightarrow[\text{chlorophyll}]{\text{light energy}} \text{sugar} + \text{oxygen}$$

The equation shows that plants use carbon dioxide for photosynthesis. In the process, they also release oxygen. Most organisms could not live without the oxygen made by plants.

Study the diagram to see how a leaf is adapted to carry out photosynthesis.

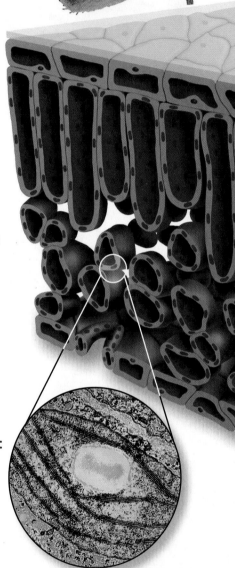

Chlorophyll is found in the structures of this chloroplast. Sugar made during photosynthesis may be changed into starch. The large light-colored structure in this chloroplast is holding starch.

Standards Focus 5LS2.f Students know plants use carbon dioxide (CO_2) and energy from sunlight to build molecules of sugar and release oxygen.
5LS2.g Students know plant and animal cells break down sugar to obtain energy, a process resulting in carbon dioxide (CO_2) and water (respiration).

Leaf Structure

A waxy layer may cover a leaf and reduce water loss.

A layer of cells covers the top and bottom of the leaf. This thin layer lets light pass into the middle of the leaf.

Photosynthesis takes place in the middle of the leaf. The tall, thin cells there absorb sunlight entering the leaf. These cells have the chloroplasts that a plant needs to make sugar.

Xylem and phloem are in the veins of a leaf. The xylem carries water and minerals into the leaf. Phloem carries sugar made by the leaf to the rest of the plant.

Cells in this part of the leaf are spread apart. The spaces around the cells let carbon dioxide move through the leaf.

Most leaves have tiny openings on the bottom where they exchange water vapor, carbon dioxide, and oxygen. Less light reaches under the leaf. This keeps the lower leaf cooler and less water is lost.

1. ✓ **Checkpoint** Describe three ways in which a plant's leaf is adapted for photosynthesis.

2. Why can't animals make their own food?

Energy from Food

Plants can make more sugar than they need. This extra sugar is changed into other kinds of sugars and starches that are stored in the plant. Plants must break down the stored food to release the energy it contains when they need it.

The process by which cells break down sugar to release energy is called **cellular respiration.** Plants and animals must break down food to release the stored energy. You may have heard the term *respiration* when people talk about breathing in through the lungs. Cellular respiration is not the same as breathing. You will learn about the lungs and the respiratory system in Chapter 4.

During cellular respiration, sugar starts to be broken down through a series of reactions that take place mostly in the mitochondria. The process makes carbon dioxide and water, and releases energy. The process of cellular respiration can be summarized by this equation:

$$C_6H_{12}O_6 + 6O_2 \longrightarrow 6CO_2 + 6H_2O + Energy$$

sugar + oxygen ⟶ carbon dioxide + water + energy

Cellular Respiration

The blue structure in this electron microscope image is a mitochondrion. Chemical reactions take place on the many folds in the mitochondrion.

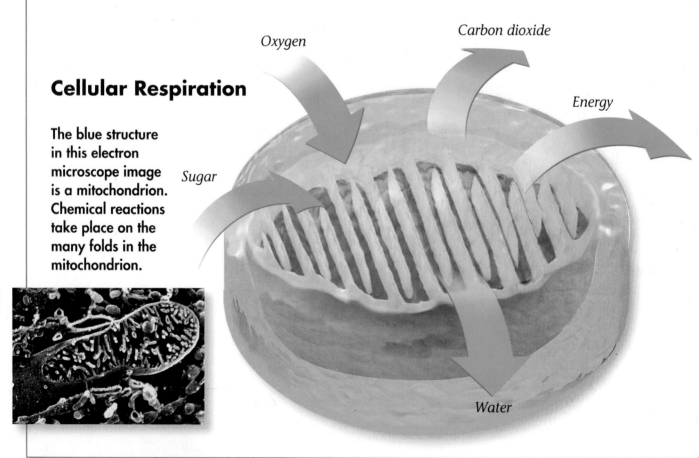

Oxygen

Carbon dioxide

Energy

Sugar

Water

Carbon Dioxide–Oxygen Cycle

Did you notice that the equations for photosynthesis and cellular respiration look alike? Look at the two equations again.

Both plants and animals give off carbon dioxide during cellular respiration.

$$\text{carbon dioxide + water} \xrightarrow[\text{chlorophyll}]{\text{light energy}} \text{sugar + oxygen}$$

$$\text{sugar + oxygen} \longrightarrow \text{carbon dioxide + water + energy}$$

The two processes are almost the reverse of each other. Materials made during one process are the same as those needed for the other process. In other words, they form a cycle. Together, photosynthesis and cellular respiration form the carbon dioxide–oxygen cycle.

Animals breathe oxygen from the air. Plants take in oxygen and carbon dioxide through their leaves. During respiration, both plants and animals use oxygen to change food into energy that they can use. At the same time, they give off carbon dioxide. When animals use food, they release carbon dioxide into the blood. It is then transported to the lungs. During photosynthesis, plants use energy to change water and carbon dioxide into more food and oxygen. The carbon dioxide–oxygen cycle provides living things with the oxygen and carbon dioxide they need.

✓ Lesson Review

1. What do plants need to carry on photosynthesis?

2. How do plants get and use energy?

3. **Make Generalizations** How does the role of energy differ in photosynthesis and cellular respiration?

TARGET SKILL

111

Large Numbers of Small Cells

The number of cells in the human body has been estimated to be in the trillions! It would take about 35,000 red blood cells to fill an area of 0.035 cm². That's about half the space inside a printed zero on this page.

You can think of one trillion as one thousand billion, or one million million. In standard form, one trillion is written as 1,000,000,000,000.

hundred trillions	ten trillions	trillions	hundred billions	ten billions	billions	hundred millions	ten millions	millions	hundred thousands	ten thousands	thousands	hundreds	tens	ones	tenths	hundredths	thousandths
		1	0	0	0	0	0	0	0	0	0	0	0	0	0	0	0
										3	5	0	0	0	0	0	0
														0	0	3	5

DIGITAL

Write each underlined number in standard form.

1. It has been estimated that the number of cells in a person's body is between 10 trillion and 100 trillion.

2. The human brain has been estimated to contain more than 100 billion nerve cells.

3. It has been estimated that the amount of heat produced by your muscle cells each day could boil almost 943 milliliters, or 943 thousandths of a liter, of water for an hour.

4. The part of the brain called the gray matter is a layer about two and five tenths millimeters thick.

5. A cell is mostly water. About 70 hundredths of the material in a typical cell is water.

6. There are about 250 million red blood cells in a single drop of blood.

Lab zone Take-Home Activity

Copy the place-value chart on page 112. Write the underlined numbers from the questions above in the chart. Find more data about human cells and write those numbers in the chart also.

Investigate How do plants use carbon dioxide?

You can measure what happens when plants take in carbon dioxide (CO_2). A chemical called BTB turns greenish yellow when the level of carbon dioxide is high. It turns blue when the level of carbon dioxide is low.

Materials

safety goggles

graduated cylinder

water with BTB

plastic wrap

cup and drinking straw

elodea

timer or clock with a second hand

What to Do

1 **Measure** 100 mL of water with BTB. Put the liquid into a cup. Cover with plastic wrap.

Be careful!

Wear safety goggles. Do not drink water with BTB in it.

100 mL

2 Push the straw through the plastic wrap into the water. Gently breathe *out* through the straw into the water. Stop as soon as the color starts to change.

Be careful!

Use the straw to breathe out only! Do not breathe in.

Process Skills

When you conduct a scientific **investigation,** you carry out a careful procedure and make observations to answer a question.

 5LS2.f Students know plants use carbon dioxide (CO_2) and energy from sunlight to build molecules of sugar and release oxygen. **5IE6.a** Classify objects (e.g., rocks, plants, and leaves) in accordance with appropriate criteria. **5IE6.f** Select appropriate tools (e.g., thermometers, metersticks, balances, and graduated cylinders) and make quantitative observations.

3 **Observe** the color of the water. Record how the color changes.

4 Put the elodea into the water. Put the cup in a bright place.

5 Measure the time it takes for the water to change back to blue.

BTB indicates how much carbon dioxide is in the water.

greenish yellow = high level of carbon dioxide

blue = low level of carbon dioxide

	Color of Water with BTB	Time (quantitative observation)
Before breathing out into the water		
After breathing out into the water		
Immediately after adding elodea to the water	greenish-yellow	0 minutes
When the water turns blue	blue	_____ minutes

Explain Your Results

1. What made the color change when you breathed into the water?

2. What made the color change when you added elodea? What quantitative **observation** did you record?

Go Further

Elodea is an aquatic plant. Use your library-media center resources to **classify** 20 plants based on their habitat needs.

115

Focus on the BIG Idea

Cells are the basic units that make up structures needed for transporting materials and carrying out life processes.

Lesson 1

What makes up multicellular organisms?

- Cells are the smallest living parts of plants and animals.
- Cells make up structures inside multicellular organisms.
- Some of these structures help transport nutrients to other parts of the organism; some help transport wastes away.

Lesson 2

How do materials move through plants?

- Vascular plants have leaves that produce sugar and stems that support the plant, hold leaves high, and transport water, nutrients, and wastes. They also have roots that get nutrients from the soil and store food.
- In a vascular plant, xylem tissue carries materials from the plant's roots to its leaves. Phloem carries sugars made in the plants leaves to the rest of the plant.

Lesson 3

How do cells get and use energy?

- A plant's leaves are adapted to use the Sun's energy and carbon dioxide to produce the plant's own food by photosynthesis.
- Plant and animal cells break down sugar to produce energy.

Cross-Curricular Links

English–Language Arts

Building Vocabulary

Look again at pages 90–91. Identify the picture behind the terms *tissue* and *cellular respiration*. Write a paragraph about each term. Tell how each term relates to the picture.

Mathematics

Growing Corn

A single corn plant can release 245 liters of water in one growing season. How much water must be available in the soil during the growing season to replace the water in a field of 10,000 corn plants?

Visual and Performing Arts

Cells

Compare and contrast plant and animal cells by drawing pictures or a Venn diagram to show what parts plant cells have, what parts animal cells have, and what both types of cell have.

Challenge!

History–Social Science

Plants in History

Research the plants used by early United States settlers. Write a report or make a poster to show what you find out.

Chapter 3 Review/Test

Use Vocabulary

cellular respiration (p. 110)	**photosynthesis** (p. 108)
chlorophyll (p. 108)	**tissue** (p. 98)
chloroplast (p. 108)	**vacuole** (p. 96)
organ (p. 98)	**vascular** (p. 102)
phloem (p. 103)	**xylem** (p. 102)

Fill in the blanks with the correct vocabulary terms. If you have trouble answering a question, read the listed page again.

1. During ____, cells of organisms release energy from food.

2. ____ carries water and minerals throughout a plant.

3. During ____, plants make sugar and release oxygen.

4. A group of cells that work together to perform the same function is called a(n) ____.

5. The plant cell structure that has chlorophyll is called a(n) ____.

6. The ____ is a cell structure that stores water and other substances.

7. ____ is a green substance that is needed by plants to make food.

Think About It

8. What are some ways cells help an organism?

9. **Process Skills** **Communicate** Explain the role of phloem in plants and how phloem forms bark on a tree.

10. **Infer** A greenhouse is filled with air that contains more carbon dioxide than normal air has. How might photosynthesis and plant growth be affected?

11. **TARGET SKILL** **Make Generalizations** Suppose you are looking at a cell through a microscope. The cell is surrounded by a thick outer structure. Inside the cell, you see a nucleus, a large vacuole, and several small structures that are green. Use the graphic organizer below to generalize about whether you are looking at a plant cell or an animal cell.

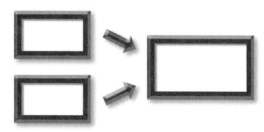

12. **Writing in Science** **Expository** Suppose that you are in a science club. Write an article for the club's newsletter that explains how photosynthesis and cellular respiration are related.

California Standards Practice

Write the letter of the correct answer.

13. Which of the following is an animal's smallest structure?

A organ

B cell

C tissue

D carbon dioxide

14. Which of the following can be described as the reverse of photosynthesis?

A mitochondria

B xylem

C chlorophyll

D cellular respiration

15. A leaf can best be described as

A an organ.

B a tissue.

C wide.

D small.

16. Which of the following is a plant organ?

A cell

B root

C phloem

D xylem

17. Which structure is present only in plant cells?

A a nucleus

B a cell wall

C a mitochondrion

D a cell membrane

18. What process is carried out by a system of organs?

A vacuole formation

B digestion

C photosynthesis

D cellular respiration

19. What is transported by xylem?

A carbon dioxide

B sugar

C water and minerals

D oxygen

20. In the cell shown, what is the job of the structure labeled A?

A protecting the cell

B directing the cell

C storing starch

D making energy for the cell

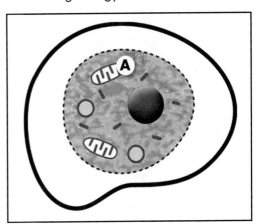

Rosalind Franklin

Rosalind Franklin was a key figure in what many call the most important discovery of the 20th century. She helped unlock the secrets of DNA!

Franklin had made a name for herself in the 1940s. This English scientist was one of the world's top experts on X-ray diffraction. In this technique, a powerful X-ray beam is aimed at a crystal, producing an image on film. Franklin perfected the technique when studying the structure of coal.

Then in 1951, Franklin turned her attention to DNA. In the early 1950s, scientists knew that DNA was the substance that carries traits from parents to offspring. But how did DNA actually pass on this genetic information? To answer that, scientists needed to know what DNA looked like. What was its structure?

Through careful investigation, the breakthrough came in 1953. Franklin produced her best X-ray photo of DNA. It showed clues to the DNA structure. A co-worker showed the photo to James Watson, who was trying to figure out DNA's structure by building models with his partner, Francis Crick. The photo gave Watson and Crick the clues they needed to finish their model correctly. They discovered the structure of DNA and were able to explain how it works. But Franklin's work was the key part to the puzzle.

Lab zone Take-Home Activity

The quest to figure out DNA's structure was an intense competition in the early 1950s. Make a poster that shows the role each of these scientists played in that quest: Rosalind Franklin, Maurice Wilkins, Linus Pauling, James Watson, and Francis Crick.

Chapter 4
Human Body Systems

CALIFORNIA Standards Preview

5LS2.0 Plants and animals have structures for respiration, digestion, waste disposal, and transport of materials. As a basis for understanding this concept:

5LS2.a Students know many multicellular organisms have specialized structures to support the transport of materials.

5LS2.b Students know how blood circulates through the heart chambers, lungs, and body and how carbon dioxide (CO_2) and oxygen (O_2) are exchanged in the lungs and tissues.

5LS2.c Students know the sequential steps of digestion and the roles of teeth and the mouth, esophagus, stomach, small intestine, large intestine, and colon in the function of the digestive system.

5LS2.d Students know the role of the kidney in removing cellular waste from blood and converting it into urine, which is stored in the bladder.

5IE6.0 Scientific progress is made by asking meaningful questions and conducting careful investigations. As a basis for understanding this concept and addressing the content in the other three strands, students should develop their own questions and perform investigations. (Also **5IE6.a**, **5IE6.b**, **5IE6.c**, **5IE6.d**, **5IE6.e**, **5IE6.f**, **5IE6.g**, **5IE6.h**)

Standards Focus Questions

- How does blood circulate?
- What is the respiratory system?
- What are the digestive and urinary systems?

How do the systems in your body help keep you alive?

artery

vein

capillary

air sacs

bronchiole

122

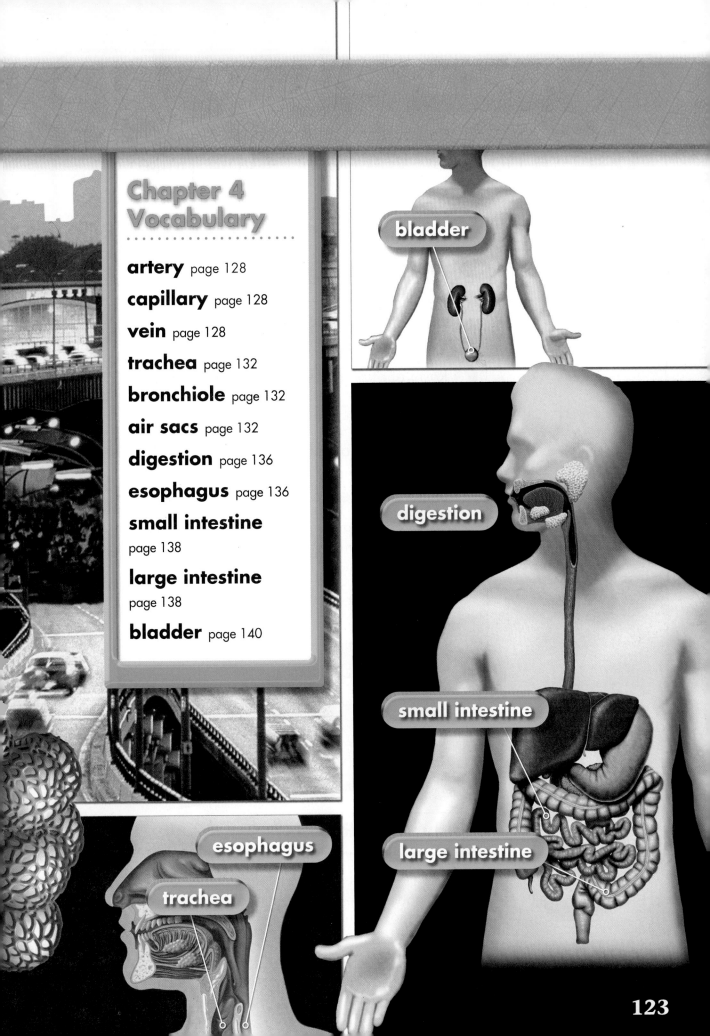

Chapter 4 Vocabulary

bladder

digestion

small intestine

large intestine

esophagus

trachea

123

Explore How can you observe your pulse?

When your heart beats, it pumps blood into the arteries. The wall of the arteries stretch. You feel this as your pulse.

Materials

plastic straw

clay

What to Do

1 Insert one end of the straw into a ball of clay. Flatten the bottom of the clay.

2 Rest your hand on a flat surface with the palm side up.

3 Place the bottom of the clay on the thumb side of your wrist. Move the clay around until you **observe** the straw start to move.

Do you wonder how exercise might affect your pulse?
Develop your own question.
Perform an investigation to answer your question.

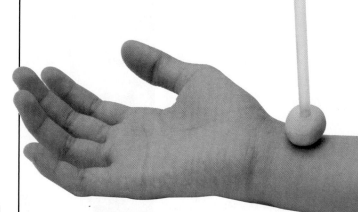

Explain Your Results

1. Describe the movements of the straw you **observed.**
2. What caused the straw to move?

Process Skills

Scientific progress is made by asking meaningful questions, conducting careful investigations, and **observing** carefully.

5LS2.b Students know how blood circulates through the heart chambers, lungs, and body and how carbon dioxide (CO_2) and oxygen (O_2) are exchanged in the lungs and tissues. **5IE6.0** Scientific progress is made by asking meaningful questions and conducting careful investigations. As a basis for understanding this concept and addressing the content in the other three strands, students should develop their own questions and perform investigations.

Reading Skills

Sequence

The order in which events happen is the **sequence** of those events. Sequence can also mean the steps we follow to do something.

- You might **observe** a sequence. Clue words such as *first, then, next,* and *finally* also can help you find the sequence of events.

- Some events take place at the same time. Clue words such as *while, meanwhile,* or *during* signal this.

Read the public message below. Clue words have been highlighted to help you identify the order in which things happen.

Public Message

Help Save Lives!

People save lives every day by donating blood. First, you must fill out a questionnaire. These questions make sure that it is healthy for you to give blood and that your blood is safe to give to others. People with certain diseases or who take certain medications cannot give blood. Next, if you meet all the requirements, a health care professional removes a unit of blood. Then, some of the blood is sent to be tested. Finally, your blood is given to a person who needs it.

Apply It!

Make a graphic organizer like the one shown. **Observe** the steps for donating blood in the message above. Then write the **sequence** of steps in the correct boxes.

First

↓

Next

↓

Then

↓

Finally

125

You Are There!

As you stand by a busy highway, you see cars, trucks, and buses moving from one part of town to another. A transportation system is important to a city. A city needs to move food, water, gasoline, garbage, and much more to meet the needs of its citizens. The same is true of your body. Your body needs to transport food, water, oxygen, and wastes in order to stay healthy. How does your body do these jobs?

DIGITAL

How does blood circulate?

Your body has structures and systems that serve special functions. The circulatory system moves material around your body. The parts of the circulatory system are the heart, the blood, and tubes called blood vessels.

The Body's Transportation System

A city needs many systems to stay healthy and grow. A system is a group of parts that work together to get a job done. No one part does everything by itself. The transportation system of a city has roads, buses, trucks, and cars to move people and supplies. The water system has drains, pipes, and pumps to move water through the city. The garbage system has trucks and dumps to keep the city clean. Many different systems meet the needs of a city's people.

Like the people in a city, all of your cells have needs that must be met. How do they get food and oxygen? How do wastes get carried away? Like a city, your body has many systems to take care of its cells.

The body has a transportation system that moves food and oxygen to each cell. It then takes away cell wastes. This system is the circulatory system. It includes the heart, blood, and blood vessels. The blood vessels are tubes that carry blood through the body. As with all systems, each part of the circulatory system has structures to help get the job done.

1. ✔Checkpoint) What is the job of the circulatory system?
2. How are the cells in your body like the people in a city?

Arteries, Capillaries, and Veins

Blood vessels are like roads for blood cells. The three kinds of blood vessels are arteries, capillaries, and veins.

Most arteries carry blood with lots of oxygen. **Arteries** are blood vessels that carry blood away from the heart to other parts of the body. Arteries have thick, muscular walls. These walls stretch as the heart pushes blood into them. Arteries branch many times into smaller and smaller tubes.

The smallest arteries branch to become capillaries. A **capillary** is the smallest kind of blood vessel. Side by side, ten capillaries would be barely as thick as one hair! Some capillaries are so narrow that red blood cells must flow through them in a single-file line.

Capillary walls are only one cell thick. Gases can pass through these thin walls. Oxygen and glucose sugar move from the blood cells in the capillaries to your body's cells. Carbon dioxide and other wastes move from cells to the blood in the capillaries.

Capillaries join together to form your smallest veins. **Veins** are blood vessels that transport blood toward the heart. Tiny veins join many times to form larger veins.

Unlike arteries and capillaries, veins have valves. Valves are flaps that act like doors to keep blood flowing in only one direction. Valves open to let blood flow to the heart. Valves close if the blood starts flowing away from the heart.

1. ✓**Checkpoint** How are the jobs of a vein and an artery the same? How are they different?

2. Why do capillaries have such thin walls?

Veins and Arteries
Veins have thinner walls than arteries, but thicker walls than capillaries.

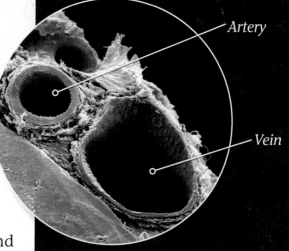

Artery

Vein

Capillaries
This capillary is as wide as only a few red blood cells.

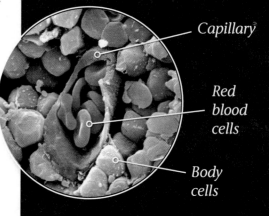

Capillary

Red blood cells

Body cells

In drawings of the circulatory system, arteries are usually colored red because they transport blood with lots of oxygen. Veins are usually blue because they transport blood with less oxygen. Veins are not truly this color. They are more maroon in color. Coloring veins blue makes them easier to see in diagrams.

The Circulatory System

Huge numbers of blood vessels form a network throughout your body. If all the blood vessels were laid end-to-end, they would stretch around Earth more than twice!

It would be impossible to show all the blood vessels in a person's body. This picture shows only some of the larger blood vessels.

DIGITAL

Look for Active Art animations at www.pearsonsuccessnet.com

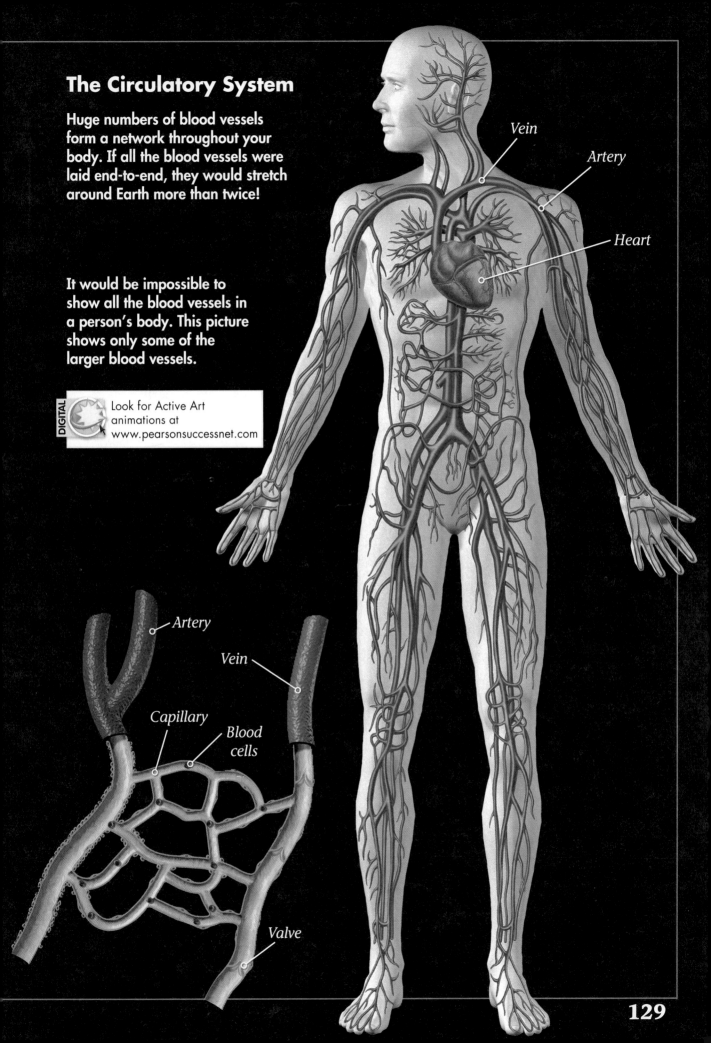

Vein

Artery

Heart

Artery

Vein

Capillary

Blood cells

Valve

Parts of the Heart

Your heart began pumping before you were born. It will keep pumping as long as you live. The heart is divided into two sides. Each side works as a separate pump and sends blood along different paths. The right side pumps blood to the lungs. In the lungs, the blood gets oxygen and gives up carbon dioxide. The blood then flows to the left side of the heart. The left side pumps the blood through arteries to all the tissues of the body.

Each side of the heart has two parts. The upper part of each side is called an atrium. The lower part is a ventricle. Each ventricle is larger and stronger than an atrium.

The parts of your heart pump in a repeating pattern. The left and right atrium pump first, and then the two ventricles pump. After a brief rest, the pattern repeats.

The muscles of your heart have many small blood vessels. The blood in these vessels gives your heart oxygen, food, and water. In one form of heart disease, these blood vessels get clogged, keeping blood from reaching heart muscles.

During your life, your heart might beat almost 3 billion times. When you are running, your heart pumps faster to give your muscles extra oxygen. It pumps more slowly when you sit quietly or sleep.

Not all hearts are alike. The hearts of most reptiles have only three parts, or chambers. Fish hearts have only two chambers.

✓ Lesson Review

1. What parts make up the circulatory system?

2. What is the job of your heart's left ventricle?

3. **Sequence** Draw a diagram of the parts of the circulatory system to show the sequence in which blood flows through the body. Write captions that describe how the parts of the system work together.

In this drawing of the heart, the veins from the lungs are colored red because they contain oxygen-rich blood. Arteries and veins going to the lungs are colored blue because they contain blood with less oxygen.

Valve
Like your veins, your heart has valves that keep the blood flowing one way.

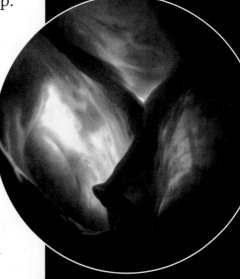

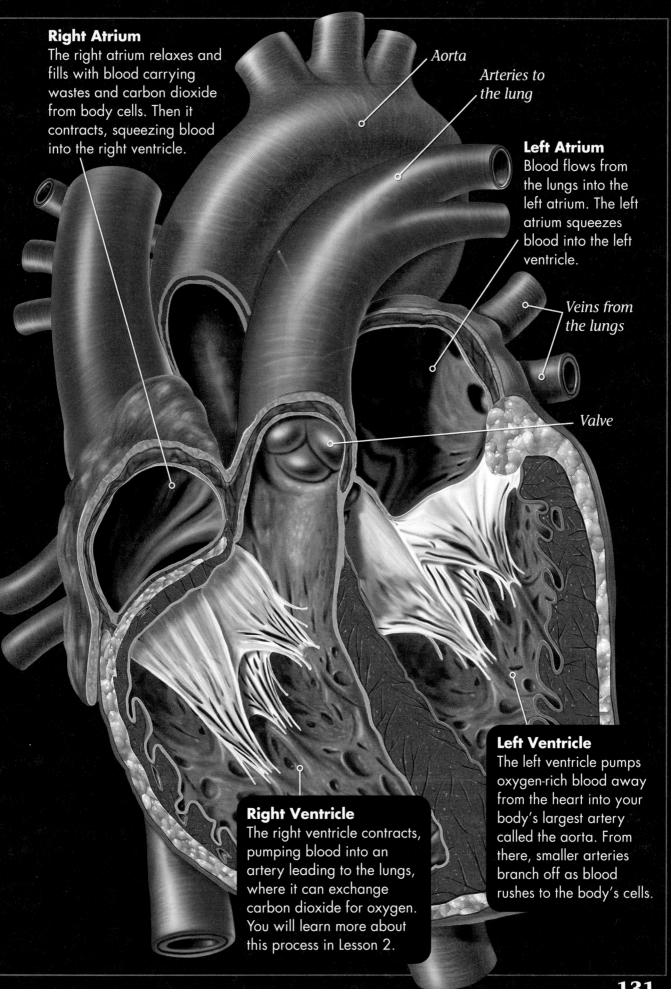

Right Atrium
The right atrium relaxes and fills with blood carrying wastes and carbon dioxide from body cells. Then it contracts, squeezing blood into the right ventricle.

Aorta

Arteries to the lung

Left Atrium
Blood flows from the lungs into the left atrium. The left atrium squeezes blood into the left ventricle.

Veins from the lungs

Valve

Left Ventricle
The left ventricle pumps oxygen-rich blood away from the heart into your body's largest artery called the aorta. From there, smaller arteries branch off as blood rushes to the body's cells.

Right Ventricle
The right ventricle contracts, pumping blood into an artery leading to the lungs, where it can exchange carbon dioxide for oxygen. You will learn more about this process in Lesson 2.

131

Lesson 2

What is the respiratory system?

The job of your respiratory system is to move oxygen and carbon dioxide between the outside air and your blood.

Parts of the Respiratory System

Take a long, slow breath. Now, breathe out. Can you feel your respiratory system at work? You take in air through your nose and mouth. Sinuses warm and moisten the air. Many parts of the respiratory system are coated with mucus. Mucus is a sticky, thick fluid. Its job is to trap dust, germs, and other things that may be in the air. With its hairs and layer of mucus, the nose traps most dust and germs. Air moves from the sinus to the back of the throat and into the larynx. The larynx contains the vocal cords.

The **trachea** is a tube that carries air from the larynx to the lungs. The trachea leads to two branches called bronchi that go into the lungs. In the lungs, the bronchi branch into smaller and smaller tubes called **bronchioles.** Asthma is a disease in which these tubes may become swollen. This keeps air from moving easily through the lungs.

The bronchioles end in clusters of tiny thin-walled air sacs in the lungs. The **air sacs** are where oxygen enters the blood and carbon dioxide leaves the blood.

1. **✓Checkpoint** Why are many parts of your respiratory system covered with mucus?

2. What is the job of air sacs?

How You Breathe

Inhale (Breathe In)

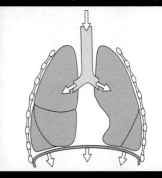

Exhale (Breathe Out)

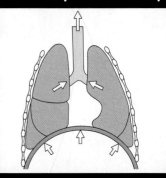

Several muscles work together when you breathe. When you inhale, the dome-shaped muscle called the diaphragm contracts and moves down, making more space in your chest. Your rib muscles may also pull your rib cage up and out, making still more space. Air quickly rushes into the lungs and takes up these new spaces. When your diaphragm and rib muscles relax, they push air out of the lungs.

Vital lung capacity is the amount of air that a person can blow out after a deep breath. The vital lung capacity for an adult is often about 3 to 5 liters.

Standards Focus 5LS2.0 Plants and animals have structures for respiration, digestion, waste disposal, and transport of materials. As a basis for understanding this concept:
5LS2.a Students know many multicellular organisms have specialized structures to support the transport of materials.
5LS2.b Students know how blood circulates through the heart chambers, lungs, and body and how carbon dioxide (CO_2) and oxygen (O_2) are exchanged in the lungs and tissues.

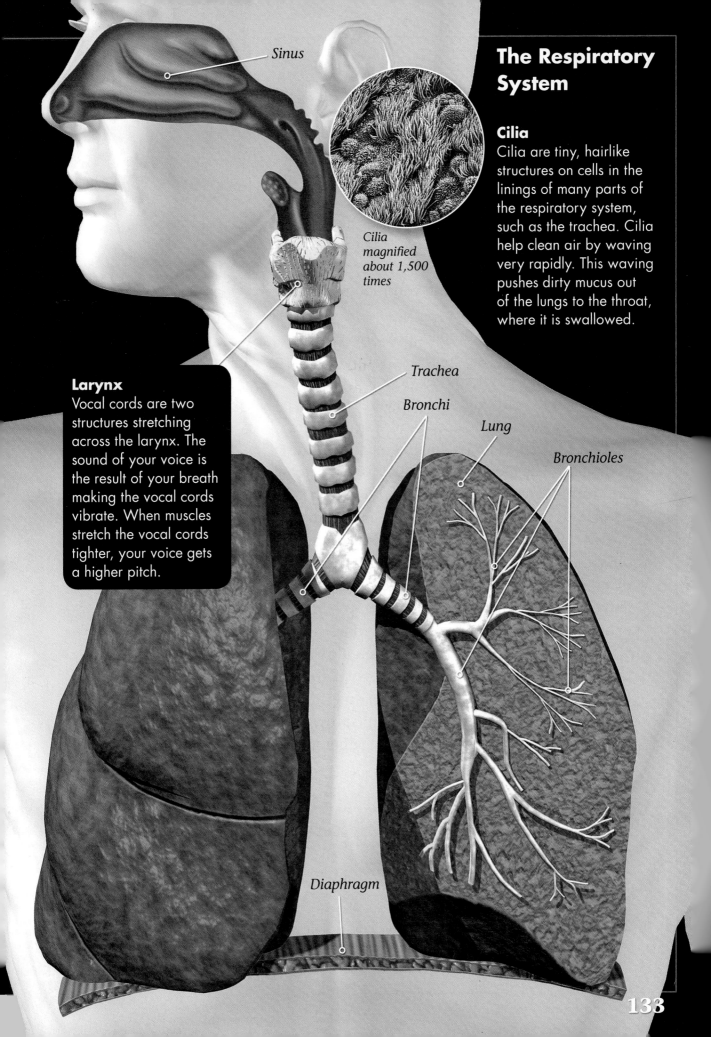

Sinus

The Respiratory System

Cilia
Cilia are tiny, hairlike structures on cells in the linings of many parts of the respiratory system, such as the trachea. Cilia help clean air by waving very rapidly. This waving pushes dirty mucus out of the lungs to the throat, where it is swallowed.

Cilia magnified about 1,500 times

Trachea

Bronchi

Lung

Bronchioles

Larynx
Vocal cords are two structures stretching across the larynx. The sound of your voice is the result of your breath making the vocal cords vibrate. When muscles stretch the vocal cords tighter, your voice gets a higher pitch.

Diaphragm

Respiratory and Circulatory Systems Work Together

All multicellular organisms need oxygen. Oxygen is used to release the energy from glucose that cells need. Insects have a respiratory system to get oxygen. Many tubes run through their bodies. These tubes have openings on the insects' sides to let air in. Worms use a circulatory system to get oxygen. Their blood absorbs oxygen through their moist skin and carries it to all parts of the body.

Your body is more complex than those of worms and insects. You have a respiratory system and a circulatory system that work together to get oxygen to your cells. Oxygen enters your body when you inhale. Your respiratory system gets the oxygen as far as the tiny air sacs inside your chest. The blood picks up the oxygen there and carries it to your heart, where it is pumped to all of your cells—all the way down to your toes!

Two things happen at the same time in the air sacs. Oxygen leaves the lungs and enters the blood. Carbon dioxide moves the other way. It leaves the blood and enters the lungs. When you exhale, you get rid of this carbon dioxide.

When you hold your breath, carbon dioxide builds up in your blood. Your brain senses this. It sends a message to the diaphragm and rib muscles telling them to breathe. In this way, several systems of your body work together to make sure your cells get oxygen.

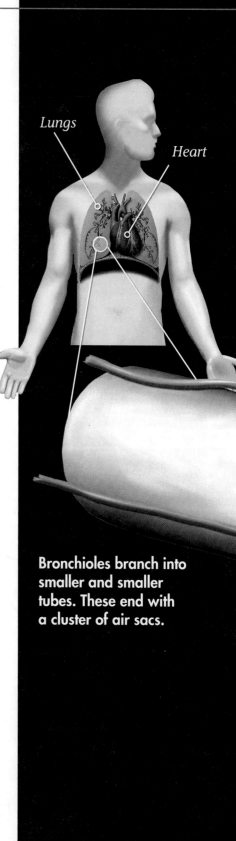

Lungs

Heart

Bronchioles branch into smaller and smaller tubes. These end with a cluster of air sacs.

✓ Lesson Review

1. Why do the cells of all multicellular organisms need oxygen?

2. How do the lungs get carbon dioxide? How does your body get rid of carbon dioxide?

3. **Sequence** What is the order of structures that oxygen passes through between your nose and bloodstream?

134

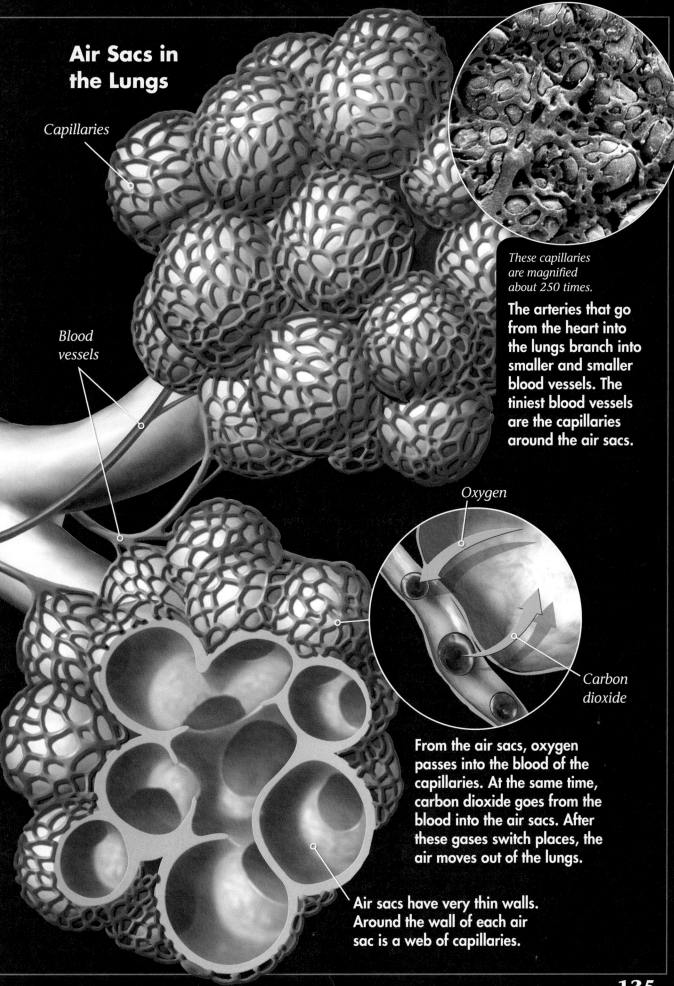

Air Sacs in the Lungs

Capillaries

Blood vessels

These capillaries are magnified about 250 times.

The arteries that go from the heart into the lungs branch into smaller and smaller blood vessels. The tiniest blood vessels are the capillaries around the air sacs.

Oxygen

Carbon dioxide

From the air sacs, oxygen passes into the blood of the capillaries. At the same time, carbon dioxide goes from the blood into the air sacs. After these gases switch places, the air moves out of the lungs.

Air sacs have very thin walls. Around the wall of each air sac is a web of capillaries.

135

Lesson 3

What are the digestive and urinary systems?

When you eat, food passes through many organs. Each organ has structures to help it do its job in the digestive system.

Digestive System

Food must be changed before your cells use it. **Digestion** is a process that changes food into forms that the body can use. During digestion, food is broken down into very small materials. Then the food can be carried in blood to your cells. Many organs work together to help you digest food. Each organ has structures that help it do its job.

The Mouth and Esophagus

Digestion starts in the mouth. When you chew, you make food small enough to swallow. Chewing also makes the job of the rest of the digestive system easier.

The **esophagus** is a tube that carries food to the stomach. Gravity does not move food to the stomach. The esophagus moves the food by squeezing rings of muscle in a pattern. Muscles behind the food contract as the lump of food passes each ring of muscle. This pushes the food through the esophagus to the stomach in about two or three seconds.

1. ✓**Checkpoint** What is the job of the saliva?

2. ✏ **Writing in Science** **Expository** A friend doesn't understand how he can swallow if he is upside-down. He says that gravity should keep the food in his mouth. Write an explanation to your friend telling how swallowing upside-down is possible.

Taste bud

Surface of tongue magnified many hundreds of times

Tongue
The tongue does more than just help you taste food. The tongue moves food so it can be chewed. It also moves food to the back of the mouth where it is swallowed. Tiny taste buds on your tongue have special nerves in them.

Standards Focus 5LS2.0 Plants and animals have structures for respiration, digestion, waste disposal, and transport of materials. As a basis for understanding this concept:
5LS2.a Students know many multicellular organisms have specialized structures to support the transport of materials.
5LS2.c Students know the sequential steps of digestion and the roles of teeth and the mouth, esophagus, stomach, small intestine, large intestine, and colon in the function of the digestive system.
5LS2.d Students know the role of the kidney in removing cellular waste from blood and converting it into urine, which is stored in the bladder.

The Digestive System

Teeth
Most adults will have as many as 32 teeth. Front teeth have a thin shape to cut food when you bite. Flatter teeth in the back of the mouth crush food as you chew. Teeth are not simply rocklike structures. They contain live cells, blood vessels, and nerves.

Salivary glands
Salivary glands make saliva. Saliva has chemicals that digest food. The water added in saliva also makes food easier to swallow.

Epiglottis
The epiglottis moves to cover your trachea when you swallow. This prevents food from going into the lungs. It makes food go down the esophagus.

Surface of esophagus magnified many hundreds of times

Esophagus
The surface of the esophagus is covered with tiny ridges.

Trachea

DIGITAL

NSTA SciLinks

keyword: **digestion** code: gr5p136

Stomach

There is a tight round muscle at the bottom of your esophagus. When you swallow, this muscle relaxes and opens to let food into your stomach. The muscle then closes to keep the food from moving back into your esophagus.

Your stomach is under your ribs on the lower left. The stomach's walls can stretch to store all of the food from a meal. The stomach releases acids that help break down food. As strong muscles in the stomach walls squeeze, the food and acids mix. The mixture becomes a soupy paste and is now ready to leave the stomach.

Intestines

Partly digested food is squeezed from the stomach into the small intestine. The **small intestine** is a narrow, winding tube. Here, food is made less acidic and broken down into small particles that the blood can absorb. Muscles of the small intestine move food in one direction. Your liver and pancreas are organs that send chemicals to the small intestine to help you digest food.

When digestion is finished, some food particles move into blood vessels in the walls of the small intestine. Tiny finger-shaped structures called villi cover the walls of the small intestine. Villi give the small intestine more surface area to absorb food.

Food that cannot be digested in the small intestine moves into a wider tube called the large intestine, often called the colon. Sections of the **large intestine** perform different jobs. One part recovers some water from the indigestible parts of food. Another part stores this waste until it is removed from the body.

The Stomach

Small intestine

Villi
The villi seen in this magnified picture are actually about one millimeter tall. Beneath the villi's thin walls is a web of capillaries. Why do you think it is helpful to have capillaries here?

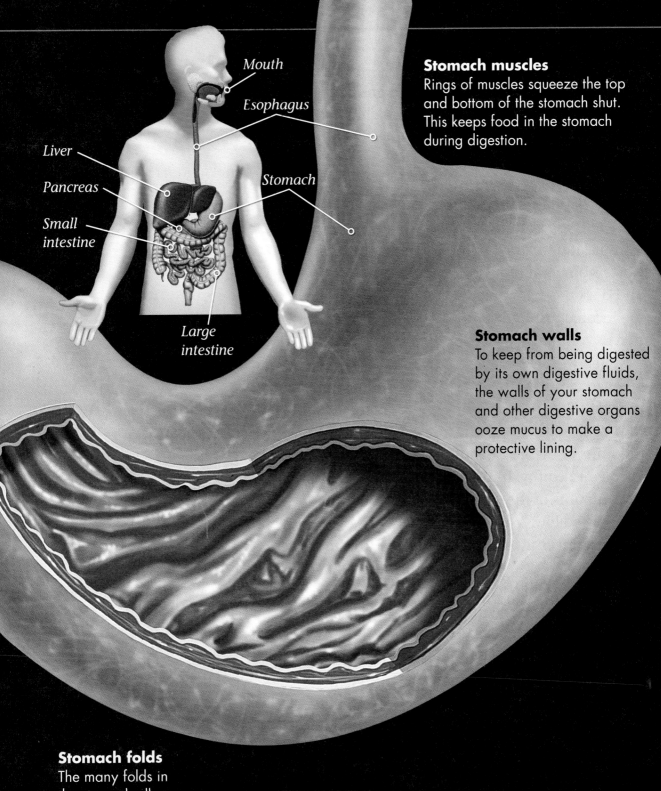

Mouth

Esophagus

Liver

Pancreas

Small
intestine

Stomach

Large
intestine

Stomach muscles
Rings of muscles squeeze the top
and bottom of the stomach shut.
This keeps food in the stomach
during digestion.

Stomach walls
To keep from being digested
by its own digestive fluids,
the walls of your stomach
and other digestive organs
ooze mucus to make a
protective lining.

Stomach folds
The many folds in
the stomach allow
it to expand when
you eat a big meal.

1. **✓Checkpoint** What parts of the structure of the small
intestine are specially shaped to help the intestine do its job?

2. **Writing in Science** **Narrative** Write a story from
the perspective of a berry that is being eaten. This berry is
writing to tell other berries what to expect when they travel
through the digestive system. Use all of these words in the
correct sequence: *colon, esophagus, large intestine, mouth,
small intestine, stomach, teeth.*

139

The Urinary System

Your body cells make wastes that enter your blood. These molecules of wastes cannot be changed into other compounds. They can poison your body. In fact, you could not live for long if your body did not get rid of these wastes. For this reason, organisms have structures that remove waste from the blood. In your body, this job is done mostly by the urinary system.

Your kidneys are a pair of organs that remove waste from your blood. Kidneys have the shape and dark red color of kidney beans. Your kidneys are located just under your lowest ribs on either side of your backbone.

When wastes are filtered out of the blood, many other materials also leave the blood. These materials include salt, calcium, nutrients, and other chemicals that your body needs. The kidneys put the right amounts of these materials back into your blood to keep you healthy. In this way, the kidneys help keep the amounts of these materials from getting too high or too low.

The kidneys take out some water with the wastes. This mix of wastes and water is urine. A tube carries urine away from each kidney to the urinary bladder. The **bladder** is a sac that collects and stores urine formed by the kidneys. At the bottom of the bladder is a tight round muscle that keeps urine inside until it is removed from the body by urination.

The kidneys are not the only organs that get rid of your cells' wastes. Remember that carbon dioxide is a waste product removed by the lungs. Sweat glands in the skin also release a small amount of waste in sweat.

Other organisms have different structures for removing wastes. For example, plants store wastes in a large central vacuole in each plant cell. The vacuole is like a garbage dump that is filled gradually as the cell ages.

Urinary System

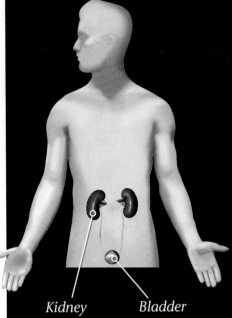

Kidney   *Bladder*

Blood filters
Blood passes through this part of the kidney. These ball-shaped structures filter wastes out of the blood and into the attached tube. The tube puts some materials back into the blood. The wastes left in the tube then drain out of the kidney.

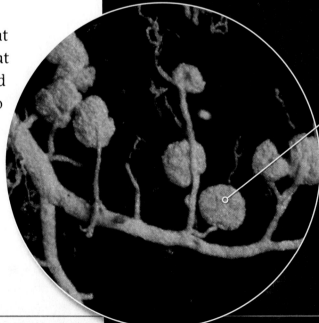

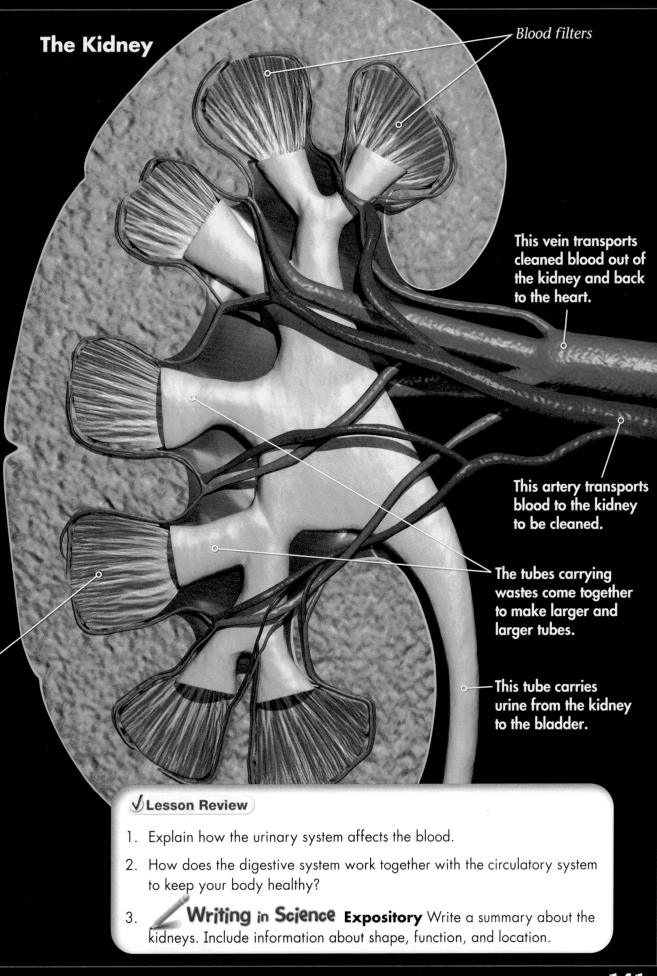

The Kidney

Blood filters

This vein transports cleaned blood out of the kidney and back to the heart.

This artery transports blood to the kidney to be cleaned.

The tubes carrying wastes come together to make larger and larger tubes.

This tube carries urine from the kidney to the bladder.

✓ Lesson Review

1. Explain how the urinary system affects the blood.

2. How does the digestive system work together with the circulatory system to keep your body healthy?

3. **Writing in Science** **Expository** Write a summary about the kidneys. Include information about shape, function, and location.

Making and Using a Graph

Your heart muscles work your entire life without stopping, pumping blood to the entire body. With each heartbeat, your heart muscles push blood out into blood vessels. You can feel these pushes as a pulse at certain points in the body.

Scientists make graphs to visualize data. Visualizing data can help you make inferences.

A bar graph has several parts. A graph needs a title so you know what kind of data is presented. A bar graph has two axes. In the graph on this page, the vertical axis shows how many times each organism's heart beats in one minute. The different organisms are listed along the horizontal axis.

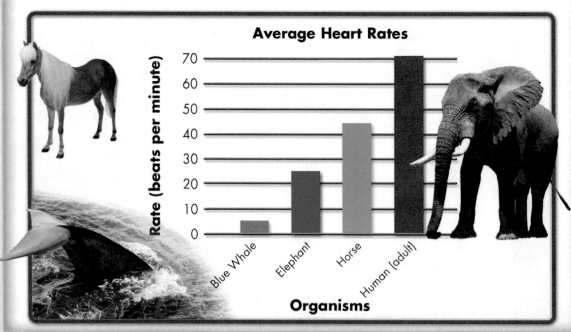

Average Heart Rates

1 Look at the chart and bar graph on page 142. How does the heart rate of human adults compare to the heart rate of the other organisms?

2 Which of the following can you infer using this graph?
   A. The larger the organism, the faster the heart rate.
   B. The larger the organism, the slower the heart rate.
   C. Size and heart rate do not have any relationship.
   D. Small organisms have a slightly slower heart rate than larger organisms.

3 Use the information in the chart below to make a bar graph. Remember to include a title and axis labels.

Organisms	Heart Rates
Dog	115
Rabbit	205
Chicken (adult)	300

Lab zone **Take-Home Activity**

Use a clock that has a second hand, and count your pulse for 20 seconds. Multiply this number by 3 to calculate your resting heart rate. Try different activities, such as walking, running, or bicycling for one minute. Calculate your heart rate after each activity. Record your results in a bar graph.

Investigate What is your lung capacity?

When you breathe, your lungs exchange oxygen in the air for carbon dioxide. How much air can you blow out? The amount varies with age, body size, and level of fitness. In this activity you can measure the amount in a simple way.

Materials

safety goggles

trash bag

tape

graduated cylinder with bubble solution

straws

metric ruler

Process Skills

You can make **inferences** about the data in a bar graph.

What to Do

1 Tape the trash bag over the top of a desk. Pour 50 mL of bubble solution onto the bag.

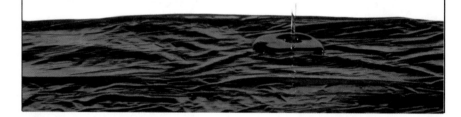

2 Spread the solution around on the bag with your hand. Dip a straw in the jar of bubble solution. Touch the straw to the solution on the bag. Take a deep breath and slowly blow as much breath as you can into the straw. **Observe** a bubble forming.

Be careful!

Do not inhale through the straw! Wear safety goggles.

5LS2.b Students know how blood circulates through the heart chambers, lungs, and body and how carbon dioxide (CO_2) and oxygen (O_2) are exchanged in the lungs and tissues. **5IE6.f** Select appropriate tools (e.g., thermometers, metersticks, balances, and graduated cylinders) and make quantitative observations.
5IE6.g Record data by using appropriate graphic representations (including charts, graphs, and labeled diagrams) and make inferences based on those data.
5IE6.h Draw conclusions from scientific evidence and indicate whether further information is needed to support a specific conclusion. (Also **5IE6.c**)

Diameter of Ring (centimeters)	Lung Capacity (liters)
14	0.7
15	0.9
16	1.1
17	1.3
18	1.5
19	1.8
20	2.1
21	2.4
22	2.8
23	3.2

3 Let the bubble burst. Measure the diameter of the ring left on the bag. Record. Use the chart to estimate the amount of air you exhaled.

4 Make a bar graph of the lung capacities of all the students in your class.

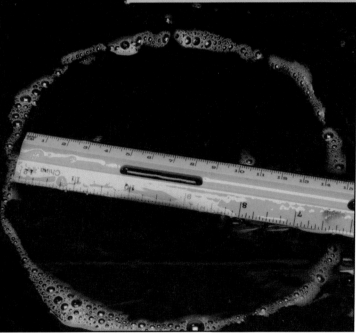

Graph axis:
Number of Students (y-axis: 0 to 15)
Lung Capacity (liters) (x-axis: 0–1, 1–2, 2–3, 3–4)

Explain Your Results

1. Make an **inference** using the data in your bar graph. State your conclusion.

2. Examine your conclusion. Do you have enough information to make this conclusion? What else would you need to know? How would you gather this information?

Go Further

Does posture affect how much air you can breathe in and out? Make and carry out a plan to investigate this or another question.

Focus on the BIG Idea

The systems in your body help keep you alive by transporting sugar and oxygen to your cells, and removing wastes and carbon dioxide.

Lesson 1

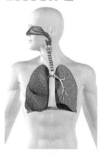

How does blood circulate?

- The circulatory system moves blood through the body. It includes the heart, the blood, and the blood vessels.
- Blood from the heart is pumped to the lungs, where it picks up oxygen and gives up carbon dioxide. The oxygen-rich blood then returns to the heart to be pumped through the body through arteries and capillaries.

Lesson 2

What is the respiratory system?

- The respiratory system carries gases between the air and the blood. It includes the nose and mouth, trachea, bronchi, and the bronchioles and air sacs in the lungs.
- The respiratory and circulatory systems work together to provide cells with the materials they need for cellular respiration.

Lesson 3

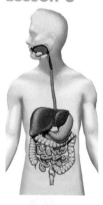

What are the digestive and urinary systems?

- The digestive system changes food into forms the body can use. The digestive system includes the mouth, esophagus, stomach, small intestine, large intestine, and colon.
- The urinary system is the body system that removes wastes from the body. The kidneys, bladder, and tubes that carry urine to and away from the bladder make up the urinary system.

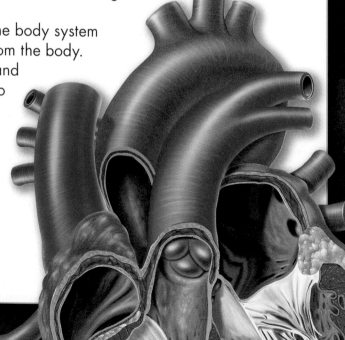

Cross-Curricular Links

English–Language Arts

Building Vocabulary

Look again at pages 114–115. Identify the pictures behind the terms *digestion*, *small intestine*, and *large intestine*. Write a paragraph about each term. Tell how each term relates to the picture and to the other terms.

Mathematics

How Much Blood?

A person is born with about 0.25 liters of blood. An adult has about 20 times this amount. About how much blood does an adult have?

Health

Exercise!

Using what you have learned about the needs of cells, why do you suppose your heart rate and breathing rate increase when you exercise?

Challenge!

English–Language Arts

Digestion

Are different types of food digested differently? Use research materials to find out. Then write a story describing what happens to a meal as it passes through the digestive system.

Chapter 4 Review/Test

Use Vocabulary

air sacs (p. 132)	**esophagus** (p. 136)
artery (p. 128)	
bladder (p. 140)	**large intestine** (p. 138)
bronchiole (p. 132)	**small intestine** (p. 138)
capillary (p. 128)	**trachea** (p. 132)
digestion (p. 136)	**vein** (p. 128)

Fill in the blanks with the correct vocabulary terms. If you have trouble answering a question, read the listed page again.

1. The tube that carries air inside a lung is the ____.

2. The large tube that moves air from the larynx to the bronchi is the ____.

3. Food is moved from the mouth to the stomach by the ____.

4. A(n) ____ carries blood from the heart to the body.

5. Food leaving the stomach moves into the ____.

6. A sac that collects and stores urine after it is filtered by the kidneys is the ____.

7. The process by which the body breaks food down into usable forms is ____.

8. The parts in the lungs where oxygen enters the blood are the ____.

Think About It

9. How do the digestive and circulatory systems work together to provide your cells with the materials they need?

10. **Process Skills** **Communicate** Think about the systems in an insect or worm. Explain how cells in your body benefit from having different systems work together.

11. **Sequence** Make a graphic organizer like the one shown below. In the boxes, write in order the parts of the respiratory system through which inhaled air passes. Use the terms in the list below.

Bronchioles
Bronchi
Trachea
Nose
Air sacs
Larynx

12. **Writing in Science**
Descriptive Write a description of how the structure of the villi helps them do their job in the digestive system.

California Standards Practice

Write the letter of the correct answer.

13. Which body systems help to exchange oxygen and carbon dioxide?

A respiratory and digestive

B circulatory and digestive

C respiratory and circulatory

D digestive and urinary

14. Which organ removes wastes from blood?

A heart

B stomach

C large intestine

D kidney

15. Which of the following is true about the heart?

A The right ventricle sends blood to the brain.

B The left ventricle receives oxygen-poor blood from the body.

C The heart pumps slower when you exercise.

D The left side of the heart pumps blood to the body.

16. Which body system transports needed materials to cells and carries cell wastes away from cells?

A circulatory system

B digestive system

C urinary system

D respiratory system

17. Which vessels carry blood from the body toward the heart?

A arteries   C bronchi

B veins   D valves

18. Which body system includes the kidneys and bladder?

A circulatory system

B digestive system

C urinary system

D respiratory system

19. In the human body, carbon dioxide moves

A from the lungs to the blood.

B from the blood to the body's cells.

C from the lungs to the body's cells.

D from the blood to the air sacs.

20. What is the function of the organ system shown in the drawing?

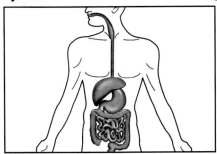

A remove wastes from the body

B move oxygen into the lungs

C break food down into forms the body can use

D transport materials needed by the body to the cells

The Human Body in Space

Your body systems are used to the tug of Earth's gravity. When astronauts don't feel the pull of gravity, their bodies start to change. NASA is concerned about these changes because astronauts spend weeks and months at work in the International Space Station.

Since the astronauts' bodies do not have to push and pull against gravity, their bones and muscles get weaker. After very long stays in space, they can get very weak. Some astronauts have a hard time walking when they return to Earth.

Astronauts' hearts also get weaker. This happens for two reasons. Since the astronauts' bodies are not working hard, their hearts do not have to pump hard. Also, as the astronauts adapt to space travel, the amount of blood in their body decreases. Therefore, there is less blood for the heart to pump, and the heart does not have to work as hard as on Earth. It slowly becomes weaker.

Standards Focus 5LS2.b Students know how blood circulates through the heart chambers, lungs, and body and how carbon dioxide (CO_2) and oxygen (O_2) are exchanged in the lungs and tissues.

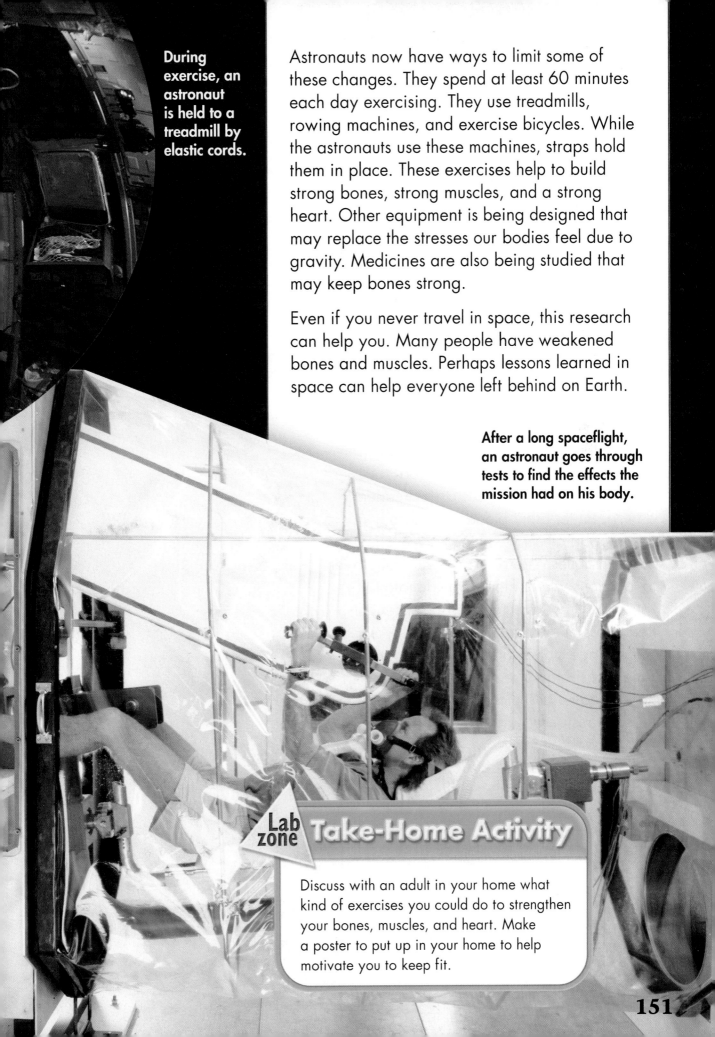

During exercise, an astronaut is held to a treadmill by elastic cords.

Astronauts now have ways to limit some of these changes. They spend at least 60 minutes each day exercising. They use treadmills, rowing machines, and exercise bicycles. While the astronauts use these machines, straps hold them in place. These exercises help to build strong bones, strong muscles, and a strong heart. Other equipment is being designed that may replace the stresses our bodies feel due to gravity. Medicines are also being studied that may keep bones strong.

Even if you never travel in space, this research can help you. Many people have weakened bones and muscles. Perhaps lessons learned in space can help everyone left behind on Earth.

After a long spaceflight, an astronaut goes through tests to find the effects the mission had on his body.

Lab zone Take-Home Activity

Discuss with an adult in your home what kind of exercises you could do to strengthen your bones, muscles, and heart. Make a poster to put up in your home to help motivate you to keep fit.

Charles Drew

Around the world, many people owe their lives to the work of Dr. Charles Drew. He found ways of preserving blood in blood banks.

After graduating from medical school, Dr. Drew became interested in studying blood. In particular, he studied the problem of storing blood. Healthy people gave their blood to be stored until a patient needed it. The problem was that blood spoiled in a matter of days. Dr. Drew learned that plasma could be stored longer than whole blood and could sometimes be given to a patient instead of whole blood.

During World War II, Dr. Drew headed a program that sent blood and plasma to Great Britain. It was his idea to have "bloodmobiles"—refrigerated trucks that went to locations where blood was donated. Later, Dr. Drew directed the first American Red Cross Blood Bank.

A postage stamp, part of the "Great Americans" stamp series, had his name and picture. Indeed, this great African American helped save millions of lives.

Lab zone Take-Home Activity

Make a poster persuading more adults to donate blood. Go to your local public library or other public building and see if they have a community bulletin board where you could hang your poster.

Unit B Summary

Chapter 3

How do cells help an organism?

- Cells deep inside multicellular organisms have needs for food and oxygen and, in animals, to have wastes removed.
- Vascular plants have xylem and phloem tissue to transport nutrients. Xylem transports water and minerals from roots to the leaves. Phloem transports sugar made in the leaves to the roots.
- Chlorophyll in plant cells is used during photosynthesis, along with energy from the Sun, carbon dioxide, and water. Photosynthesis produces sugar and oxygen.
- Plant and animal cells use sugar and oxygen to gain energy. This process, called cellular respiration, results in water and carbon dioxide.

Chapter 4

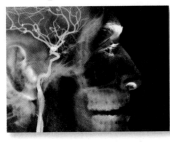

How do the systems in your body help keep you alive?

- The circulatory system moves material around the body.
- Oxygen-poor blood flows in veins into the right side of the heart. This blood is sent to the lungs, where it gets rid of carbon dioxide and receives oxygen. This oxygen-rich blood goes to the left side of the heart. It is then pumped through arteries to the rest of the body.
- The digestive system, including the mouth, esophagus, stomach, small intestine, large intestine, and colon, breaks down food into materials cells can use.
- Kidneys filter wastes from blood. Combined with water, these wastes make up urine. Urine is stored in the bladder until it is removed by urination.

Be careful!

Let your teacher know if you have trouble exercising because of a health condition.

Experiment How does exercise affect heart rate?

Materials

timer or clock with a second hand

Ask a question.

How does running affect heart rate?

State a hypothesis.

If a person exercises, then will the person's heart rate increase, decrease, or stay about the same?

Identify and control variables.

Exercise is the **variable** you change. The variable that you **observe** and **measure** is heart rate. Everything else must be **controlled,** or kept the same. Make sure you measure your heart rate for the same amount of time before and after running.

Process Skills

An **experiment** begins with a testable question.

DIGITAL

Lab zone

5LS2.b Students know how blood circulates through the heart chambers, lungs, and body and how carbon dioxide (CO_2) and oxygen (O_2) are exchanged in the lungs and tissues. **5IE6.0** Scientific progress is made by asking meaningful questions and conducting careful investigations. As a basis for understanding this concept and addressing the content in the other three strands, students should develop their own questions and perform investigations. **5IE6.b** Develop a testable question. **5IE6.d** Identify the dependent and controlled variables in an investigation. **5IE6.e** Identify a single independent variable in a scientific investigation and explain how this variable can be used to collect information to answer a question about the results of the experiment. **5IE6.g** Record data by using appropriate graphic representations (including charts, graphs, and labeled diagrams) and make inferences based on those data. (Also **5IE6.c, 5IE6.f, 5IE6.h**)

Variables

An *independent variable* is what you change in an experiment.

A *dependent variable* is what you measure or observe.

A *controlled variable* is what *could be* changed but must not be changed for the experiment to be a fair test.

What is the independent variable?

What is the dependent variable?

What is one controlled variable?

How does identifying a single independent variable help you collect information to answer questions about the results of your experiment?

Test your hypothesis.

1 Before beginning, practice finding your pulse.
Place 2 fingers lightly on the inside of your wrist.

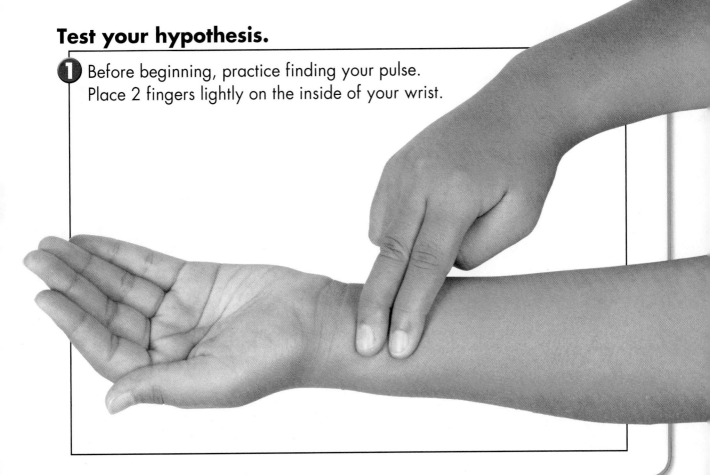

2 Sit quietly. Measure your heart rate by taking your pulse for 30 seconds. Have a member of your group keep track of the time.

3 Run in place for one minute. Have a member of your group keep track of the time.

4 Measure your heart rate for 30 seconds again. Have a member of your group keep track of the time.

5 Repeat for each member of your group.

Collect and record data.

Record your heart rate while sitting and after exercise. Share with other groups. Record data on all students in your class.

Student	Before Exercise		After Exercise	
	Number of Beats in 30 Seconds	*Pulse (beats per minute)	Number of Beats in 30 Seconds	*Pulse (beats per minute)
Student 1				
Student 2				

*Pulse = 2 × Number of Beats in 30 Seconds

Interpret your data.

Make and use graphs to help you interpret and **make inferences** based on your data.

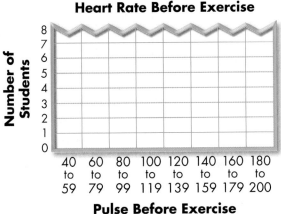

Heart Rate Before Exercise

Number of Students

8 7 6 5 4 3 2 1 0

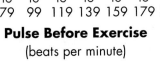

40 to 59   60 to 79   80 to 99   100 to 119   120 to 139   140 to 159   160 to 179   180 to 200

Pulse Before Exercise
(beats per minute)

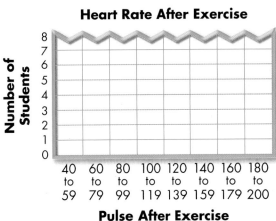

Heart Rate After Exercise

Number of Students

8 7 6 5 4 3 2 1 0

40 to 59   60 to 79   80 to 99   100 to 119   120 to 139   140 to 159   160 to 179   180 to 200

Pulse After Exercise
(beats per minute)

State your conclusion.

Compare your results and hypothesis. Make an **inference** based on your data. How does exercise affect your heart rate? **Communicate** your conclusion.

Go Further

Predict How might exercising for more than one minute affect your heart rate? Use this question or develop another testable question. Plan and conduct a simple investigation. Write instructions others could follow.

157

Make a Concept Map

Review the roles of the digestive, respiratory, and circulatory systems. Make a table that lists the main organs of each system and their jobs. Then use the information from your table to make a concept map for each body system that traces the movement of materials (food, oxygen, carbon dioxide, and blood) through the organs in each system.

Classify Objects in Nature

Take a walk around your neighborhood and look at the different plants that grow there. Photograph or make drawings of at least ten plants. For each plant you observe, take notes describing the shape of its leaves, whether its stem is woody, and whether the plant has flowers. Use your notes and pictures to classify the plants you observe into groups with similar characteristics. Try repeating this activity with other objects in nature, such as rocks.

Write a Story

Write a story from the perspective of an oxygen atom that is moving through the environment in the oxygen-carbon dioxide cycle. The atom should tell other oxygen atoms what to expect as they take part in cellular respiration and photosynthesis. As you write your story, remember to:

- Establish a plot, point of view, setting, and conflict
- Show, rather than tell, the events of the story

carbon dioxide molecule

Read More About Life Sciences

Look for other books about Life Sciences in the library-media center. Here is one you may want to read.

Guts: Our Digestive System
by Seymour Simon

Have you ever wondered how the foods you eat travel through your digestive system? How does your body turn food into nutrients for your body? In this book, Seymour Simon describes the journey through your digestive system and how it is sometimes affected when you are sick. The colorful pictures show the organs in your digestive system and how they move food through your body.

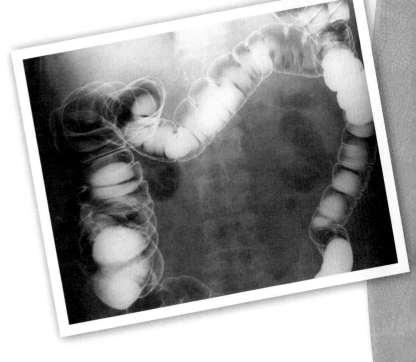

Science Fair Projects

How can you estimate a cell's size?

You can estimate the size of a plant cell by comparing it to the width of your hair.

Idea: Prepare a microscope slide with a piece of your hair and a moss leaf. Using a microscope, locate the hair and moss cells. Find out how many moss cells can fit across the width of your hair. A strand of hair is about 0.1 mm wide. Use this information to estimate how large the moss cells are.

How do fertilizers affect plant growth?

You have read that plants make their own food through photosynthesis. If this is true, what do fertilizers provide to plants? Do fertilizers improve plant growth?

Idea: Do research to find out what substances fertilizers provide to plants. State a hypothesis about how fertilizers affect plant growth. Then design an experiment to test your hypothesis.

How does exercise affect respiratory rate?

When you inhale, you bring oxygen into your body. During cellular respiration, your body uses this oxygen to provide your cells with energy.

Idea: Your respiratory rate is a measure of how many times you inhale per minute. Investigate how exercise affects your respiratory rate.

Using Scientific Methods

1. Ask a question.
2. State a hypothesis.
3. Identify and control variables.
4. Test your hypothesis.
5. Collect and record your data.
6. Interpret your data.
7. State your conclusion.
8. Go further.

Unit B California Standards Practice

Write the letter of the correct answer.

1. **What are the basic building blocks of all living things?**
   A cells
   B organs
   C organ systems
   D tissues

2. **In humans, what cells are responsible for carrying oxygen to all parts of the body and carrying away carbon dioxide?**
   A nerve cells
   B blood cells
   C skin cells
   D xylem cells

3. **In most plants, what system carries water, food, and minerals?**
   A digestive system
   B respiratory system
   C urinary system
   D vascular system

4. **To what human body system do the organs shown belong?**

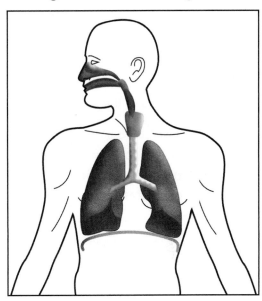

   A digestive system
   B respiratory system
   C urinary system
   D vascular system

5. **What structures of the circulatory system carry blood containing carbon dioxide from the body back to the heart?**
   A air sacs
   B arteries
   C capillaries
   D veins

Unit B California Standards Practice

6. **What happens to blood containing wastes and carbon dioxide from cells after it returns to the heart?**

    A It is pumped back to the body.

    B It is pumped to the lungs.

    C It remains in the heart.

    D It is pumped to the stomach.

7. **Which of the following correctly traces the path of food through the digestive system?**

    A esophagus, mouth, stomach, large intestine, small intestine

    B esophagus, small intestine, stomach, large intestine

    C mouth, esophagus, stomach, small intestine, large intestine

    D mouth, stomach, large intestine, esophagus, small intestine

8. **Which part of the digestive system collects and stores indigestible parts of food until they are removed from the body?**

    A large intestine

    B liver

    C small intestine

    D stomach

9. **Which structure shown in the diagram is the esophagus?**

    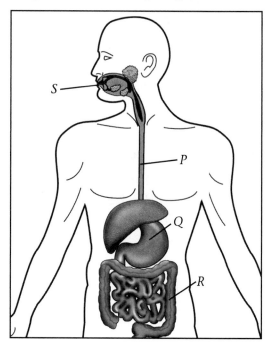

    A structure P

    B structure Q

    C structure R

    D structure S

10. **In what part of the human body are cellular wastes filtered from the blood?**

    A bladder

    B colon

    C kidneys

    D small intestine

11. What part of a plant cell collects and stores wastes made by the plant?

A cell membrane

B cell wall

C cytoplasm

D vacuole

12. What organ of the body collects and stores the urine made by the kidneys until it can be removed from the body?

A air sacs

B bladder

C colon

D vacuole

13. What plant tissue is responsible for transporting water and minerals from the roots to the leaves of a vascular plant?

A chloroplast

B large intestine

C phloem

D xylem

14. Which term best completes the chart below?

Part of a Vascular Plant	Function
chloroplast	aids in photosynthesis
root	stores extra sugar and provides stability
phloem	?
cell wall	provides rigid support for plant cells

A stores wastes

B transports sugar from leaves to the rest of the plant

C aids in cellular respiration

D stores wastes

15. What process is summarized by the equation shown?

$$\text{Light Energy}$$
$$6CO_2 + 6H_2O \longrightarrow C_6H_{12}O_6 + 6O_2$$
$$\textbf{Chlorophyll}$$

A cellular respiration

B digestion

C photosynthesis

D circulation

16. Where does most photosynthesis take place in a plant?

A in the leaves

B in the roots

C in the stem

D in the vascular tissue

17. Which of the following gases do plants produce during photosynthesis?

A carbon dioxide

B hydrogen

C nitrogen

D oxygen

18. What process is summarized by the equation shown?

$$C_6H_{12}O_6 + 6O_2 \longrightarrow 6CO_2 + 6H_2O$$

A cellular respiration

B circulation

C digestion

D photosynthesis

19. Which process do living things use to release energy from food?

A cellular respiration

B decomposition

C photosynthesis

D urination

20. Which of the following gases do cells use in cellular respiration?

A carbon dioxide

B hydrogen

C oxygen

D water vapor

Earth Sciences

THE SAN JOSE/SANTA CLARA
Water Pollution
Control Plant

Alviso, California

As you get ready for school, you stand in the shower, washing your body and hair. The water swirls down the drain and you wonder: where does it go? In most cases, the water you use flows through pipes to a wastewater treatment plant. The San Jose/Santa Clara Water Pollution Control Plant in Alviso is one of California's largest wastewater treatment plants. It can treat 167 million gallons of wastewater each day!

Water that flows into the plant is first filtered to remove solid waste. The water flows into basins called clarifiers. Some solids float to the top of the clarifier. Other solids sink to the bottom of the water. These solids get separated from the water and sent to containers to be broken down by bacteria. The water may then flow through very small filters to remove harmful organisms. Most of the treated water flows into San Francisco Bay. Some is recycled and used in farming and industry.

Find Out More

Research to find out more about wastewater treatment plants in California.

- **Find out where wastewater in your community is treated. Share your findings with the class.**

- **If possible, arrange to take a tour of a local wastewater treatment plant. Learn about the methods used to separate wastes from the water. Write a report of your findings.**

Alviso

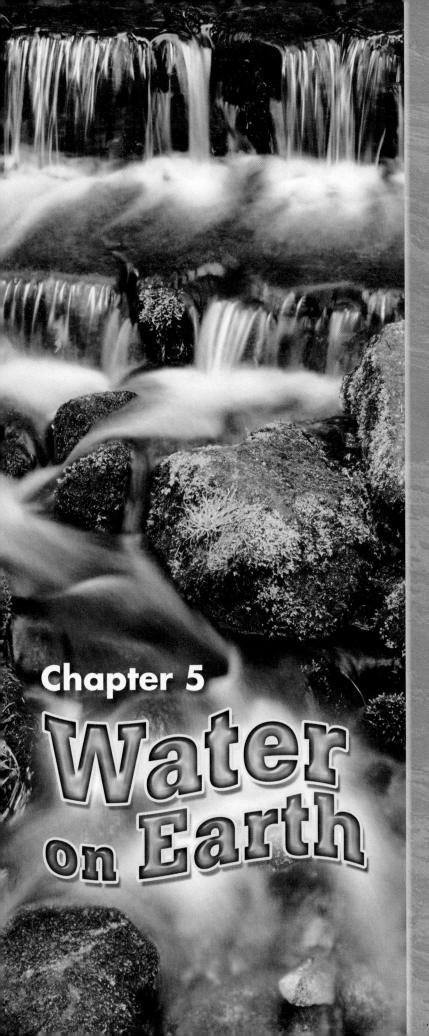

Chapter 5
Water on Earth

CALIFORNIA Standards Preview

5ES3.0 Water on Earth moves between the oceans and land through the processes of evaporation and condensation. As a basis for understanding this concept:

5ES3.a Students know most of Earth's water is present as salt water in the oceans, which cover most of Earth's surface.

5ES3.b Students know when liquid water evaporates, it turns into water vapor in the air and can reappear as a liquid when cooled or as a solid if cooled below the freezing point of water.

5ES3.c Students know water vapor in the air moves from one place to another and can form fog or clouds, which are tiny droplets of water or ice, and can fall to Earth as rain, hail, sleet, or snow.

5ES3.d Students know that the amount of fresh water located in the rivers, lakes, underground sources, and glaciers is limited and that its availability can be extended by recycling and decreasing the use of water.

5ES3.e Students know the origin of the water used by their local communities.

5ES4.0 Energy from the Sun heats Earth unevenly, causing air movements that result in changing weather patterns. As a basis for understanding this concept:

5ES4.b Students know the influence that the ocean has on the weather and the role that the water cycle plays in weather patterns.

5IE6.0 Scientific progress is made by asking meaningful questions and conducting careful investigations. As a basis for understanding this concept and addressing the content in the other three strands, students should develop their own questions and perform investigations. (Also **5IE6.f**, **5IE6.g**, **5IE6.h**)

Standards Focus Questions

- How can oceans be described?
- Where is fresh water found?
- What are some California water sources?
- What is the water cycle?
- How do clouds form?

Focus on the BIG Idea

How does water move through the environment?

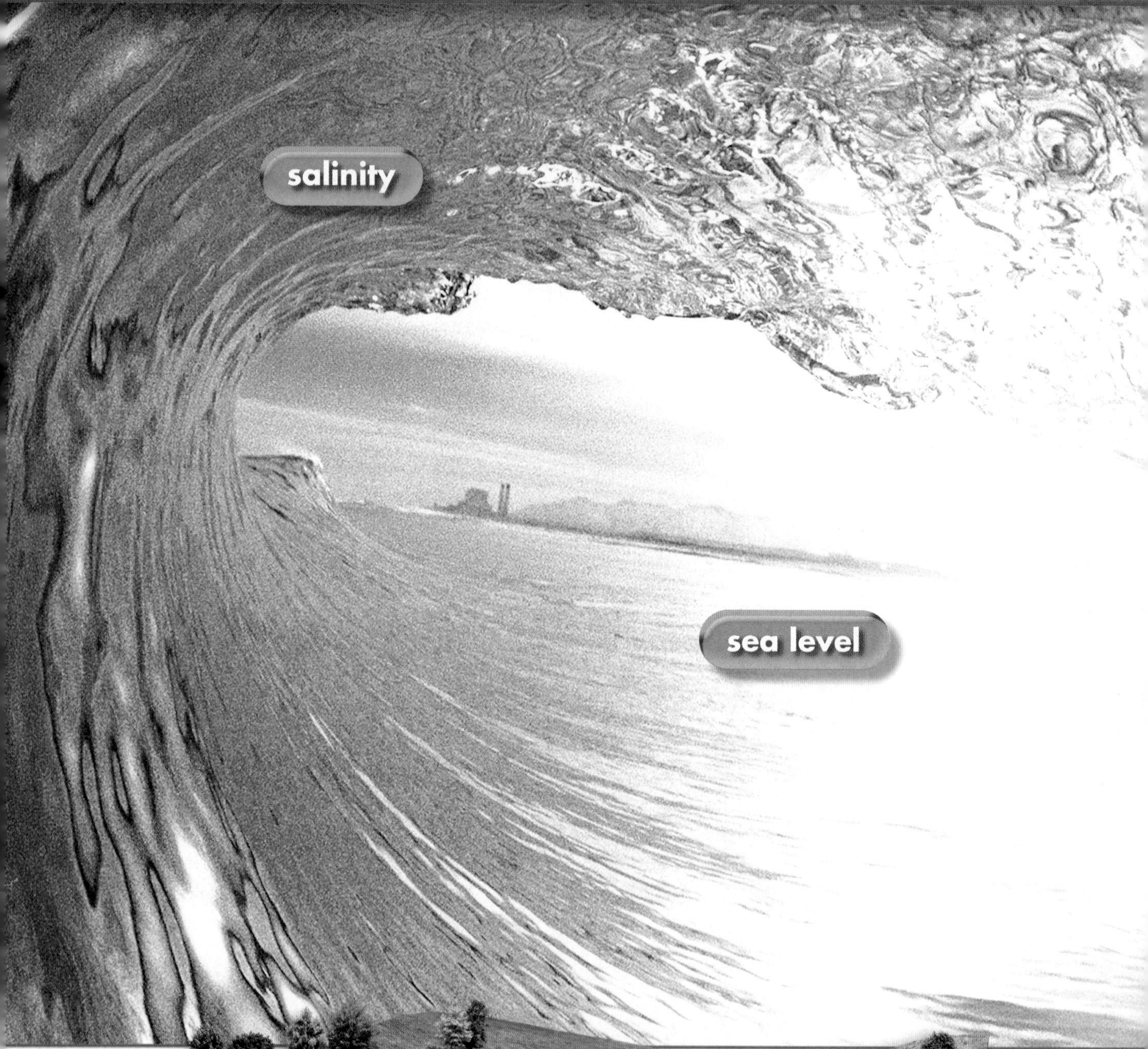
salinity
sea level

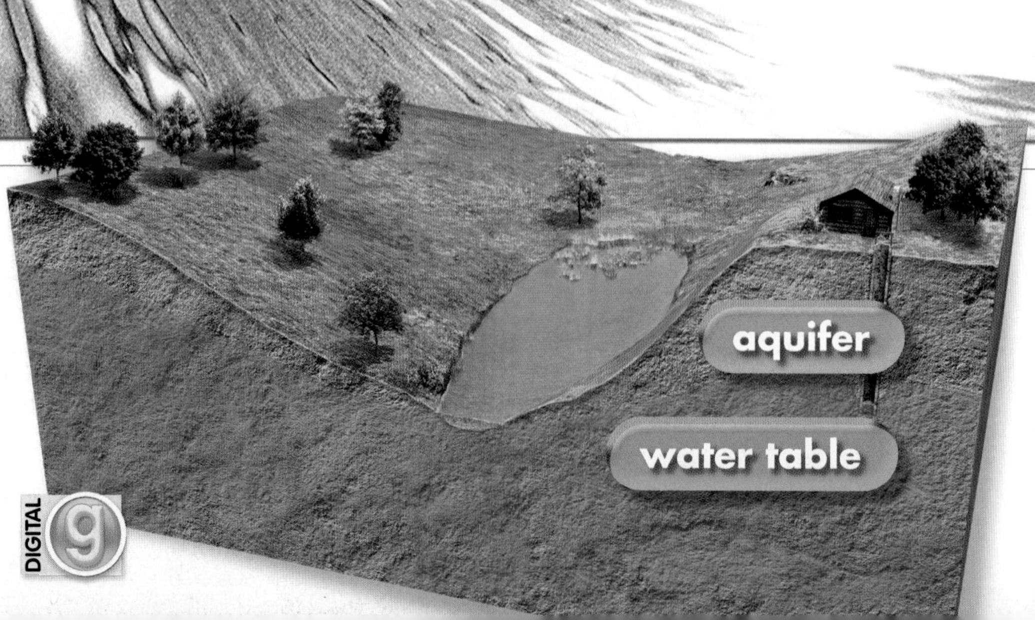
aquifer
water table

DIGITAL

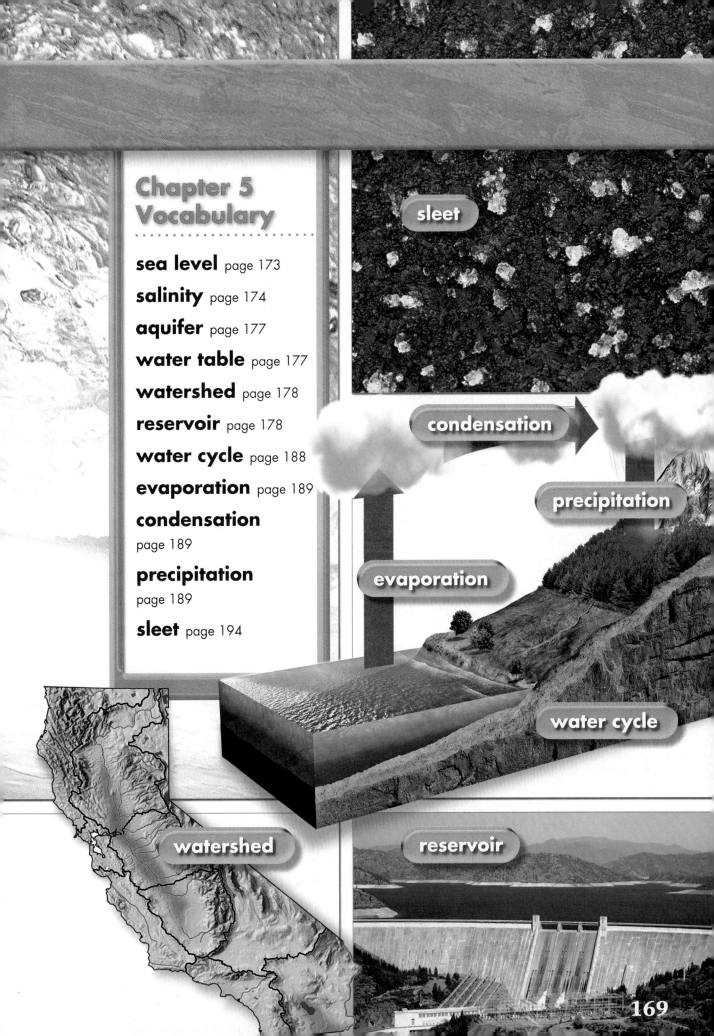

Chapter 5 Vocabulary

sleet

condensation

precipitation

evaporation

water cycle

watershed

reservoir

Explore Where is Earth's water?

Earth's Water	Amount of Water (total = 2200 mL)
Atmosphere (fresh water)	about $\frac{1}{2}$ drop
Lakes, rivers, streams (fresh water)	about 4 drops
Groundwater (fresh water)	13 mL
Icecaps and glaciers (fresh water)	47 mL
Oceans and seas (salt water)	2139 mL

Materials

2 L plastic bottle filled with water

4 cups

dropper and masking tape

funnel and graduated cylinder

What to Do

① Label the cups.

② Look at the chart. Find the amount of water shown for the atmosphere. Take out that much water from the bottle. Put it in the atmosphere cup.

Hold the bottle with both hands.

③ Repeat for the other places water is found. Select a tool to **measure** the water.

④ Label the bottle *salt water—oceans and seas.*

Explain Your Results

Infer based on your model, draw a conclusion about the need to conserve fresh water. Explain.

5ES3.a Students know most of Earth's water is present as salt water in the oceans, which cover most of Earth's surface. **5IE6.f** Select appropriate tools (e.g., thermometers, metersticks, balances, and graduated cylinders) and make quantitative observations. **5IE6.h** Draw conclusions from scientific evidence and indicate whether further information is needed to support a specific conclusion.

Process Skills

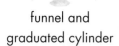

Conclusions often are based on **inferences.** Before you draw a conclusion, determine if you have enough information.

DIGITAL Lab zone

How to Read Science

Reading Skills

Main Idea and Details

Learning to find **main ideas** and **details** can help you understand and remember what you read. Details can help you to **infer** the main idea.

The main idea and the details are marked in the article below.

• Write down the main idea in your own words.

• Write down the details as sentences or as a list.

Science Article

Getting a Drink

Before the water you drink comes out of your tap, it needs to go through a treatment process. Depending on where you live, the water you drink can come from a well, a river, a lake, or another source. Water is collected from these sources, and in the case of surface sources, it gets pumped to a treatment plant. There, the water is treated with chemicals and filters to remove any pollutants that might be in it. The water is sent to a water tower and is then piped into homes and schools.

Apply It!

Make a graphic organizer like the one shown below. List the **main idea** and **details** from the article in your organizer.

```
┌─────────────────────────────────────────┐
│              Main Idea                   │
└─────────────────────────────────────────┘
     ↑            ↑              ↑
┌─────────┐  ┌─────────┐  ┌─────────┐
│ Detail  │  │ Detail  │  │ Detail  │
└─────────┘  └─────────┘  └─────────┘
```

You Are There!

On a warm summer day, you lie on a surfboard, enjoying the waves. Each time a large wave curls over you, the sunlight shines through the spray. You take a deep breath before the water crashes over you. A moment later you start paddling your board back to shore. You're happy that you live near the ocean and can have fun at the shore even if you can't drink the water. Why does the ocean water leave white grains on your skin?

Standards Focus 5ES3.a Students know most of Earth's water is present as salt water in the oceans, which cover most of Earth's surface

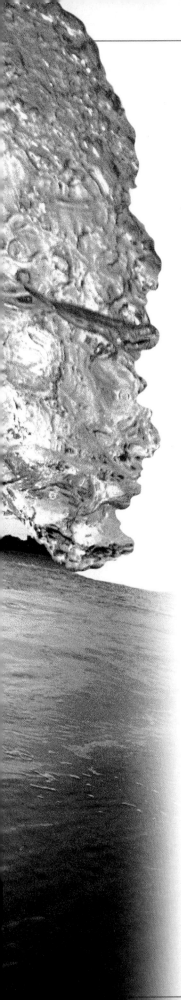

How can the oceans be described?

Earth is sometimes called the blue planet. It gets this name because it is covered mostly by water. Water makes Earth appear blue from space. Most of Earth's water is in its salty oceans.

The Hydrosphere

What body of water is closest to where you live? More than half the people in the United States live within 80 kilometers of an ocean. Many people live near other bodies of water, such as rivers and lakes. Bodies of water play a huge role in our lives. They give us a way to travel, places to catch food, and beautiful sights to visit. What are some ways that oceans or lakes have affected your life?

All of the waters of Earth make up the hydrosphere. Almost all of the hydrosphere is ocean water. Only $\frac{3}{100}$, or 3 percent, of the hydrosphere is in places other than the oceans. The hydrosphere covers three-fourths of Earth's surface. The Pacific Ocean is the largest ocean, followed by the Atlantic Ocean, the Indian Ocean, the Southern Ocean, and the Arctic Ocean. On a map or globe, you can see that the oceans are all connected.

The Pacific Ocean is both the largest and deepest ocean. Its average depth is about 4,000 meters. In its deepest place, it is more than 11,000 meters deep.

The oceans are all a bit different from one another. Some have more storms than others. Many properties of the water are different, such as the amount of salt in the water or the average temperature. Even **sea level,** the level of the ocean's surface, differs slightly from ocean to ocean.

1. **✓Checkpoint** How much of Earth's surface is covered by water?

2. List the oceans in order from smallest to largest.

Earth's Oceans

Have you ever had a taste of seawater while swimming in the ocean? If you have, you know that it tastes salty. Ocean water contains many kinds of salt. Ocean water not only tastes bad, it is also bad for your health if you drink too much of it.

The oceans get salt from rivers. Rain falls over the oceans and land. When rain falls over land, it dissolves salts and other minerals, which are then carried to the oceans by rivers. When water evaporates from the surface of the ocean, the dissolved salts are left behind in the ocean water.

Salinity is a measure of the amount of salt in water. Ocean water is saltier in some places than in others. Places where rivers pour fresh water into the ocean have low salinity. In warm, dry areas, ocean water evaporates fairly quickly. Salt is left behind, and the ocean water has higher salinity.

Cold, salty water is heavier than the same amount of water that is either warmer or has lower salinity. Look at the cups below. The blue water is at room temperature and holds one-half spoonful of salt. The red water is warm but has no salt. The clear water is cold and holds two spoonfuls of salt.

If drops of the blue water are added to the clear water, the blue water forms a layer on top of the clear water. The warmer blue water with lower salinity is lighter than the clear water. The red water is even warmer and has lower salinity, so it will form a layer on top of the blue water.

30 mL room-temperature water with blue food coloring and one-half spoonful of salt

blue water

30 mL warm water with red food coloring

red water

blue layer

30 mL cold water with 2 spoonfuls of salt

Salt is left behind when ocean water in these shallow ponds evaporates.

Ocean Temperatures

The temperature of ocean water differs from place to place. Ocean water near the equator is about 30°C. Near the poles, ocean water can be as cold as −2°C.

The temperature of ocean water does not only vary according to how close it is to the poles. Some currents carry warm water toward the poles. The Gulf Stream is such a current. It moves warm water from the Caribbean Sea to the North Atlantic Ocean. Other currents carry cold water toward the equator. The California Current carries cold water southward along the west coast of the United States. You will learn more about ocean currents in Chapter 6.

Ocean Resources

Much of the salt that people add to food comes from the ocean. One way to get this salt is by evaporating ocean water. People who process the salt allow ocean water to flow into shallow ponds. The water evaporates, and the salt is left.

Materials such as magnesium and drinking water also come from ocean water. Ocean water can be made drinkable by removing the salt. This process is expensive, so it is not done in many places.

The ocean is the source of many useful products. Do you like tuna fish? Tuna is just one of many foods that come from the ocean.

Ocean water near the mouth of the Nile River has less salinity than ocean water farther away.

✓ Lesson Review

1. How does salt get into the ocean?

2. **Writing in Science** Descriptive
   Suppose that you are on a raft in the ocean near an area where a river flows into it. Describe how the salinity of the water changes as you float away from the river.

175

Where is fresh water found?

Only $\frac{3}{100}$ of Earth's water is fresh water. This is the water that we use for drinking, cooking, and cleaning. We also use this water to grow crops, make electricity, and make many products.

Fresh Water

Drinking water is also called fresh water. Fresh water has some dissolved salts but much less than seawater. After playing hard on a warm day, a cool glass of fresh water can be very refreshing. Where does this fresh water come from?

Almost all of Earth's fresh water starts as rain or snow. Some of this fresh water sinks into the ground. Some collects in rivers and lakes. Some is frozen in ice sheets and glaciers.

Fresh water is not evenly spread over the world. Some places have much more fresh water than others. Some areas have more available fresh water in some seasons than in others. But no matter where you are, the amount of fresh water is limited. Water should be used wisely. The water supply can be extended by recycling or by using less water whenever possible.

Scientists can help communities use water wisely. The scientists can give people information about the location of underground water and about the water's quality. They can also provide technology that reduces the amount of water a community needs.

Some water falling on the ground seeps into spaces in the soil and rocks.

The water table is rarely level. It usually follows the slope of the land. It is higher beneath hills and lower in valleys.

Standards Focus 5ES3.d Students know that the amount of fresh water located in rivers, lakes, underground sources, and glaciers is limited and that its availability can be extended by recycling and decreasing the use of water. **5ES3.e** Students know the origin of the water used by their local communities.

Groundwater

Rain or melted snow that soaks into the ground is called groundwater. This water fills spaces between particles of soil and rock. Groundwater keeps sinking until it reaches a layer of rock or clay it cannot move through. Some layers of rock or clay act like a dam to keep the water from moving deeper. The water can slowly flow over these layers.

The layer of rock and soil that groundwater flows through is an **aquifer.** The top level of groundwater in an aquifer is the **water table.** The level of a water table changes during the year. It rises when water is added by rain or melting snow. It gets lower when there is a drought.

Many people get their water from wells that go into an aquifer. The water table gets lower if people pump water out of the aquifer faster than it is replaced. People must use groundwater wisely to keep aquifers from becoming dry.

If too much water is pumped out of an aquifer, the water table in the area will drop. That can cause lakes like this one to dry up and wells to go dry.

1. ✓**Checkpoint** Identify three places in which fresh water is found.

2. **Main Idea and Details** What is the main idea of the last paragraph on page 176? List some details that support the main idea.

Pollution from the surface can seep into the groundwater in the same way that rain does.

A lake, pond, stream, or swamp forms where the water table meets the surface.

The water table is lower in places where people are using groundwater from an aquifer faster than it can be refilled.

177

Rivers

Surface waters include rivers, streams, and lakes. Melting snow, rainwater, and groundwater all help form Earth's surface waters. Water from rain and melting snow flows downhill in small creeks. These small creeks join to form larger streams and rivers. Most rivers flow into the ocean. Groundwater also seeps into rivers. The area from which water drains into a river is called the river's **watershed.**

What happens on the land in a watershed can affect places far away. If chemicals or pollutants are placed in the watershed, they may be carried by water to rivers. Rainwater may erode soil from fields and construction sites. This soil can run into the rivers and cause changes to the ecosystems downstream. Many researchers are studying how these and other issues affect watersheds.

Lakes

Sometimes water flows into a place that is surrounded by higher land or blocked by a dam. Lakes form when the water collects in a low spot. A **reservoir** is usually an artificial lake that forms behind a dam.

Water that forms a lake is not trapped. Water can leave a lake by flowing into a river, seeping into the ground, or evaporating into the air.

This dam forms the Hetch Hetchy Reservoir in Yosemite National Park.

Map Fact

Rivers and creeks sometimes flow over cliffs, forming waterfalls. Yosemite National Park in central California has many waterfalls. Yosemite Falls is the fifth tallest falls in the world. It is about 739 meters high. Water usually starts to flow slowly over the falls in the autumn. As snow above the falls starts to melt in spring, the water comes roaring down.

Map Fact

This iceberg is floating in Disko Bay in Greenland. Only $\frac{1}{10}$ of the iceberg floats above the water. You cannot see the $\frac{9}{10}$ that is underwater.

Ice

About seven-tenths of Earth's fresh water is frozen into ice. Because most of Earth's fresh water is frozen and far from cities, it is hard for people to use.

Much of Earth's ice is on Greenland and Antarctica. In these places, huge ice sheets cover most of the land. The ice sheets are several kilometers thick in some places. The ice at the North Pole floats on the ocean. There is no land under it.

Glaciers

Smaller areas of ice are called glaciers. Valley glaciers are found in the valleys of high mountains. Valley glaciers are long stretches of ice that flow slowly downhill. As they flow, they scrape and move rock. This changes the shape of the valley bottom.

Glaciers and ice sheets form over time if snowfall is greater than the amount of snow that melts. The weight of new snow squeezes the snow underneath into ice.

In places where glaciers and ice sheets are in contact with the ocean, large pieces of ice can break off. These floating ice pieces are icebergs. One iceberg that broke off the Antarctic ice sheet was twice the area of the state of Rhode Island.

1. ✓ **Checkpoint** Where is most of Earth's fresh water located?

2. ✏️ **Writing in Science** **Persuasive**
Write a letter to the editor of a farm magazine encouraging farmers to keep rivers that flow through their farms clean. Explain how farmers' actions can affect many people.

179

Water Treatment Plant

Screens keep out large objects.

Chemicals are added to stick to pollutants.

The water and chemicals are mixed.

Heavy pollutants fall to the bottom of the settling tank.

Water flows through sand to filter small particles.

Getting Water to Homes

Does your town have a water tower? Do you know how water gets into the tower? A water tower is often the tallest structure in a small town. Water towers are only part of the system that gets water to homes and businesses.

Some towns in the United States get their water from groundwater. Other towns use surface waters as a source of fresh water. But surface water might have harmful bacteria. Because water easily dissolves many materials, it is easily polluted. Harmful chemicals that wash off farm fields, city streets, and even lawns can end up in rivers and lakes. Even groundwater may have pollutants. Because of these problems, water must be treated before it is used.

The process of treating water is shown in the diagram. First, water is pumped from a river or lake through screens to a tank in a treatment plant. Next, chemicals are added to the water. The chemicals cause small particles to stick together and form larger particles. The larger particles become heavy enough to sink to the bottom of the tank.

Pumping station

Chlorine, fluoride, or other chemicals may be added at the end of treatment.

The treated water is pumped to the top of a water tower.

Gravity pulls water down from the tank.

Water flows through pipes to homes and businesses in the community.

The water then passes through filters. Some filters are formed by layers of sand and gravel. These filters remove small particles that did not settle earlier.

After the filters remove harmful materials from water, more chemicals are added to the water. Many treatment plants add a small amount of chlorine to kill harmful bacteria. Other treatment plants use other ways to kill bacteria. Many towns add fluoride to water. This chemical helps your teeth resist decay. Water is then pumped to a water tower for storage.

As you can see, getting water to your home is not easy! This is why people should take care not to waste water. The chart on this page shows the average amount of water a person uses in a day. You will learn about conserving water in the next lesson.

Average Daily Water Use (Per Person)	
Toilet flush	71 L
Laundry	57 L
Shower/bath	49 L
Other	38 L

✓ Lesson Review

1. On an average day, how does a person use the most water?

2. Why does water need to be treated before it can be used?

Lesson 3

What are some California water sources?

Californians get fresh water from lakes, rivers, and groundwater. Because the amount of fresh water is limited, it is important to use water wisely.

This dam in northern California creates a reservoir of fresh water.

Snow melting off the Sierra Nevada provides drinking water to many Californians.

Too Much or Not Enough?

Does your town get plenty of rain? Or do you live in a dry area? Not all parts of California get the same amount of rain. In the northern coastal region of the state, about 250 centimeters of rain falls each year. In the same period, the deserts of southeastern California get only about 10 centimeters of rain. Because most fresh water starts as rain or snow, the supply of fresh water in southern California is very limited. This area uses about two-thirds of all the fresh water used in California. Getting enough water to meet the needs of all areas of California is a challenge.

Much of the water in California falls as snow in the winter. As temperatures rise in the spring, the snow melts to form fresh water. This water runs off the mountains to feed nearby streams and lakes. This water can be collected and transported to all parts of the state for use during the entire year.

Standards Focus 5ES3.d Students know that the amount of fresh water located in rivers, lakes, underground sources, and glaciers is limited and that its availability can be extended by recycling and decreasing the use of water. **5ES3.e** Students know the origin of the water used by their local communities.

Transporting Water Throughout California

Many Californians depend on aqueducts to bring them fresh water. An *aqueduct* is a system of pipes that carries water from a river or lake to the area where it is needed. The California Aqueduct carries fresh water from the mouth of the Sacramento River to people living more than 400 kilometers to the south.

The Los Angeles Aqueduct provides some of the fresh water used by the city of Los Angeles. The first part of the system was built about 100 years ago. It transports water from the Owens River on the east side of the Sierra Nevada to Los Angeles. Later, more pipes were added to get water from some streams that supplied Mono Lake. In 1970, a second aqueduct was added to the system.

The Colorado River Aqueduct provides much of San Diego's fresh water. This aqueduct begins at Lake Havasu at the border of Arizona and California. It carries water nearly 390 kilometers to Lake Mathews in Riverside County before it heads south to San Diego.

Aqueduct systems like this one carry fresh water from rivers and lakes to people living many kilometers away.

1. **✓Checkpoint** Why are aqueducts important to Californians?

2. **✏ Writing in Science** **Descriptive** Using library-media center resources, find out about the history of the Los Angeles Aqueduct and why it has been important to the growth of Los Angeles. Write a brief report of your findings.

Local Water Sources

You have learned that a watershed is the land that water flows across or under on its way to a stream, lake, river, or ocean. No matter where you live, you live in a watershed. The map on the next page shows California's watersheds. In which watershed do you live?

The amount of water available to an area depends on how much water is collected in the watershed. It also depends on how much water is used. This water falls as rain or snow and collects on the surface in streams, rivers, and lakes. It also soaks into the soil and becomes groundwater. The water that collects on the surface, along with groundwater that is pumped to the surface, is available for people to use.

Water quality also affects how much fresh water is available to people. The way land in a watershed is used affects water quality. For example, harmful chemicals can be carried in water that runs off farms or city streets. Soil is carried in water that flows over land disturbed by construction, projects that control rivers, or farming. Using land wisely in these areas can help keep water safe for use. Federal, state, and local governments have laws to help keep water safe.

This farm uses reclaimed water for irrigation to help conserve water.

Conserve Water!

Conservation is using a resource such as water wisely so that it lasts longer. Here are some ways you can conserve water.
- Take shorter showers.
- Use a low-flow showerhead.
- Don't let the water run while brushing your teeth.
- Fix leaky faucets and toilets.
- Use a water displacement device in toilet tanks.

Reclamation

Water used in homes and businesses can be recycled and used again, or reclaimed. In *reclamation*, wastewater from homes or businesses is carried to a wastewater treatment plant. After the water is treated, it can be used for purposes other than drinking. Some of it is used to water lawns. Some is sent to streams, where it is pumped onto farms and other lands to water crops.

California Watersheds

North Coast
North Lahontan
Sacramento River
San Joaquin River
South Lahontan
Colorado River
San Francisco Bay
Central Coast
Tulare Lake
South Coast

1. **✓Checkpoint** Identify three ways people can reduce and recycle the water they use.

2. **Main Idea and Details** List some details for the following main idea: The way land in a watershed is used affects water quality.

Goose Lake

Klammath River

Pit River

Shasta Lake

Eagle Lake

1

California Lakes and Rivers

Eel River

1

Clear Lake

2 Lake Tahoe

3 Mono Lake

Merced River

San Joaquin River

Owens Lake (Dry)

Salinas River

Cities
- Sacramento
- San Francisco
- Barstow
- Los Angeles
- San Diego

Kern River

Salton Sea

Colorado River

Finding Out About Local Water Sources

As you read in Lesson 2, some people get their fresh water from wells dug into aquifers. Others get their water from lakes, streams, or rivers. These bodies of water may be located close to where you live. Your community may also use aqueducts to bring water from lakes or streams located far away. This water may be collected and stored in reservoirs located near your home.

The map on page 186 shows the locations of some of California's larger lakes and rivers. The amount of water in each of these sources is limited by how much rain and snow falls there. Seasonal activities, such as irrigation, can also affect how much water is available. Using water wisely can help keep the demand for water resources in balance with the available supply.

Where does your community's water come from? The source of your water depends both on where you live and on how much water your community needs. You can find the source of your water supply by contacting your local water company. Information about your water source may also be found in the library-media center or by contacting the Association of California Water Agencies or another local water agency.

✓ Lesson Review

1. Look at the map on page 186. Identify the nearest lake and/or river that could provide fresh water to your community.

2. ✎ **Writing in Science** **Descriptive** Use the library-media center to find out where and how your community gets water. Write a report that traces the journey of the water from its source to your home.

Lesson 4

What is the water cycle?

Earth's water does not stay in one place. It changes form and moves from one place to another.

Water in the Air

Look around the room you are in now. Can you see water around you? Even if you do not see it, water surrounds you all the time. This water is not in a liquid form as in rivers or a solid form as in glaciers. This water is an invisible gas called water vapor. Air always has some water vapor in it, even air in the driest deserts. This water vapor was liquid water at some time in the past. It may have been water inside a plant, in a tropical river, or in the Arctic Ocean.

Water vapor makes up only a small fraction of the gases in the air. The particles of water vapor, like the particles of other gases, are always moving.

The Water Cycle

Water on Earth moves between the oceans and land through the processes of the water cycle. The **water cycle,** or the hydrologic cycle, is the repeated movement of water through the environment in different forms. The steps of the water cycle include evaporation, condensation, and precipitation. These steps are affected by temperature and pressure. A simple diagram of a water cycle is shown here.

Evaporation

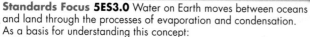

DIGITAL

Look for Active Art animations at www.pearsonsuccessnet.com

Standards Focus 5ES3.0 Water on Earth moves between oceans and land through the processes of evaporation and condensation. As a basis for understanding this concept:
5ES3.b Students know when liquid water evaporates, it turns into water vapor in the air and can reappear as a liquid when cooled or as a solid if cooled below the freezing point of water.
5ES3.c Students know water vapor in the air moves from one place to another and can form fog or clouds, which are tiny droplets of water or ice, and can fall to Earth as rain, hail, sleet, or snow.

Evaporation is the changing of liquid water to water vapor. Liquid water evaporates into invisible water vapor when it is heated by the Sun. In **condensation,** air cools and some of the water vapor turns into a liquid, such as water droplets in clouds or fog. These water droplets are so small they remain suspended in air. In **precipitation,** air cools further so the water droplets grow large enough to fall from clouds as rain, hail, sleet, or snow.

Water can take many different paths through the water cycle. For example, condensation does not form only clouds. Condensation also forms dew, like that shown in the photograph.

It is important to note that precipitation does not always fall over land as it does in the simple water cycle below. Evaporation, condensation, and precipitation occur over all areas of Earth, including land and ocean.

Condensation forms dew.

Condensation

Precipitation

Water that falls over land may join bodies of water, or it may sink into the ground and become groundwater.

Water vapor on a cold surface may freeze without first becoming liquid water. The ice crystals that form are called frost.

1. **✓Checkpoint** How are evaporation and condensation the same? How are they different?

2. Trace the path of water through the simple water cycle shown here. List the stages water passes through, starting with water in a lake or an ocean.

Many Paths of the Water Cycle

A detailed picture of the water cycle is shown here. Water is not always in the nonliving portion of the environment. You know that living things use and make water. Plants break down water as they make sugar during photosynthesis. Plants and animals release water during respiration.

As water vapor rises, it may form a cloud.

Because salts are left behind when water evaporates, the oceans remain salty.

Water vapor turns into frost or dew. Frost and dew often form in the morning and evaporate soon after sunrise.

Water evaporates from oceans, lakes, and puddles faster with warm temperatures and winds.

Animals take in water. All animals also produce water in respiration. Animals that sweat give off water vapor.

Energy in the Water Cycle

The Sun has a major effect on the water cycle. The energy of sunlight causes melting, evaporation, and sublimation, or changing from solid ice directly to water vapor. Energy is needed to raise water vapor to the clouds and move it with winds. This energy originally comes from the Sun.

Water vapor releases energy as it condenses into liquid water. This energy is heat that warms nearby air or water. During evaporation, water takes in heat energy. This cools nearby air and water. This heating and cooling of air and water can change weather patterns.

Very slowly, snow and ice can turn into water vapor by sublimation.

Raindrops and snowflakes fall to Earth. Most precipitation falls on the oceans.

Water also evaporates from plants.

Plants take in water from the soil.

Water runs off the land into streams and rivers that flow into lakes and the oceans.

Some rain or melted snow soaks into the ground and becomes groundwater.

Groundwater slowly moves through aquifers into rivers, lakes, and the ocean. This can take thousands of years.

√ Lesson Review

1. How does the water cycle affect weather patterns?

2. ✐ **Writing in Science Narrative** Write a story from the point of view of a drop of water. In your story, describe how the water changes as it moves through the water cycle. Describe how the water drop forms precipitation.

191

Lesson 5

How do clouds form?

Clouds have an important role in the water cycle. Clouds bring precipitation to all parts of the world. Without clouds, rivers and lakes would dry up.

Temperature and Pressure

Have you ever watched a cloud get larger and larger? Have you tried to see shapes in the clouds? Clouds come in many shapes and sizes.

Clouds form when water vapor condenses to form tiny water droplets or ice crystals. Forming of clouds is a major part of the water cycle.

Whether a cloud is made of water droplets or ice crystals depends partly on the air's temperature. The temperature of air high in the clouds is often much lower than that of air near the ground. Even on summer days, many clouds are made of ice crystals.

Air pressure also affects the forming of clouds. Clouds often form when air moves upward to areas of lower air pressure. Saucer-shaped clouds like those in the picture on this page can form when winds blow over a mountain. When air moves up, the air pressure is less. With less pressure, the air expands and cools. If the air cools enough at this new air pressure, water vapor will form droplets or ice crystals. You will learn more about air pressure in Chapter 6.

1. ✓**Checkpoint** What are clouds made of?
2. Why are clouds important?

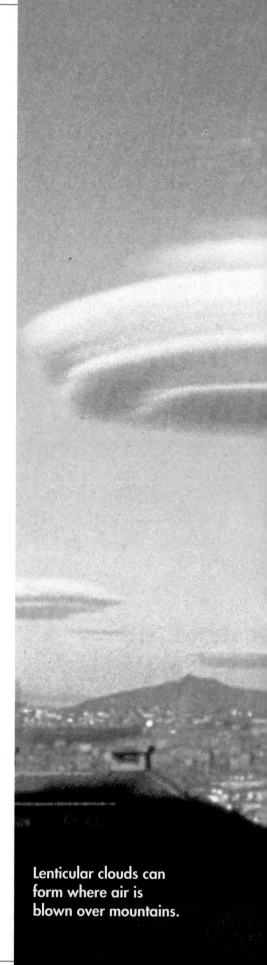

Lenticular clouds can form where air is blown over mountains.

Types of Clouds

High-altitude clouds form more than 6,000 m above the ground. This region overlaps the region for mid-altitude clouds. Cirrus clouds are high-altitude clouds that are thin, wispy, and white.

Clouds that grow vertically have rising air inside them. The bases of these clouds may be as low as 1,000 m above the ground. The rising air may push the tops of these clouds higher than 12,000 m up. Vertical clouds are sometimes called thunderheads because they often cause thunderstorms.

The bases of mid-altitude clouds are between 2,000 m and 7,000 m above the ground. Altocumulus clouds are mid-altitude clouds that look like small, puffy balls. The bottoms of the clouds can look dark because sunlight may not reach them. The sides of the clouds are white because sunlight is reflecting off them.

Low-altitude clouds are often seen less than 2,000 m above the ground. Stratus clouds are low-altitude clouds that cover the whole sky. They look dark because little sunlight gets through the layer of clouds.

Fog is a cloud at ground level. It can form in several ways. One kind of fog can form on clear, cool nights with no wind. Air near the ground cools. If the air cools enough, water vapor condenses into tiny droplets and forms a cloud at or near the ground. As more droplets form and get larger, the fog appears thicker.

Daily Weather

Day	Conditions
Monday	Temperature: 17°C Humidity: 90% Precipitation: Light rain
Tuesday	Temperature: 18°C Humidity: 80% Precipitation: Light rain

Exploring Weather Data

Explore the relationship among humidity, temperature, and the likelihood of rainfall or snowfall. Using news reports, record the daily humidity and the temperature for two weeks. Also record if it rains or snows. After two weeks, graph your data. Examine your results. Look for relationships among humidity, temperature, and whether it rained or snowed. Describe what you learned.

Upward winds carry hail through a cloud many times.

Precipitation

You may be surprised to learn that most rain in the United States starts as snow. The temperature of the air high above the ground is often below 0°C. Clouds of ice crystals form in the cold air. The ice crystals grow larger until they start to fall as snowflakes. As they fall, the crystals may stick to other crystals and form larger snowflakes. If the temperature of the air between the cloud and the ground is less than 0°C, the ice crystals fall to the ground as snow.

Ice crystals from a cloud may change as they fall through different layers of air. If the ice crystals fall into air that is warmer than 0°C, they will melt and fall as rain. If the air near the ground is very cold, the rain may freeze before it hits the ground. These frozen raindrops are **sleet.** Sleet, freezing rain, and hail are not the same. They form in different ways. Freezing rain, or an ice storm, forms from rain that freezes as soon as it hits the ground or other cold objects.

Hail Formation

Hail forms when very strong winds blow upward into a cloud. The winds blow raindrops back up into the freezing air at the top of a cloud. The raindrops freeze into small bits of ice. As the ice is blown back up into the cloud many times, many layers of water freeze on it. Hailstones fall when they become too heavy for the upward winds to lift them.

✓ Lesson Review

TARGET SKILL

1. Summarize how snow, rain, and sleet form.

2. **Main Idea and Details** List four details to support the following main idea: Almost all precipitation in the United States starts as snow.

Types of Precipitation

Rain

Most clouds over North America are made of ice crystals.

Ice crystals melt as they fall through warmer air. They fall to the ground as rain.

Freezing Rain

Ice crystals fall from clouds.

Ice crystals melt to form raindrops as they fall through warm air.

A layer of air close to the ground is colder than 0°C. This cold air makes the ground, trees, and other objects very cold. Rainwater freezes when it lands.

Sleet

Ice crystals melt as they fall through a thin layer of warm air high above the ground.

If raindrops fall for a longer time through cold air, they freeze before they hit the ground. Frozen raindrops are called sleet.

Snow

Ice crystals will fall as snow if the air between the clouds and ground has a temperature below 0°C.

Estimating the size of a lake

You know how to find the area of geometric shapes. But most things in nature have irregular shapes. Finding their exact areas may be hard. Making a good estimate of their areas is easy!

Area is the number of square units that a figure covers. So, one way to find the area of an odd shape is to use a grid that divides the shape into square units. Then count the number of square units. To get a better estimate, you can combine half-squares and add them to your count.

Suppose you want to find the area of the lake shown on the map below. On this map, 1 unit represents a distance of 1 kilometer. This means that a square unit represents an area of 1 square kilometer.

Six squares are completely or almost completely covered. Eight squares are about half covered, making 4 more whole squares. A good estimate for the area of the lake is 10 square kilometers.

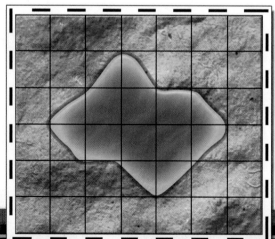

Answer each question.

1. What is the area of the blue shape in square units?
   A. 4
   B. 5
   C. 6
   D. 7

On the maps on the right, each square unit represents one square kilometer.

2. What is the best estimate of the area of the middle lake in square kilometers?
   A. 6
   B. 13
   C. 17
   D. 24

3. Estimate the area of the bottom lake shown in the map. Explain how you estimated.

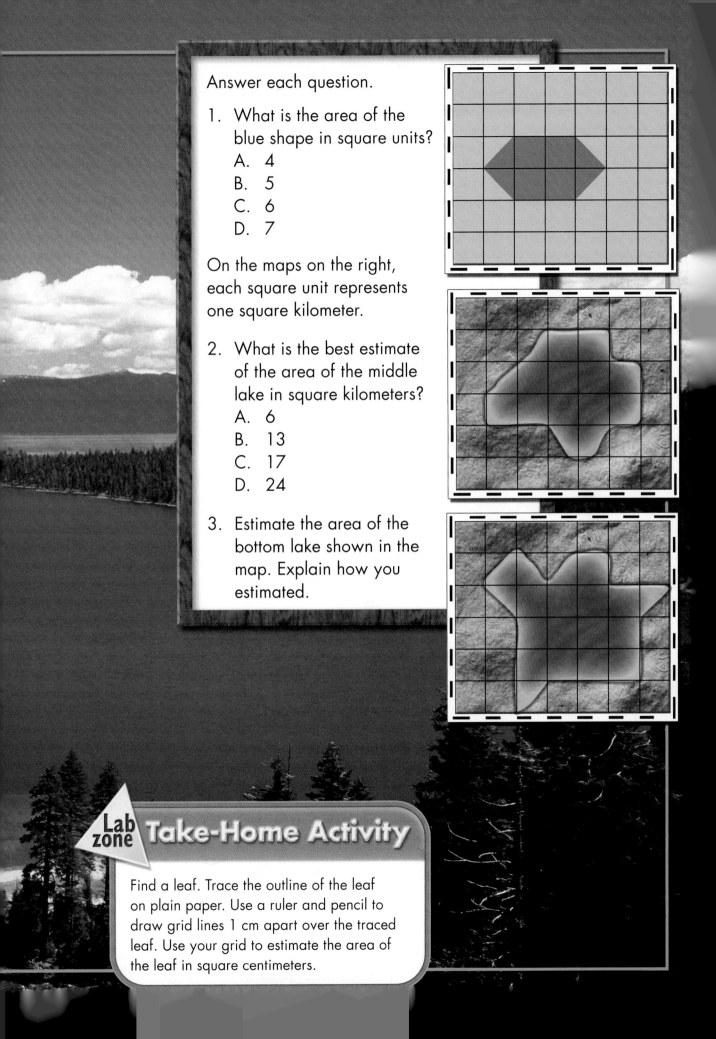

Lab zone Take-Home Activity

Find a leaf. Trace the outline of the leaf on plain paper. Use a ruler and pencil to draw grid lines 1 cm apart over the traced leaf. Use your grid to estimate the area of the leaf in square centimeters.

Investigate What is a cloud?

Tiny droplets of water (and sometimes tiny pieces of ice) make up a cloud. The water droplets form when moisture in the air collects on dust and other particles. In this activity, look for tiny droplets to form on the top and side of the bowls, not in the air. The moisture inside the bowls has no tiny particles on which to collect.

Materials

ice cubes

2 plastic bowls with lids

warm water

graduated cylinder

What to Do

1 **Measure** 150 mL warm water. Put the water into a bowl and cover it.

Be careful!

Wipe up spills right away.

warm water ————

2 Leave the other bowl empty. Close its lid.

Process Skills

Making and using a model can help you learn about a process, such as how clouds form.

5ES3.b Students know when liquid water evaporates, it turns into water vapor in the air and can reappear as a liquid when cooled or as a solid if cooled below the freezing point of water. **5ES3.c** Students know water vapor in the air moves from one place to another and can form fog or clouds, which are tiny droplets of water or ice, and can fall to Earth as rain, hail, sleet, or snow. **5IE6.f** Select appropriate tools (e.g., thermometers, metersticks, balances, and graduated cylinders) and make quantitative observations. (Also **5IE6.g**)

3 Put ice cubes on the lids.

Put the same number of ice cubes on each lid.

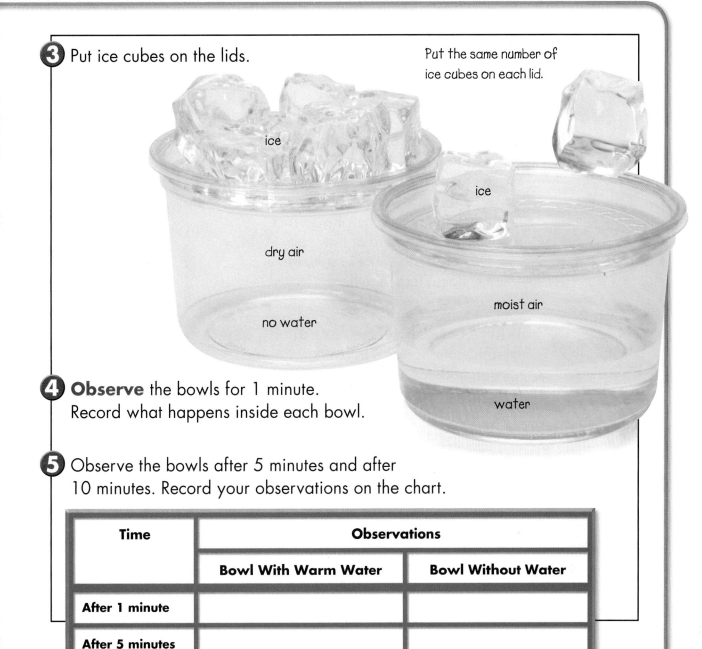

ice

dry air

no water

ice

moist air

water

4 **Observe** the bowls for 1 minute. Record what happens inside each bowl.

5 Observe the bowls after 5 minutes and after 10 minutes. Record your observations on the chart.

Time	Observations	
	Bowl With Warm Water	**Bowl Without Water**
After 1 minute		
After 5 minutes		
After 10 minutes		

Explain Your Results

1. Make an **inference** based on your **models.** Is water vapor in the air when clouds form? Explain.

2. Use your results to describe conditions necessary for clouds to form.

Go Further

Does temperature have an effect on the results? Design and conduct a scientific investigation to answer this question or one of your own. Describe and demonstrate how to perform your investigation safely.

Chapter 5 Reviewing Key Concepts

Focus on the BIG Idea Water moves through the water cycle. Evaporation, condensation, and precipitation are the parts of the water cycle.

Lesson 1

How can the oceans be described?
- Most of Earth's water is salt water in the oceans, which cover most of Earth's surface.
- Salinity is a measure of how salty water is. Ocean water is saltier in some places than in others.

Lesson 2

Where is fresh water found?
- Fresh water is found in rivers, lakes, underground sources, and glaciers.
- The amount of fresh water is limited. Its availability can be extended by recycling and decreasing the use of water.

Lesson 3

What are some California water sources?
- Sources of fresh water in California include streams, rivers, lakes, and underground sources.
- In many parts of California, pipelines called aqueducts carry water long distances from rivers or lakes to local communities.

Lesson 4

What is the water cycle?
- The water cycle is the repeated movement of water through the environment in different forms.
- In the water cycle, liquid water evaporates from Earth to form water vapor in the air that moves from place to place. In time this water vapor cools and condenses to form water that falls back to Earth.

Lesson 5

How do clouds form?
- In the water cycle, water vapor in the air can cool to form clouds, which are tiny droplets of water or ice. These droplets can fall back to Earth as rain, hail, sleet, or snow.

Cross-Curricular Links

English–Language Arts

Building Vocabulary

Look again at pages 168–169. Identify the picture behind the terms *salinity* and *sea level*. Write a paragraph about each term. Tell how each term relates to the picture.

Mathematics

Water Use

Look at the chart on page 181. How much water would an average family of four people use in a week?

Visual and Performing Arts

Conserving Water

Brainstorm ways to conserve water. Use research materials to help. Make an illustrated poster that shows three things people can do to conserve water.

Challenge!

English–Language Arts

Different Clouds and Weather

Are certain types of clouds linked to certain types of weather? Use research materials to find out. Then write an expository composition that describes the relationship between cloud types and weather.

Chapter 5 Review/Test

Use Vocabulary

aquifer (p. 177)	**sea level** (p. 173)
condensation (p. 189)	**sleet** (p. 194)
evaporation (p. 189)	**water cycle** (p. 188)
precipitation (p. 189)	**watershed** (p. 178)
reservoir (p. 178)	**water table** (p. 177)
salinity (p. 174)	

Fill in the blanks with the correct vocabulary terms. If you have trouble answering a question, read the listed page again.

1. _____ is a measure of how salty water is.

2. _____ is the level of the surface of an ocean.

3. A _____ is a lake that forms behind a dam.

4. _____ forms when raindrops freeze before they hit the ground.

5. The layer of rock and soil that groundwater flows through is a(n) _____.

6. The _____ is the top level of groundwater in an aquifer.

7. The area from which water drains into a river is called the river's _____.

8. The repeated movement of water through the environment is the _____.

Think About It

9. Describe the oceans and explain how the water cycle affects the salinity of the ocean.

10. Explain how clouds usually form rain over the United States.

11. **Process Skills** **Communicate** Summarize the roles of evaporation, sublimation, and condensation in the water cycle.

12. **Main Idea and Details** Make a graphic organizer like the one shown below. List some details for the main idea in the box below. Look at Lesson 4 if you need help.

Water changes form and moves around Earth in the water cycle.

13. **Writing in Science**

Descriptive List and describe three different sources that local communities use for fresh water. Choose one and describe how water gets from the source to a person's home.

California Standards Practice

Write the letter of the correct answer.

14. What is one way you can conserve water?

   A take long showers

   B dig wells

   C fix leaky faucets

   D swim in the ocean

15. Which kind of cloud touches the ground?

   A altocumulus

   B fog

   C cirrus

   D lenticular

16. Where is most of Earth's water located?

   A rivers

   B groundwater

   C oceans

   D lakes

17. Warm water is moved from the Caribbean Sea to the North Atlantic Ocean by

   A an ocean current.

   B the water cycle.

   C the water table.

   D an aquifer.

18. What is the process that changes water vapor into clouds or fog?

   A evaporation

   B sublimation

   C condensation

   D runoff

19. Which of the following is an example of evaporation?

   A Water on land sinks into soil.

   B A layer of ice forms on a puddle.

   C Rain falls from a cloud.

   D Water in a puddle slowly disappears.

20. In the diagram of the water cycle, which arrow shows that condensation is taking place?

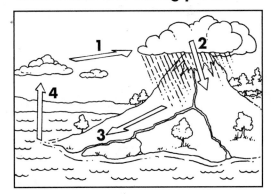

   A 1

   B 2

   C 3

   D 4

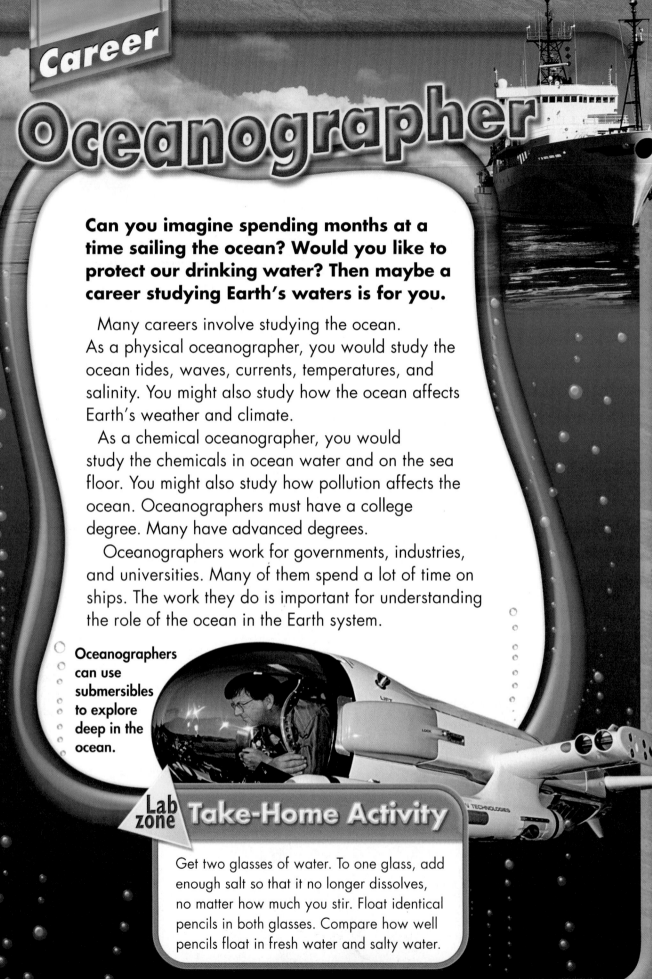

Oceanographer

Can you imagine spending months at a time sailing the ocean? Would you like to protect our drinking water? Then maybe a career studying Earth's waters is for you.

Many careers involve studying the ocean. As a physical oceanographer, you would study the ocean tides, waves, currents, temperatures, and salinity. You might also study how the ocean affects Earth's weather and climate.

As a chemical oceanographer, you would study the chemicals in ocean water and on the sea floor. You might also study how pollution affects the ocean. Oceanographers must have a college degree. Many have advanced degrees.

Oceanographers work for governments, industries, and universities. Many of them spend a lot of time on ships. The work they do is important for understanding the role of the ocean in the Earth system.

Oceanographers can use submersibles to explore deep in the ocean.

Lab zone Take-Home Activity

Get two glasses of water. To one glass, add enough salt so that it no longer dissolves, no matter how much you stir. Float identical pencils in both glasses. Compare how well pencils float in fresh water and salty water.

Chapter 6

WEATHER

5ES4.0 Energy from the Sun heats Earth unevenly, causing air movements that result in changing weather patterns. As a basis for understanding this concept:

5ES4.a Students know uneven heating of Earth causes air movements (convection currents).

5ES4.b Students know the influence that the ocean has on the weather and the role that the water cycle plays in weather patterns.

5ES4.c Students know the causes and effects of different types of severe weather.

5ES4.d Students know how to use weather maps and data to predict local weather and know that weather forecasts depend on many variables.

5ES4.e Students know that the Earth's atmosphere exerts a pressure that decreases with distance above Earth's surface and that at any point it exerts this pressure equally in all directions.

5IE6.0 Scientific progress is made by asking meaningful questions and conducting careful investigations. As a basis for understanding this concept and addressing the content in the other three strands, students should develop their own questions and perform investigations. (Also **5IE6.f**, **5IE6.g**)

Standards Focus Questions

- How does air move?
- What are air masses?
- What causes severe weather?
- How are weather forecasts made?

Focus on the BIG Idea

Why does the weather change?

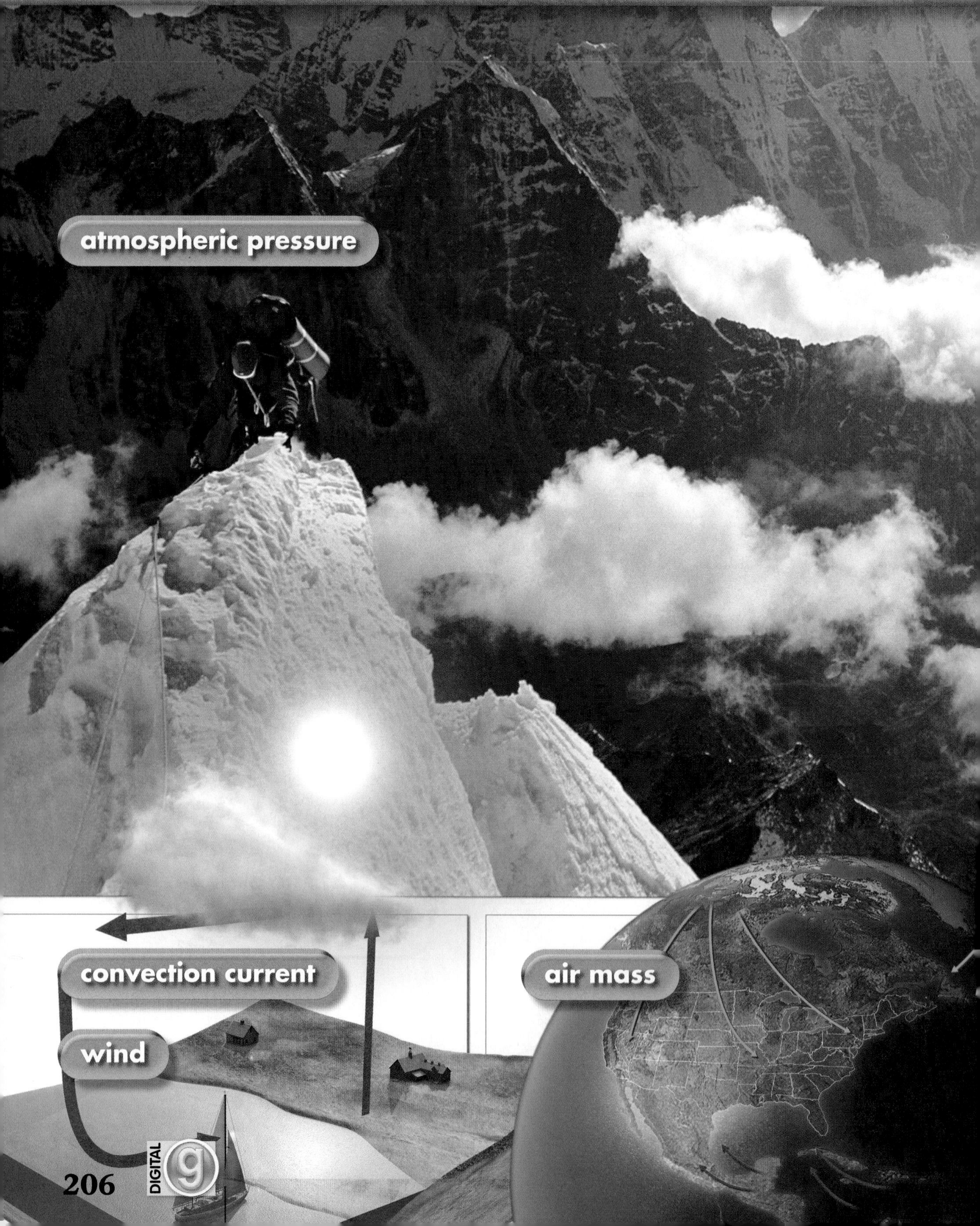
atmospheric pressure
convection current
wind
air mass

DIGITAL

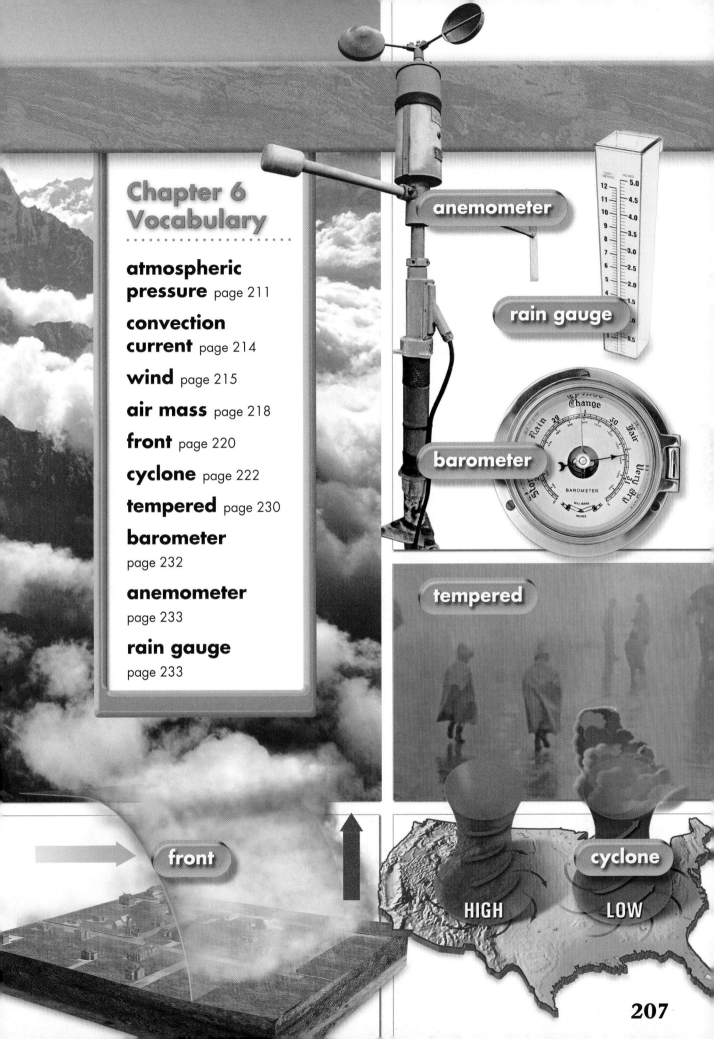

Chapter 6 Vocabulary

anemometer

rain gauge

barometer

tempered

front

cyclone

HIGH

LOW

Explore How can you demonstrate that warm air rises?

In this chapter you will learn how different parts of the Earth are heated unevenly. The process of warm air rising and cool air sinking can cause local winds and global air currents. In this activity you will demonstrate that warm air rises.

Materials

pencil

lightweight cardboard

metric ruler

scissors and thread

masking tape

bowl with very warm water

thin markers (optional)

What to Do

1 Draw a 12 cm circle with a spiral inside it. Cut out the circle and cut along the spiral.

Tape the thread to the center of the spiral. Hold the thread so the bottom of the spiral is about 2 cm above the bowl.

Be careful! Don't use water too hot to be safe!

2 Describe what happens to the spiral.

3 **Observe.**

Explain Your Results

Make a labeled diagram to record your **observations.** Explain your observations.

5ES4.a Students know uneven heating of Earth causes air movements (convection currents). **5IE6.g** Record data by using appropriate graphic representations (including charts, graphs, and labeled diagrams) and make inferences based on those data.

How to Read Science

TARGET SKILL

Draw Conclusions

Learning to **draw conclusions** can help you evaluate what you read and **observe.**

- As you read, put together facts and then extend them to form a conclusion or to make an **inference.**

- Sometimes you may have more than one conclusion.

- You might change your conclusions when you get more facts.

Science Article

Rising to the Heights

Soon after people started flying in hot-air balloons, they began measuring air conditions above Earth's surface. Researchers who wanted to understand weather rose high into the air. But these flights were dangerous. At higher altitudes, air pressure can be dangerously low. In 1862, a pair of researchers rose so high they barely survived their flight. One passed out due to a lack of oxygen at the high altitude. The other could barely move for the same reason. He used his teeth to operate the balloon's controls and bring it down.

Apply It!
Make a graphic organizer like this one. List facts from the science article and **draw a conclusion.**

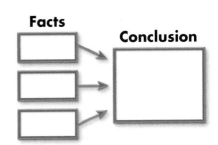

Facts

Conclusion

You Are There!

A cold wind blows around you as you climb higher up the ice-covered mountain. You spend a moment adjusting the tank on your back. At this altitude, you need an oxygen tank to help you breathe. As you look at the clouds below, you think about all the planning that went into your climb. You are thankful that the weather forecasters could tell that this would be a good week for the climb. How were they able to predict this good weather?

Standards Focus 5ES4.0 Energy from the Sun heats Earth unevenly, causing air movements that result in changing weather patterns. As a basis for understanding this concept:
5ES4.a Students know uneven heating of Earth causes air movements (convection currents).
5ES4.e Students know that Earth's atmosphere exerts a pressure that decreases with distance above Earth's surface and that at any point it exerts this pressure equally in all directions.

DIGITAL

How does air move?

Air is a mixture of gases in constant motion. Differences in air temperature cause wind.

Under Pressure

The atmosphere is all of the air around Earth. Earth's atmosphere has several layers. Most weather takes place in the layer nearest Earth's surface.

As you go up through the atmosphere, temperature and pressure change. Temperature changes because Earth's surface and the layers of the atmosphere get energy from the Sun. **Atmospheric pressure,** or air pressure, is the weight of air pushing down on an area. Atmospheric pressure changes with height because the amount of air above each level is different.

As you go higher in the atmosphere, there is less air above you to push down on you. Air pressure decreases as you go up. Lower air pressure means fewer air particles in a given location.

Air pressure is lowest where air particles are farthest apart.

Higher in the atmosphere, air particles can spread farther apart. Air pressure is lower.

Air pressure is highest near Earth's surface, where air particles are squeezed close together by the weight of the air above.

1. ✓**Checkpoint** What is atmospheric pressure?

2. Explain why atmospheric pressure decreases with increasing altitude.

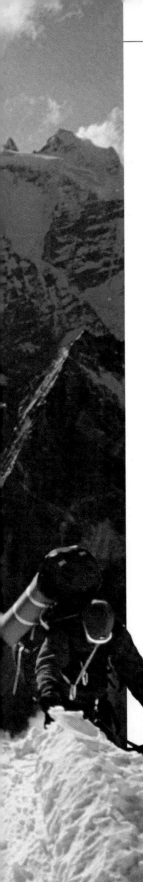

More About Atmospheric Pressure

You know that air is matter. Air is invisible, and it is difficult to weigh. But like all matter, air has mass and takes up space. Air is pulled toward Earth's center by gravity. You may remember that weight is a measure of the pull of gravity on an object. Because air is pulled by Earth's gravity, air has weight.

Air pressure is a result of Earth's gravity. Gravity pulls the air toward Earth's surface, just as gravity pulls you down on a bathroom scale. The weight of Earth's air causes air pressure.

Particles of air are always moving in every direction. As you move away from Earth's surface, the air particles become more spread out. This means that high in the atmosphere, air pressure is lower than it is at Earth's surface.

Because particles of air move in all directions, air pressure pushes equally on objects in all directions. Objects, such as closed paper bags, don't collapse under this pressure because the air inside also pushes out. You don't feel air pressure for the same reason. The pressure inside your body balances the air pressure outside your body.

Knowing that air pressure decreases as you go higher above Earth's surface is helpful to airplane pilots. Instruments called altimeters can help pilots determine how high they are flying. Altitude is a measure of distance above sea level. It may surprise you to learn that an altimeter actually measures air pressure, not altitude!

As you know, air pressure decreases with height. This is true even for a small object, such as a balloon. The air pressure is a little bit greater at the bottom of the balloon than at the top of the balloon.

1. ✓ **Checkpoint** What does an altimeter measure? What information does it provide to pilots?

2. ✎ **Writing in Science** **Narrative** Suppose that you are a mountain climber traveling from the base to the top of the world's tallest mountain. Describe and explain the changes in atmospheric pressure that you experience as you move higher.

An altimeter measures atmospheric pressure to show altitude.

The air pressure on the bottom of the balloon is slightly greater than the air pressure on the top of the balloon.

213

Convection Currents

Even at the same height in the atmosphere, gas particles in cool air are closer together than those in warm air. This causes cool air to be heavier than an equal volume of warm air. When cool air and warm air are next to each other, the cool air will sink and force the warm air to rise.

Have you ever walked over hot sand to get to the cool water of a lake or an ocean? Land heats more quickly in sunlight than water does. This uneven heating of Earth's surface causes air to be at different temperatures. At night, land cools faster than water does. This causes air over land and over water to have different temperatures.

These temperature differences cause convection currents to form. A **convection current** is the rising and sinking of matter in a circular pattern. Temperature differences in air cause wind, storms, and all types of weather.

Rising air will cool. It stops rising when it is the same temperature as surrounding air. This cooled air is pushed over the water by the rising air below it.

The warm land makes air above it warm. This warm air is forced up by the cool air, causing sea breezes.

The cool water will not warm the air above it as much as the land warms the air above it. So, the cool air sinks below the warm air.

Cool, sinking air causes high air pressure at the surface.

Warm, rising air causes low air pressure at the surface.

As the cool air moves under the warm air, wind is created. Wind occurs as air moves from a place of high air pressure to a place of low air pressure.

214

Wind is movement of air that happens because of differences in air pressure caused by temperature differences. The diagram on page 214 shows how convection currents form wind near large bodies of water during the day. At night, a different convection current flows in the opposite direction. This pattern of sinking cool air and rising warm air repeats over and over again. The circular path of moving air can also form patterns of clouds, rain, and changes in atmospheric pressure.

Convection does not happen only in air. It also affects ocean water and the rock deep beneath Earth's surface. Some currents on the ocean surface are caused by wind. But deeper ocean currents form when cold, salty water sinks under warmer water. Ocean currents can affect climate. For example, the warm water of the Gulf Stream makes northern countries, such as Scotland much warmer than they would be otherwise. Convection currents also move heat inside Earth. As hot rock slowly flows, heat is moved from deep in Earth toward Earth's surface.

Gas particles in cool air

Gas particles in warm air

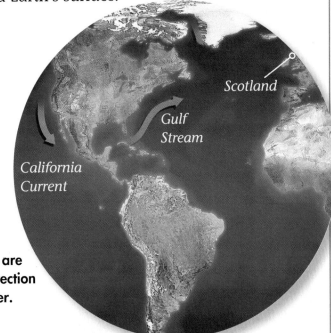

Scotland

Gulf Stream

California Current

Ocean currents are caused by convection currents in water.

1. ✓**Checkpoint** What causes convection currents?

2. ✏️ **Writing in Science** **Expository** Suppose you need to teach a fourth grader about convection currents. Do research and write a paragraph explaining how differences in temperature affect different parts of Earth.

DIGITAL NSTA SciLinks keyword: convection current code: gr5p214

Uneven Heating Due to Earth's Tilt

Energy from the Sun heats Earth's surface and atmosphere. However, all parts of Earth are not heated evenly. The resulting temperature differences cause convection currents, both locally and around the world.

Huge convection currents form in the air above Earth. One reason that these currents form is that tropical areas are warmer than other parts of Earth. The movement of air in the huge convection currents and Earth's rotation cause regional wind patterns. In most parts of the United States, regional winds blow from west to east.

Latitude is a measure of how far a place is north or south of the equator, which has a latitude of 0°. Temperatures on Earth change with latitude. Places near the equator get much more energy from the Sun than do places near the poles. These differences in the amount of energy received are related to the angle at which sunlight strikes Earth.

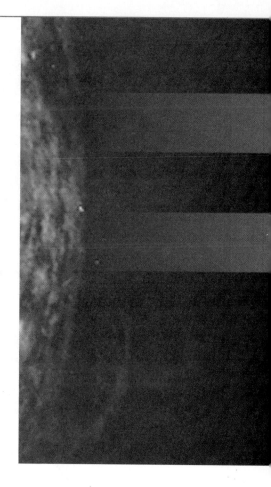

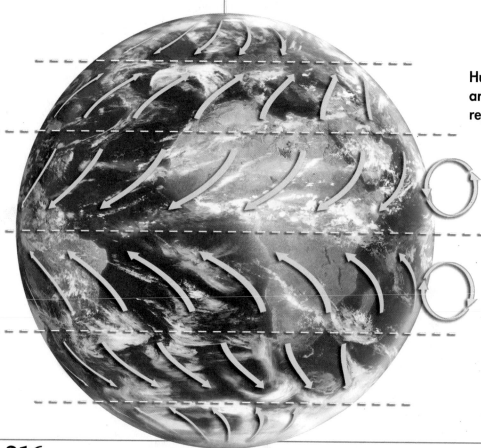

Huge convection currents around Earth result in regional wind patterns.

Near the poles, the Sun's rays are more spread out.

Near the equator, the Sun's rays are more concentrated.

Earth spins around its axis. This axis is tilted at about 23.5° to Earth's orbit around the Sun. Because Earth's axis is tilted, energy from the Sun hits places near Earth's equator more directly than places near Earth's poles. The diagram above shows how the angle at which the Sun's rays hit Earth changes from place to place. Near the equator, the Sun is high in the sky. The Sun's rays hit these areas at a direct angle. Near the poles, the Sun is low in the sky. The Sun's rays hit these areas at a less direct angle.

The angle at which the Sun's rays hit determines how warm a place will be. Near the poles, where the Sun's rays hit at a less direct angle, the Sun's energy is spread out over a large area. This is why polar regions are cold. Near the equator, where the Sun's rays hit more directly, the Sun's energy is concentrated in a smaller area. These areas are warm all year.

✓ Lesson Review

1. How are convection currents related to weather patterns?

2. Why are temperatures warmer near the equator than near the poles?

3. **Draw Conclusions** Regional winds are sometimes stronger than normal. What conclusion can you draw about regional temperature differences during these times?

TARGET SKILL

217

Lesson 2

What are air masses?

Large bodies of air move across the globe. There are four basic kinds of air masses. The weather can change where these air masses push together.

Kinds of Air Masses

Suppose that your cousins have just returned from a trip. You want to figure out where they went. When they show you the seashells they collected, you know that your cousins were at a beach. You can figure out where air has been too. The air's temperature and amount of water vapor are clues.

If air stays over an area for some time, it takes on properties of that area and becomes an air mass. An **air mass** is a large body of air with similar properties all through it. The most important of these properties are temperature and amount of water vapor. An air mass keeps its original properties for a while as it moves to a new area.

Four kinds of air masses are shown in the picture on page 219. Generally, the kind of weather that you have at any time is a result of the air mass in your area. If you are having several warm, clear days, the weather will remain that way until a new air mass moves into the area. Some kinds of weather usually happen only at the edges of air masses.

Air masses move because of winds. These winds may be near the ground. Some air masses are guided by the jet stream, a strong air current high above the ground. If the jet stream guides an air mass from Canada to the middle of the United States, northerly winds will bring cold, dry air into that area. Storms may occur at the edge of this air mass.

1. ✔️Checkpoint How do air masses form and move?

2. ✏️ **Writing in Science** **Descriptive** In a letter, a friend wonders why the weather has been so hot and humid. Write a reply to your friend explaining the role of air masses in making the weather hot and humid.

Standards Focus 5ES4.0 Energy from the Sun heats Earth unevenly, causing air movements that result in changing weather patterns. As a basis for understanding this concept:
5ES4.c Students know the causes and effects of different types of severe weather.

218

Air Masses

① Continental Polar Air
Very little water evaporates from the land and ice near the poles. So, an air mass from this area is cold and fairly dry.

② Continental Tropical Air
A large hot desert can cause the air above it to be warm and fairly dry.

③ Maritime Polar Air
Even though the ocean near the poles is cold, water vapor evaporates into the air. An air mass forming over the ocean near the poles is cold, but relatively moist.

④ Maritime Tropical Air
Humid air has lots of moisture. Over tropical oceans or rain forests, an air mass becomes warm and very humid because water can easily evaporate there.

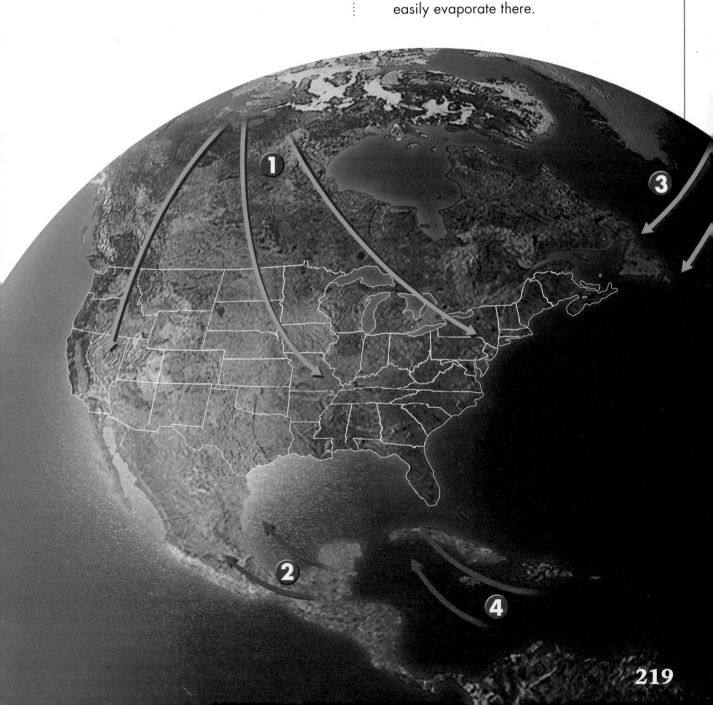

When Air Masses Meet

Have you ever seen a line of clouds move from the horizon until it is overhead? What you have probably seen is the arrival of a front. A **front** is a boundary between two air masses. Most air masses move from west to east over North America, so fronts have the same motion.

A front gets its name from the kind of air that is moving into the area. A *cold front* brings colder air into an area. A *warm front* brings warmer air into an area. Sometimes a front does not move very much, or it moves back and forth over the same area. This kind of front is called a *stationary front*.

Notice in the pictures shown here that both fronts have rising warm air. Areas of rising air near the fronts have lower pressure than areas in the middle of the air masses. Rising air at fronts often causes the rain or snow of the water cycle.

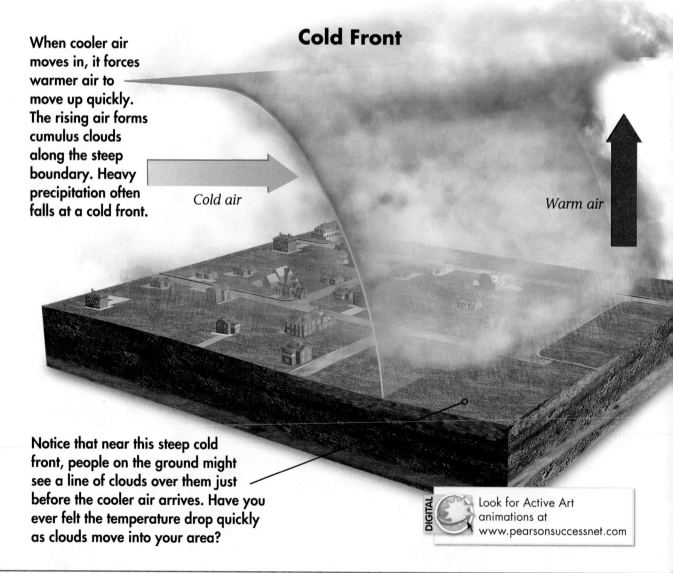

Cold Front

When cooler air moves in, it forces warmer air to move up quickly. The rising air forms cumulus clouds along the steep boundary. Heavy precipitation often falls at a cold front.

Cold air

Warm air

Notice that near this steep cold front, people on the ground might see a line of clouds over them just before the cooler air arrives. Have you ever felt the temperature drop quickly as clouds move into your area?

DIGITAL

Look for Active Art animations at www.pearsonsuccessnet.com

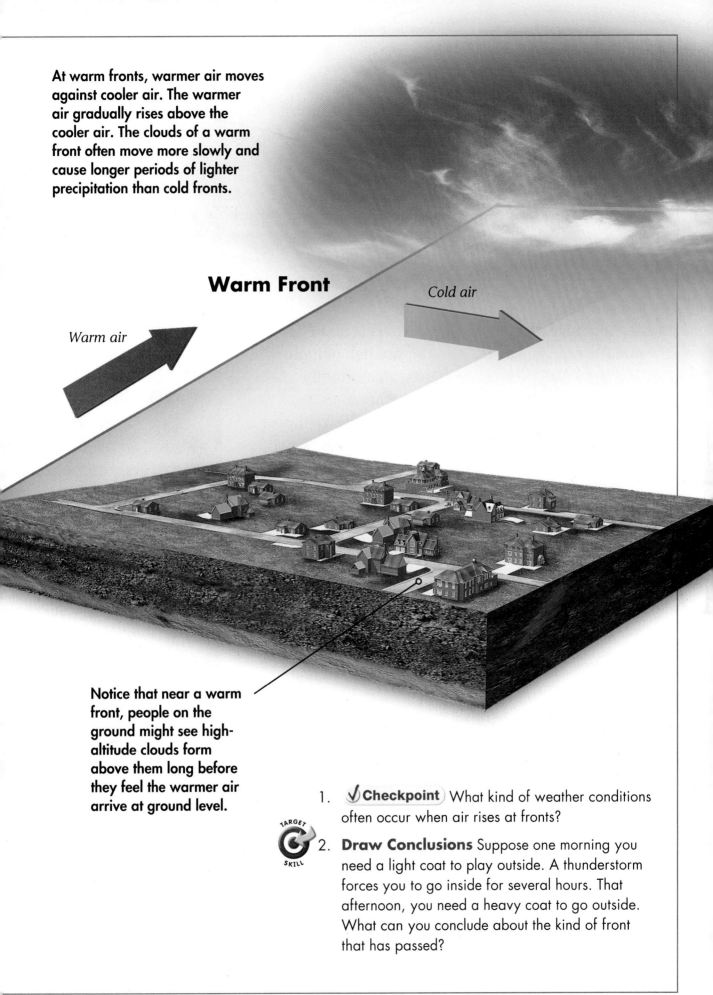

At warm fronts, warmer air moves against cooler air. The warmer air gradually rises above the cooler air. The clouds of a warm front often move more slowly and cause longer periods of lighter precipitation than cold fronts.

Warm Front

Warm air

Cold air

Notice that near a warm front, people on the ground might see high-altitude clouds form above them long before they feel the warmer air arrive at ground level.

1. **✓ Checkpoint** What kind of weather conditions often occur when air rises at fronts?

2. **Draw Conclusions** Suppose one morning you need a light coat to play outside. A thunderstorm forces you to go inside for several hours. That afternoon, you need a heavy coat to go outside. What can you conclude about the kind of front that has passed?

Highs and Lows

The Sun is the source of energy for all weather. You know that the heating of Earth by the Sun is uneven. This causes the air in some places to be warmer or cooler than the air in other places.

Air pressure is affected by air temperature. For example, air that is cool is heavier and under higher pressure than the same volume of warmer air. Differences in air pressure cause wind because air moves from areas of higher pressure to areas of lower pressure.

You have probably seen the letters H and L on weather maps. The H stands for an area of high pressure. Places under high pressure normally have fair weather. The L on a weather map is used to identify low pressure. Places under a low-pressure system are usually cloudy and windy. They may also have some kind of precipitation. Fronts are connected with low-pressure systems.

Cyclones

On Earth's surface, high-pressure air surrounds warm, low-pressure air. The high pressure causes the warm air in the center to rise. As this air rises, the high-pressure air around it flows in to take its place. This flow of air forms a wind that spirals inward and forms a weather system called a **cyclone.**

Remember that winds in the United States generally flow from west to east. Earth's rotation causes winds to move in this way. Earth's rotation also affects cyclone winds. In the United States and other places north of the equator, cyclone winds spin in a counterclockwise direction and flow inward toward the center. South of the equator, winds from cyclones flow in a clockwise direction and spiral toward the center. Areas of stormy weather are usually near cyclones. A hurricane is an example of a severe storm with cyclone winds.

Cyclones sometimes cause severe weather.

H

This symbol is used on weather maps to show a region of high pressure.

L

This symbol is used on weather maps to show a region of low pressure.

Anticyclone

Cyclone

HIGH

LOW

Winds in cyclones spin in opposite directions from those in anticyclones.

The diagram shows how air moves in a cyclone in the United States. Winds in an *anticyclone* spin in the opposite direction as in a cyclone. North of the equator, this means winds from an anticyclone flow in a clockwise direction and away from the center. Anticyclones form around areas of higher pressure. Usually, but not always, clear skies and fair weather come with these areas of high pressure.

✔ Lesson Review

1. What kind of weather conditions are likely to occur if a cold air mass moves into an area of warm, humid air?

2. How do cyclones and anticyclones affect weather?

TARGET SKILL

3. **Draw Conclusions** An air mass moves into the middle of North America. It has low humidity and high temperatures. Where can you conclude that this air mass formed?

Lesson 3

What causes severe weather?

Sometimes winds and the water cycle can lead to dangerous weather. Severe weather includes thunderstorms, tornadoes, hurricanes, and monsoons.

Thunderstorms

What kinds of severe weather happen where you live? Are there thunderstorms? Do you have tornadoes, hurricanes, or blizzards? These are all forms of severe weather that may be familiar to you. But just having very high or very low temperatures can be dangerous. If you know that severe weather is coming, you need to prepare for it.

Thunderstorms can form in different ways. Often, the first stage of a thunderstorm has strong, quickly rising currents of moist air. Clouds grow as water condenses in the rising air. The clouds have both ice crystals and water droplets.

In the storm's second stage, precipitation starts to fall. This pulls some air downward. The storm has both upward and downward currents of air.

In the storm's last stage, all of the air motion is downward, and the clouds get smaller as precipitation leaves them. Remember from Chapter 5 that the condensation and precipitation of thunderstorms are parts of the water cycle.

1. ✔**Checkpoint** Describe the three stages of a thunderstorm.

2. **Draw Conclusions** Why should you take cover as soon as possible when there is a severe storm warning?

First stage: All air currents move upward.

Second stage: Air currents are mixed.

Final stage: All air currents move downward.

Standards Focus 5ES4.b Students know the influence that the ocean has on the weather and the role that the water cycle plays in weather patterns.
5ES4.c Students know the causes and effects of severe weather.

Different areas of a thunderstorm cloud have either positive or negative electrical charges. This may be caused by the precipitation colliding in the air currents of the cloud.

Lightning is a large electrical spark moving between areas of opposite charge. Lightning can warm air to 30,000°C in a fraction of a second. This high temperature causes the air to expand so rapidly that it makes vibrations in the air. We hear these vibrations as thunder.

What we see as one flash of lightning is often many flashes of both positive and negative charges going up and down.

Lightning often hits tall objects. If you cannot get inside a building during a thunderstorm, move away from trees or high towers. Stay low, but do not lie on the ground.

The negative charges on the cloud cause positive charges to gather in the ground below.

Watches and Warnings

A **severe thunderstorm watch** means that severe thunderstorms with high winds and hail might form.

A **severe thunderstorm warning** means that severe thunderstorms have formed and you should prepare for them. Get inside as soon as possible.

How Tornadoes Form

Before thunderstorms form, winds change direction and increase in speed. Winds begin to spin.

As the thunderstorm forms, air within it rises. The spinning air begins to tilt upward.

The area of spinning grows wider.

Tornadoes

Thunderstorms can bring thunder, lightning, strong winds, and rain. In some cases, thunderstorms also bring tornadoes. A tornado is a rotating column of air that extends from clouds in a thunderstorm to the ground.

Many things must happen for a tornado to form. First, layers of wind in a storm blow at different speeds or in different directions. Between these layers, a column of air starts spinning like a log rolling on its side. Upward winds lift one end of this spinning column. Downward winds push down on the other end. The spinning column of air is called a funnel cloud. It is called a tornado when it touches the ground.

Usually, tornadoes last only a few minutes, but they can leave a path many kilometers long and hundreds of meters wide. Winds in a tornado move at hundreds of kilometers per hour. These winds can move cars and buildings around.

If you hear warning sirens or see tornado announcements on television, take cover right away. It is best to go to a basement. If you cannot do that, go to a closet or windowless room in the center of the building. Why do you think it is important to stay away from windows?

1. ✓**Checkpoint** How do tornadoes form?

2. ✏️ **Writing in Science Narrative** Write a short story about a tornado striking a small town. Describe the weather conditions leading up to the tornado and how a character learns that a tornado is coming and reacts to avoid danger.

Map Fact

About 1,000 tornadoes occur in the United States each year. Most of these occur in the central part of the United States during March, April, and May. Because it has more tornadoes than other places, this part of the country is called Tornado Alley.

Watches and Warnings

A **tornado watch** is issued when conditions are right for tornadoes to form.

A **tornado warning** is issued when a tornado has been seen. You should take cover to protect yourself from the storm.

How Hurricanes Form

Thunderstorms grow out of a tropical depression.

Air pressure at the ocean's surface drops. Surface winds blow faster and begin to swirl. A tropical storm develops.

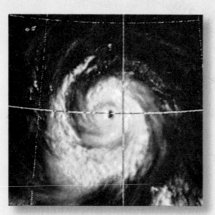

Thunderstorms begin to move in spiral bands. Air pressure drops lower, and surface winds blow faster. The tropical storm is now a hurricane.

Hurricanes

A strong cyclone that forms over warm ocean water is called a hurricane. Hurricanes get their energy from warm ocean water. When water vapor from the ocean condenses, it releases heat energy. Under the right conditions, this heat energy builds and drives the winds of a hurricane.

Even though the spinning winds of a hurricane are not as fast as those of a tornado, these ocean storms are more destructive. Do you know why? First, hurricanes last for days, possibly hitting several locations. Second, a hurricane can be hundreds of kilometers wide. Third, hurricanes can cause huge waves that cause severe damage and flood the shore. Finally, heavy rains can cause floods farther inland.

Locate these places on a map or globe. Look at the chart below for other names of hurricanes.

Other Names for Hurricanes

Atlantic and Eastern Pacific Oceans	Hurricane
Northwest Pacific Ocean	Typhoon
Southwest Pacific Ocean	Severe tropical cyclone
Southwest Indian Ocean	Tropical cyclone
North Indian Ocean	Severe cyclonic storm

Hurricane Movement

Direction of storm

The Eye

The spot in the middle of the hurricane is its eye. Winds in the eye are gentle. The eye has no rain and few, if any, clouds. It usually has the lowest air pressure of the storm. The entire hurricane spins around its eye.

Warm ocean water fuels hurricanes.

1. ✓Checkpoint What is the source of energy for a hurricane?

2. ✎ **Writing in Science**
   Persuasive Create a poster, play, or radio advertisement that would persuade people that severe weather is dangerous and tells what they can do to be safe.

Ocean Temperature Affects Weather

The ocean is important to the surface temperature all around the world. Water evaporates from the warm surface of the oceans. The water vapor is transported by winds to cooler places, where it condenses. As water vapor condenses and forms precipitation, heat is released.

The amount of precipitation an area receives depends on the temperature at the ocean's surface. Changes in the ocean's temperature, even small changes, can cause large changes in weather. *El Niño* is a warming of the eastern Pacific Ocean near the equator that happens every 4 to 12 years. This change can cause very wet and very dry seasons in many parts of the world.

You have read that land heats and cools more quickly than water. This means air above land heats and cools more quickly than air above water. Large bodies of water, such as oceans, can affect the temperature of the air above them. The air in these areas is **tempered,** or warmed in winter and cooled in summer.

Monsoons

In the United States, winds generally flow from west to east. In some areas of the world, winds change direction with the seasons. A monsoon is an example of this type of wind. Monsoons are common in southern and southeastern Asia.

In the summer, air over the ocean is cooler than air over land. The moist air over the ocean moves toward land. The summer monsoon brings strong winds and very heavy rains. People who live in this area depend on these rains to grow crops. The wind pattern reverses in the winter. Cold air over land is dry, and the winter season brings very little precipitation.

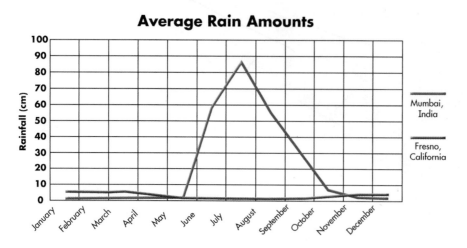

This graph shows the average rainfall for Mumbai, India, and Fresno, California. You can compare and see how much more rain falls in India during its summer monsoon season.

Map Fact

The city of Cherrapunji is located in eastern India. This area receives about 1,080 centimeters of rainfall each year. Most of this rain falls during the summer monsoon.

✔ **Lesson Review**

1. Explain ways in which the ocean influences the weather.

2. What are four types of severe weather?

231

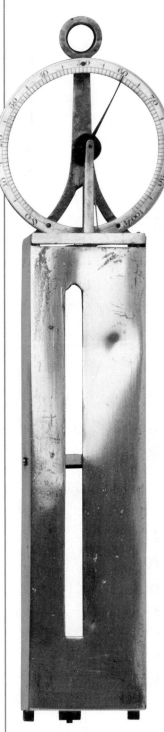

Lesson 4

How are weather forecasts made?

People use many kinds of instruments to collect weather data. Weather forecasts are based on the data collected.

Collecting Data

What exactly is weather? How would you define it? To completely describe the weather at any particular place and time, you need to describe all of its parts: temperature, moisture, clouds, precipitation, wind speed, air pressure, and wind direction. All of these parts may interact with one another and change during the course of a day. They may change even more quickly than that!

Many kinds of tools measure these changing parts of the weather, called *variables*. Some of these tools might even be in your home. Have you used a weather-measuring tool that is not shown here?

A **barometer** shows air pressure. In some barometers, air pressure pushes mercury up a tube. The barometer shown here has a small sealed container connected to a dial. When air pressure squeezes the container, the dial of the barometer moves.

A hygrometer measures the moisture in the air. Some hygrometers have a pointer connected to a horsehair. The hair gets shorter in drier air and moves the pointer.

Horsehair hygrometer

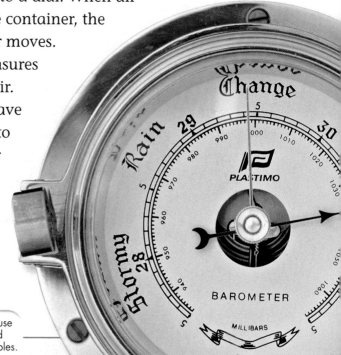

Standards Focus 5ES4.d Students know how to use weather maps and data to predict local weather and know that weather forecasts depend on many variables.

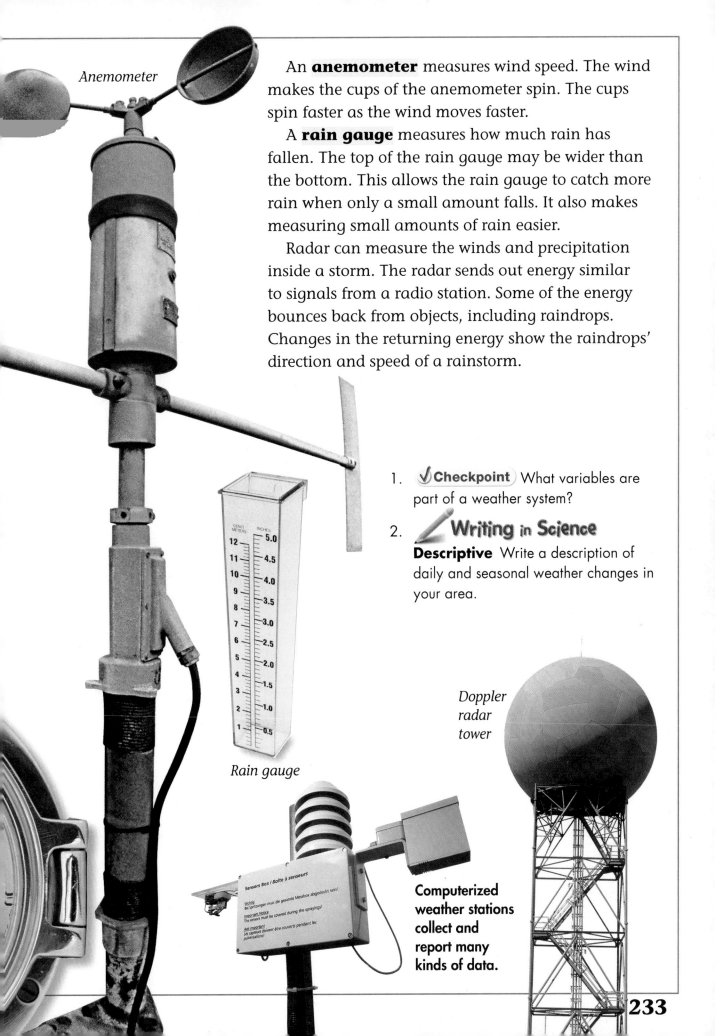

Anemometer

An **anemometer** measures wind speed. The wind makes the cups of the anemometer spin. The cups spin faster as the wind moves faster.

A **rain gauge** measures how much rain has fallen. The top of the rain gauge may be wider than the bottom. This allows the rain gauge to catch more rain when only a small amount falls. It also makes measuring small amounts of rain easier.

Radar can measure the winds and precipitation inside a storm. The radar sends out energy similar to signals from a radio station. Some of the energy bounces back from objects, including raindrops. Changes in the returning energy show the raindrops' direction and speed of a rainstorm.

1. **✓Checkpoint** What variables are part of a weather system?

2. **✏ Writing in Science**
Descriptive Write a description of daily and seasonal weather changes in your area.

Rain gauge

Doppler radar tower

Computerized weather stations collect and report many kinds of data.

233

Technology Helps Weather Forecasters

A weather forecaster is a person who predicts and reports on weather. To predict weather, weather forecasters use observations of past and present weather conditions.

Technology helps weather forecasters gather weather data. The tools you read about earlier in this lesson are some of the ways technology has been used to make weather measurements. The time line shows some other technologies used by weather forecasters and when these first came into use.

The first weather balloon carries instruments into the atmosphere.

1844   1927

The telegraph is invented and is soon used to transmit weather reports.

Weather Instrument Technology

The invention of the telegraph allowed weather forecasters in different places to share data. This made it possible to see patterns in weather that improved forecast accuracy. Today, weather reports are communicated more quickly to more people through the use of radio, television, and computer technology.

The first weather balloon was launched in 1927. Weather balloons carry instruments high into the atmosphere. The instruments measure air conditions, such as temperature and air pressure, at different altitudes. This data is transmitted to receivers on the ground.

Satellites are important for weather forecasting. Satellites orbiting Earth use cameras and other tools to show the locations of clouds. Instruments on satellites also form pictures that show temperature at different places on Earth. Satellites can even show how much water vapor is in the air. Unlike weather stations on Earth, some satellites move around Earth. This motion allows satellites to supply weather data for all parts of Earth.

Radar technology uses echoes to measure distance and motion. Some radar stations gather data about clouds and their height in the atmosphere. A newer form of radar, called Doppler radar, can measure precipitation and air motion. This technology is used to find storms and track their motions. Doppler radar is very useful for tracking tornadoes.

The first weather satellite is launched.

1960

Offices of the National Weather Service begin using Doppler radar at sites around the country.

1990s

Scientists called meteorologists use data from weather stations, radar, and satellites to forecast the weather.

1. ✓**Checkpoint** Identify weather variables that may be measured by weather balloons.

2. Use materials from the library-media center to find out about other instruments used to gather weather data. Make a poster that explains the weather variables that each instrument can measure. Be sure to include when the instrument was first used.

235

Weather Patterns in Forecasting

Weather follows patterns. For example, temperature usually rises during the day and falls at night. Temperature also changes with the seasons. Precipitation may change seasonally, bringing rain in spring and snow in winter.

Weather forecasters observe many variables to find patterns of weather change. They use this data to make inferences about how air, land, and the water cycle make weather systems. This helps forecasters better predict the weather.

Predictions are sometimes made by assuming that future weather will act the way that similar weather has in the past. The more similar the conditions are, the more likely they are to develop in the same way. The more data forecasters have, the better their predictions will be.

Weather Maps

Forecasters often display their data and predictions on weather maps. Most weather maps display air temperature, air pressure, and precipitation. Look at the weather maps on page 237. The legends beneath the maps explain the symbols and colors used.

The lines showing fronts on a weather map can tell you much about the weather. The triangles or half circles on the lines point in the direction in which the front is moving. Warm fronts bring warmer weather. Cold fronts bring colder weather. Recall that fronts are always in places of low pressure and often bring cloudy weather. They also tend to move from west to east across most of the United States. Areas of high pressure that are away from fronts often have clear skies.

Weather forecasters often use charts like this one to show long-range weather forecasts.

Seven-Day Forecast for Lake Tahoe, CA

Tuesday	Wednesday	Thursday	Friday	Saturday	Sunday	Monday
☀	☀	⛅	⛈	☀	☀	☀
High 28°C	High 26°C	High 26°C	High 26°C	High 27°C	High 26°C	High 24°C
Low 6°C	Low 4°C	Low 5°C	Low 4°C	Low 4°C	Low 4°C	Low 5°C

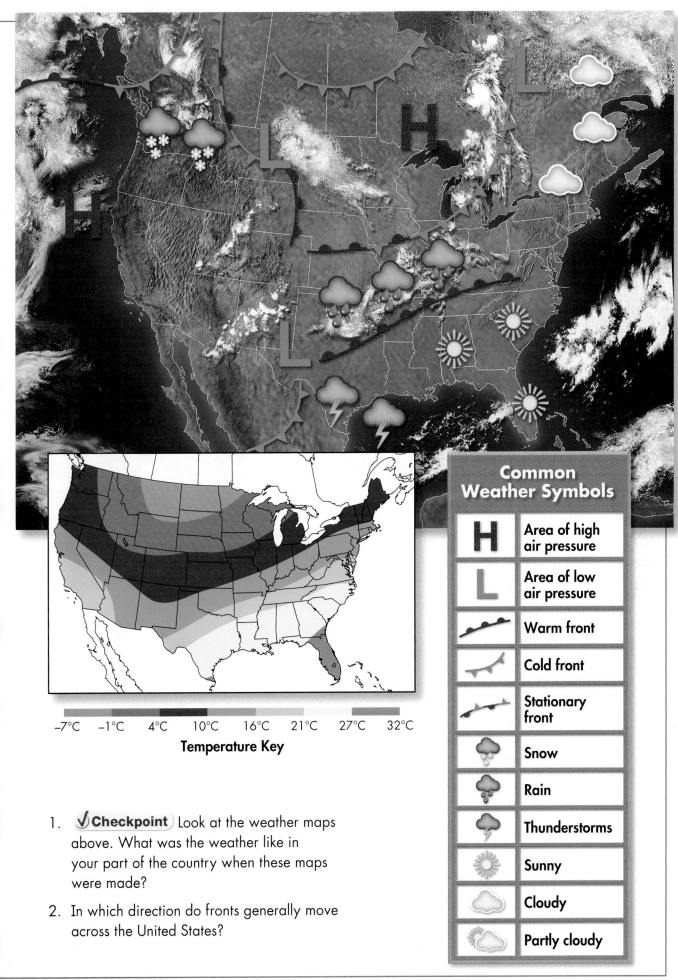

Common Weather Symbols

H	Area of high air pressure
L	Area of low air pressure
	Warm front
	Cold front
	Stationary front
	Snow
	Rain
	Thunderstorms
	Sunny
	Cloudy
	Partly cloudy

−7°C −1°C 4°C 10°C 16°C 21°C 27°C 32°C

Temperature Key

1. ✓**Checkpoint** Look at the weather maps above. What was the weather like in your part of the country when these maps were made?

2. In which direction do fronts generally move across the United States?

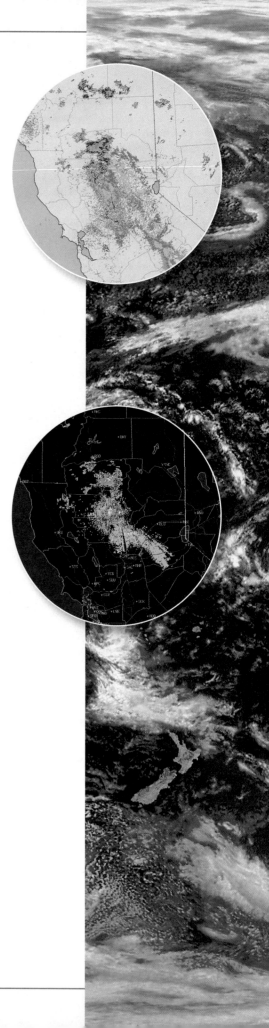

Satellite and Radar Maps

Weather forecasters use many different kinds of maps to show weather conditions and make predictions. The kind of map used depends on what is being shown. For example, satellite images can show clouds. These images can be shown on top of a map of the United States to show the clouds' locations.

Most of the maps used to show weather conditions are made by high-speed computers. Doppler radar detects precipitation and how wind affects its movement. A computer analyzes and maps these data so quickly that a real-time image is formed. This technology is very useful for alerting people to dangers from severe weather such as thunderstorms and tornadoes.

Computers also make maps that are used to forecast weather. A computer model uses data from many weather stations to predict changes in weather. Predictions from one or more models can then be shown on maps to forecast weather. Advances in technology have improved the accuracy of short-term forecasts. But, because slight changes in the weather can cause big changes later on, long-term forecasts are less reliable.

✓ Lesson Review

1. Identify three variables other than temperature that are used to make weather forecasts.

2. A weather forecaster reports that a low-pressure system is approaching your area. What kind of weather do you predict will occur?

3. **Draw Conclusions** Why is a weather map formed from Doppler radar a better indicator of current weather than one showing a forecast made with a computer model?

TARGET
SKILL

238

Try Making Your Own Weather Forecast

Explore the relationships among weather in different cities. Select two cities from states that are located east and west of each other. Using news reports, record the daily weather conditions for each city in a chart each day for two weeks. Include information about air pressure, temperature, cloud cover, and precipitation.

Examine your results. Look for patterns between the weather conditions in the two cities. Describe what you learn. Now, predict how the weather will change over the next several days. Check your predictions.

239

Analyzing Tornado Data

Somewhere in the United States, thunderstorms may produce tornadoes this month. Tornadoes happen during all times of the year, and they happen in every state. The bar graph shows the average number of tornadoes that happen each month in the United States.

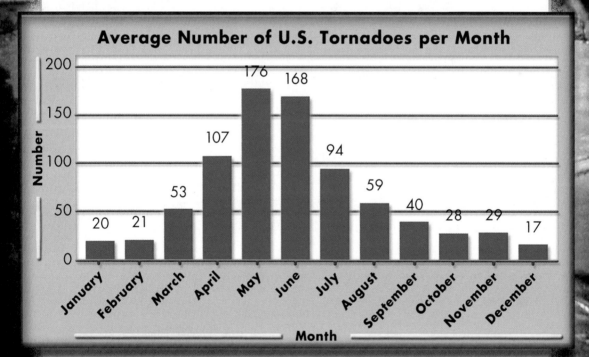

Average Number of U.S. Tornadoes per Month

One way to describe a pattern in the data above is to use ranges. Ranges show how much the data changes. A lower range shows less change. A higher range shows more change. For example, the range in the three months of January, February, and March is 53–20, or 33. The range in the three months of March, April, and May is 176–53, or 123. So, the change in the number of tornadoes each month from March through May is almost four times the change from January through March!

Use the graph to answer the following questions.

1. What is the range from June through August?
   A. 146
   B. 109
   C. 85
   D. 74

2. What is the range in the number of tornadoes from September through February?
   A. 59
   B. 40
   C. 23
   D. 19

3. Between which two months does the number of tornadoes change the most?
   A. March–April
   B. April–May
   C. May–June
   D. June–July

4. Between which two months does the number of tornadoes change the least?
   A. January–February
   B. February–March
   C. March–April
   D. April–May

5. The number of tornadoes from January through May
   A. increases by 109.
   B. decreases by 109.
   C. increases by 156.
   D. decreases by 156.

Lab zone Take-Home Activity

Record the outside air temperature throughout one day. At what time is the temperature at its highest point? lowest point? Is the greatest change in the morning, afternoon, evening, or overnight?

Guided Inquiry

Investigate What causes convection currents?

In a convection current, particles in a gas or liquid move from a warmer area to a cooler one.

Materials

4 foam cups

graduated cylinder

very warm water, ice water, room-temperature water

clear plastic tub, red and blue food coloring

timer or clock with a second hand and drawing paper

red and blue markers and metric ruler

Process Skills

You can **make and use a model** to help explain an object or event.

What to Do

1 Place the cups in 2 rows of 2.

2 **Measure** 150 mL of warm water into each of the 2 cups on the left. Measure 150 mL of ice water into each of the 2 cups on the right. Label the cups.

Be careful!

Pour water carefully.

Let the coloring slide down the side of the container.

5 cm

very warm water

3 Pour room temperature water into the tub to a depth of 5 cm. Measure the depth using a metric ruler. Balance the tub on the cups. Wait 5 minutes.

4 Put 4 drops of red coloring into the left end of the tub. Put 4 drops of blue coloring into the right end.

5ES4.0 Energy from the Sun heats Earth unevenly, causing air movements that result in changing weather patterns. **5ES4.a** Students know uneven heating of Earth causes air movements (convection currents). **5IE6.f** Select appropriate tools (e.g., thermometers, metersticks, balances, and graduated cylinders) and make quantitative observations.

5 You **made a model** of convection currents.

6 **Observe** how the food coloring moves. Using red and blue markers, draw what you see. Record your data on a chart.

Convection Currents

Time	Side View	Top View
After 1 minute		
After 2 minutes		
After 3 minutes		

ice water

Explain Your Results

1. Describe how the food coloring moved at the warm and cold ends of your **model.**

2. Relate your **observations** to warm and cold convection currents found in the air.

Go Further

Investigate further to find a way to make two convection systems in the tub.

Focus on the BIG Idea

The Sun heats Earth unevenly, causing changing weather.

Lesson 1

How does air move?
- Atmospheric pressure decreases with increasing height above sea level.
- At any one point, the force of atmospheric pressure is equal in every direction.
- Convection currents drive weather patterns.
- Uneven heating of Earth's surface can cause convection currents in the atmosphere.

Lesson 2

What are air masses?
- An air mass is described by where it comes from. The ocean tempers the air above it, which means it is warmed in the winter and cooled in the summer.
- When air masses meet to form fronts, severe weather can form.
- Four types of severe weather are thunderstorms, tornadoes, hurricanes, and monsoons.

Lesson 3

What causes severe weather?
- Four types of severe weather are thunderstorms, tornadoes, hurricanes, and monsoons.
- The ocean influences weather patterns. The ocean tempers the air above it, which means it is warmed in the winter and cooled in the summer.
- Severe weather can form from cyclones, which can form when air masses meet.

Lesson 4

How are weather forecasts made?
- Many variables are used to make weather forecasts.
- Local weather can be forecasted using weather maps and data.
- Advances in technology have allowed weather forecasters to make accurate predictions.

Cross-Curricular Links

English–Language Arts

Building Vocabulary

Look again at pages 206–207. Identify the pictures behind the terms *convection current*, *front*, and *anemometer*. Write a paragraph about each term. Tell how each term relates to the picture and to the other terms.

Mathematics

Monsoons

If $\frac{3}{4}$ of the rainfall of Cherrapunji, India, falls during the summer monsoon, what percentage of rain falls during this period?

Visual and Performing Arts

Convection Currents

Land cools more quickly than water does. This causes convection currents near shorelines to move in the opposite direction at night than during the day. Make a drawing to show how winds move at night near a shoreline.

Challenge!

Health

Breathing and Atmospheric Pressure

When you breathe, a muscle called the diaphragm contracts and relaxes, changing the size of your chest cavity. Use research materials to find out how this action affects air pressure and breathing. Write a summary of your findings.

Use Vocabulary

air mass (p. 218)	**cyclone** (p. 222)
anemometer (p. 233)	**front** (p. 220)
atmospheric pressure (p. 211)	**rain gauge** (p. 233)
barometer (p. 232)	**tempered** (p. 230)
convection current (p. 214)	**wind** (p. 215)

Fill in the blanks with the correct vocabulary words. If you have trouble answering a question, read the listed page again.

1. A(n) ____ is used to measure air pressure.

2. A boundary between two air masses is a(n) ____.

3. A(n) ____ is used to measure the amount of rainfall.

4. Wind speed is measured by a(n) ____.

5. A large body of air that generally has the same amount of moisture and temperature throughout is a(n) ____.

6. A(n) ____ is a wind that spirals inward around an area of low pressure.

7. The circular path formed by the rising and sinking of matter is a(n) ____.

8. ____ is a horizontal movement of air that results from differences in air pressure.

Think About It

9. Explain how oceans can affect the weather in an area.

10. Describe how convection currents relate to weather patterns.

11. **Process Skills** **Interpret the data** in the chart to conclude what type of front moved through the area.

Day	Noon Temperature
Monday	28°C
Tuesday	20°C

12. **Draw Conclusions** Make a graphic organizer like the one below. Use the following facts to draw a conclusion.
- Gas particles become more spread out at higher altitudes.
- At higher altitudes, there is less air above you pushing down so the air pressure is lower.
- Mountain climbers need oxygen tanks to breathe well at high altitudes.

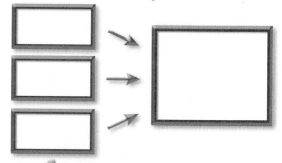

13. **Writing in Science**
Descriptive Write a description of one type of severe weather and explain how it forms. Then describe what can be done to stay safe in that kind of severe weather.

California Standards Practice

Write the letter of the correct answer.

14. What kind of weather might a cyclone bring to land if it formed over warm water?

  A cold and stormy

  B hurricane conditions

  C clear and sunny

  D monsoon conditions

15. What causes wind at Earth's surface?

  A moist air

  B dry air

  C high temperatures

  D temperature differences

16. What type of air mass comes from tropical ocean areas?

  A warm and dry

  B cold and dry

  C warm and moist

  D cold and moist

17. A weather map shows that a warm front is approaching the region where you live. You can expect

  A temperatures to drop.

  B temperatures to rise.

  C no change in temperature.

  D severe thunderstorms.

18. Which of the following *best* describes how air moves?

  A Air moves from areas of low pressure to areas of high pressure.

  B Air moves from areas of high pressure to areas of low pressure.

  C Air moves quickly.

  D Air moves from areas of higher altitude to areas of lower altitude.

19. What causes air currents?

  A uneven heating of Earth's surface

  B Earth's distance from the Sun

  C the meeting of two fronts

  D the heating of air by lightning

20. You see the symbol below on a weather map. What does the symbol show?

  A a hurricane

  B heavy rain

  C hot air

  D high pressure

El Niño and the "BIG BELCH"

Like living animals such as cows and sheep, the Earth sometimes "burps." During El Niño years in particular, the planet suddenly releases large amounts of gas, just as you might after drinking a carbonated beverage.

Every three to seven years, the temperature of the Pacific Ocean along the equator warms up a great deal. The phenomenon was given the name El Niño, or "The Child," by people in Peru. El Niño changes "normal" weather patterns around the world.

The reason scientists sometimes call the changes "a big belch" is because two greenhouse gases in the atmosphere, methane and carbon dioxide, increase significantly during El Niño years. So much gas is released that some scientists compare it to Earth having a planet-sized case of heartburn.

The image shows sea surface height relative to normal ocean conditions.

Standards Focus 5ES4.b Students know the influence that the ocean has on the weather and the role that the water cycle plays in weather patterns.

Many greenhouse gases result from people burning fossil fuels. That factor doesn't change during El Niño years, so why do methane and carbon dioxide increase so much? Scientists thought that the increase was due to a change in the life cycle of plants during El Niño years. But now NASA scientists think wildfires may get the "big belch" started. In El Niño years, large areas in the tropics become very dry, and fires can result. During the 1997–1998 El Niño, huge fires burned in Mexico and Southeast Asia, for example.

At the same time that burning plants are releasing huge amounts of carbon dioxide into the atmosphere, fewer plants are growing in the dry tropics. Plants take in carbon dioxide from the air. With less plant growth, less carbon dioxide is taken in by plants. Just a small change in the amount absorbed by plants is enough to give Earth heartburn.

Lab zone Take-Home Activity

Research the effect of greenhouse gases on Earth. Find out ways to reduce the amount of these gases in the atmosphere. Use the information to make a pamphlet that informs the public about ways to reduce greenhouse gases.

Atmospheric Scientist

Lin Chambers works with other scientists to understand how light energy flows through clouds.

When Lin Chambers was young, she and her family lived in Europe. Almost every year, they flew back to the United States for a visit. Those airplane rides inspired Chambers to study aeronautical engineering in college.

Chambers got her first full-time job at NASA. She studied how spacecraft heat up as they travel through the atmosphere. A few years later, she began to work on a project to study how light energy and heat energy move in and out of Earth's atmosphere. Chambers focuses on how light energy flows through clouds. She compares measurements from satellites with measurements taken from the ground. She runs computer models to understand how clouds can change the direction of light flow through the atmosphere.

Chambers works with many other scientists. Each scientist analyzes data in different ways. The scientists check each other's work and discuss different conclusions they can draw. Working as a team, each scientist is responsible for a different piece of the problem. The project goal is to produce accurate data about Earth's climate. Chambers says, "We rely on each other," stressing the importance of collaboration in her work.

Chambers loves studying clouds. It brings her back to the reason for her first career choice. Thinking about her experience on airplanes she admits, "The thing I enjoyed most about it was sitting at the window, looking down at the clouds."

Lab zone Take-Home Activity

Keep your own cloud journal to identify cloud types. Also find out about and look for the clouds known as contrails. Record information about the weather. Write down the date and time of your observations. Draw conclusions about cloud types and the weather, and compare your conclusions with those of a friend.

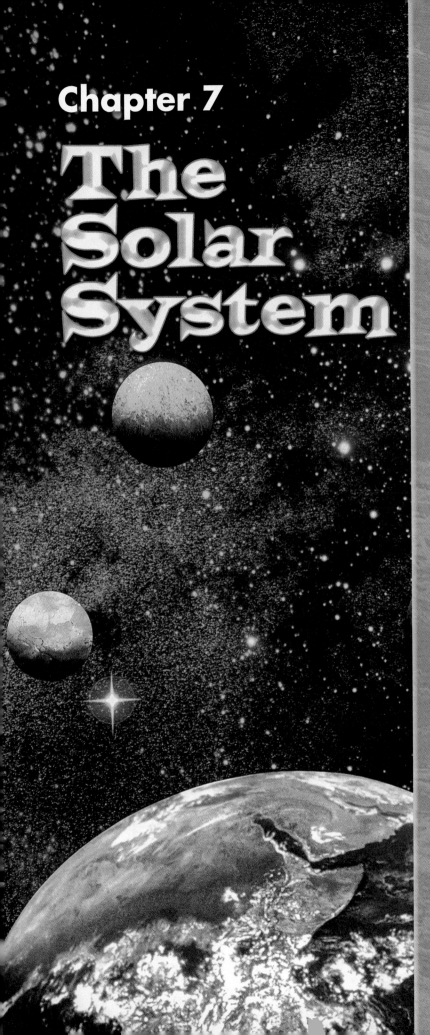

Chapter 7

The Solar System

CALIFORNIA Standards Preview

5ES5.0 The solar system consists of planets and other bodies that orbit the Sun in predictable paths. As a basis for understanding this concept:

5ES5.a Students know the Sun, an average star, is the central and largest body in the solar system and is composed primarily of hydrogen and helium.

5ES5.b Students know the solar system includes the planet Earth, the Moon, the Sun, eight other planets and their satellites, and smaller objects, such as asteroids and comets.*

5ES5.c Students know the path of a planet around the Sun is due to the gravitational attraction between the Sun and the planet.

5IE6.0 Scientific progress is made by asking meaningful questions and conducting careful investigations. As a basis for understanding this concept and addressing the content in the other three strands, students should develop their own questions and perform investigations. (Also **5IE6.b**, **5IE6.c**, **5IE6.d**, **5IE6.e**, **5IE6.f**, **5IE6.g**, **5IE6.i**)

*The California State Board of Education adopted the Science Content Standards in 1998. In 2006, the International Astronomical Union passed Resolutions 5A and 6A. In Resolution 5A, the term "planet" is defined. This definition recognizes eight planets in the solar system. Resolution 6A defines a new kind of celestial object, "dwarf planet."

Standards Focus Questions

- What is the Sun?
- Why do planets revolve around the Sun?
- What are the inner planets?
- What do we know about the outer planets and beyond?

What objects in space make up the solar system?

star

solar system

ellipse

planet

DIGITAL

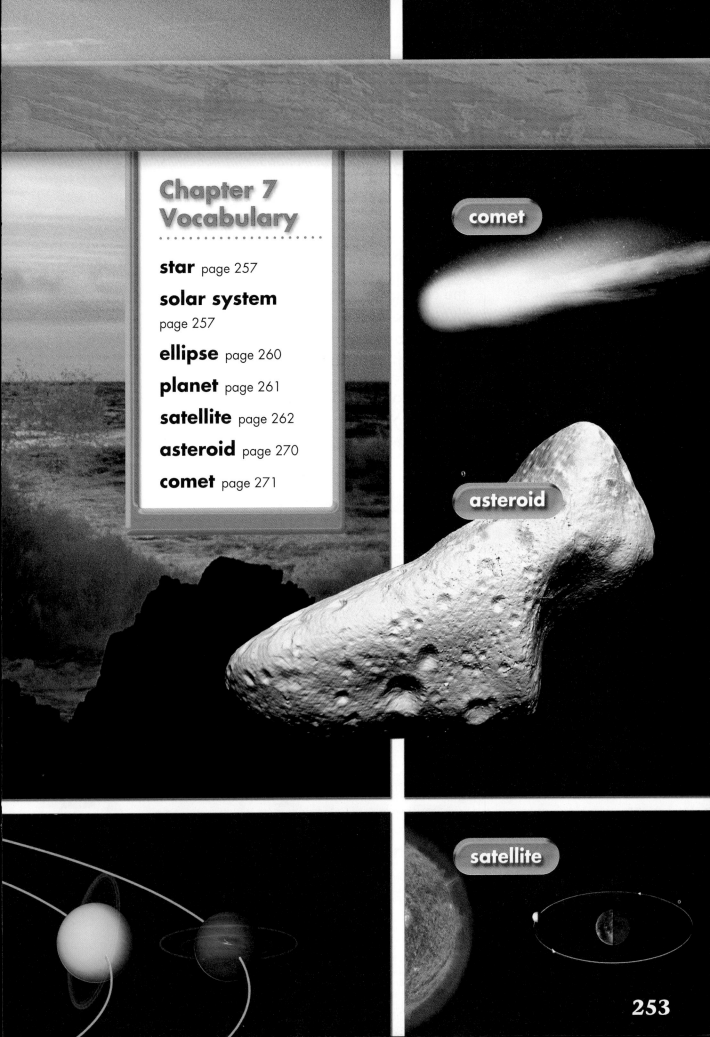

Chapter 7 Vocabulary

comet

asteroid

satellite

Be careful!

Wear safety goggles.

Explore What is the shape of a planet's path?

Materials

safety goggles

paper

heavy cardboard

tape

2 pins

metric ruler

30 cm piece of string

Process Skills

Making a model can help you make **inferences.**

What to Do

1 Tape the paper onto the cardboard. Stick a pin in the center. Tie a knot to make a loop of string. Put the loop over the pin. Use a pencil and the string to draw a circle. Hold the pencil upright against the stretched string as you draw your circle.

2 Put a second pin 5 mm away from the first. Put the loop over both pins. Try to draw another circle. **Observe** the shape. Is the length from the center to the edge the same in all directions?

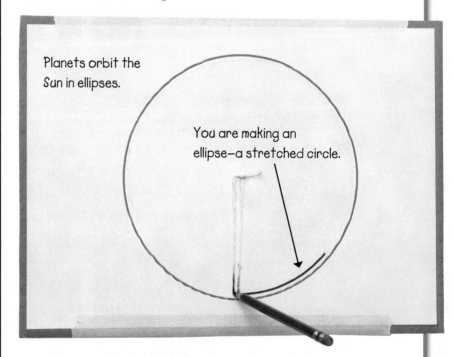

Planets orbit the Sun in ellipses.

You are making an ellipse—a stretched circle.

Explain Your Results

Infer How would moving the second pin farther from the center affect the shape of the new ellipse?

5ES5.0 The solar system consists of planets that orbit the Sun in predictable paths. **5ES5.c** Students know the path of a planet around the Sun is due to the gravitational attraction between the Sun and the planet. **5IE6.g** Record data by using appropriate graphic representations (including charts, graphs, and labeled diagrams) and make inferences based on those data.

How to Read Science

Make Inferences

A writer doesn't always tell us everything. As you read, you might have to put some facts together. When you **make an inference,** you make a guess from facts you have read or **observed.** Some facts are marked in the article below.

- Try to make an inference from the facts you read.

- Use your own experiences to help you make inferences.

Science Article

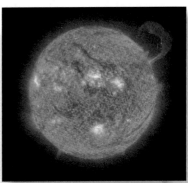

Deciding About Distance

Mercury takes 88 days to travel around the Sun. Mars takes 687 days, and Neptune takes about 164.5 years. Each planet travels in its own path and is a different distance from the Sun. Which of these three planets is farthest from the Sun?

Apply It!
Study this graphic organizer. Make a graphic organizer like this one. List the facts from the science article in your graphic organizer. Write your **inference.**

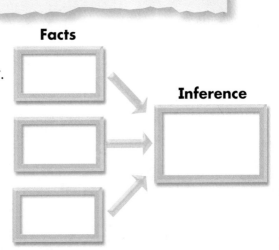

Facts

Inference

You Are There!

It's late afternoon on a beautiful autumn day. Sitting on a blanket, you dig your toes into the cooling sand. The air grows cooler as the once-blue sky fills with shades of orange and red. Suddenly, your hat is picked up by a light wind. As you place your hat back on your head, you look toward the ocean. Within minutes, the Sun disappears from view. You've just experienced the beauty of a California sunset. What do we know about the Sun and the other objects in the solar system?

DIGITAL

What is the Sun?

The Sun is an average-sized star made mostly of hydrogen and helium. This star is the central and largest body in our solar system.

The Star of Our Solar System

The Sun is a star. A **star** is a huge ball of very hot gas that gives off energy. The Sun is the center of the solar system. The **solar system** is made of the Sun and its planets, along with many moons, asteroids, and comets.

The Sun is the largest object in the solar system. Scientists have been able to calculate its mass from the shapes of the planets' orbits around it. The Sun has almost 99 percent of the mass in the solar system. The Sun is huge when compared to Earth. In fact, the Sun has about one million times the volume of Earth. If you think of the Sun as a gumball machine, it would take over one million Earth gumballs to fill the Sun gumball machine!

The Sun is an average-sized star. Stars called giants have diameters that are 8 to 100 times larger than the Sun's diameter. Supergiant stars can be more than 500 times larger than the Sun. Other much smaller stars are only about the size of Earth.

The Sun gives off large amounts of energy. Because the temperature inside the Sun's center is very high, the hydrogen particles are moving very fast. When the particles hit each other, they can combine to form particles of the element helium. This fusion of hydrogen into helium produces most of the Sun's energy.

1. **√Checkpoint** What bodies make up the solar system?

2. Which two elements make up the Sun's center?

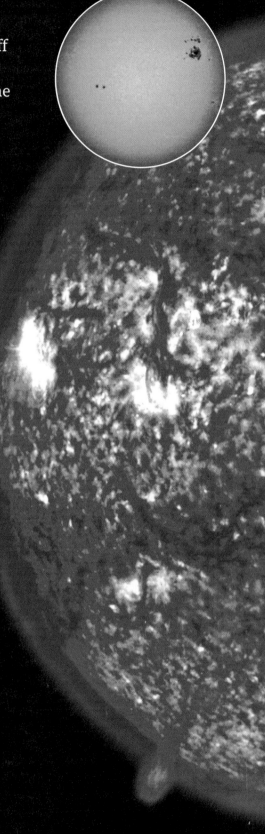

The Explosive Sun

The Sun is like a ball of hot gases with no hard surfaces. Astronomers have found that there are layers in the Sun. The part of the Sun that gives off the light energy we see is called the *photosphere.* It is the innermost layer of the Sun's atmosphere. The layer above the photosphere is the *chromosphere.* The outermost layer is called the *corona.*

The Sun may look calm—no more exciting than a giant glowing light bulb. Scientists have discovered that there is a lot of activity on the Sun. Using special instruments, Galileo noticed dark spots, called *sunspots,* on the face of the Sun. Sunspots are dark because they are not as hot as other parts of the Sun.

The number of sunspots changes in cycles of about 11 years. Sometimes there are many, and sometimes there are few.

Solar Eruptions

Two types of eruptions that take place on the Sun are prominences and solar flares. A *prominence* looks like a ribbon of glowing gases. Prominences may appear and then disappear in a few days or months.

Solar flares are similar to volcanoes here on Earth. A solar flare causes a bright spot on the Sun. Along with extra bright light, solar flares also give off other forms of solar energy. This energy may be powerful enough to interrupt radio and satellite communication on Earth. Solar flares usually last for only minutes or hours.

Prominences may rise at a speed of 1,000 kilometers per second. Some may reach a height of more than one million kilometers.

Light-Years

Light from the Sun takes only about eight minutes to reach Earth. But all the rest of the stars we see are much farther away. Scientists measure how far away stars are in light-years. A light-year is the distance light travels in one year, which is over 9.4 trillion kilometers. Not counting the Sun, the nearest star to Earth is Alpha Centauri, which is more than four light-years away. In other words, the light we see coming from Alpha Centauri started traveling from the star more than four years ago. Stars are so far away they always look like points of light, even with the largest telescopes.

Solar flares give off more light than other parts of the Sun. They also give off more X rays and other kinds of energy.

✓ Lesson Review

1. How does the Sun produce energy?

2. ✏ **Writing in Science** **Descriptive** Look again at pages 257–259. Write a description of the Sun and its features. Include information about the Sun's size, what it is made of, and its location in the solar system.

Why do planets revolve around the Sun?

The solar system includes the planets, their moons, and other objects that orbit the Sun. The planets move around the Sun in elliptical orbits.

The Solar System

The solar system includes the Sun and its eight planets, dwarf planets, moons, asteroids, and comets. Every object in the solar system revolves around the Sun in a path called an orbit. The orbits of the planets have a slightly elliptical shape. An **ellipse** is a shape like an oval.

Mercury

Venus

Earth

Mars

Asteroid belt

Jupiter

Saturn

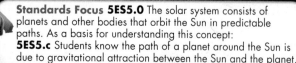

Standards Focus 5ES5.0 The solar system consists of planets and other bodies that orbit the Sun in predictable paths. As a basis for understanding this concept:
5ES5.c Students know the path of a planet around the Sun is due to gravitational attraction between the Sun and the planet.

Planet Diameters

Planet	Diameter (compared to Earth)
Mercury	0.4
Venus	0.9
Mars	0.5
Jupiter	11.0
Saturn	10.0
Uranus	4.0
Neptune	4.0

A **planet** is a large, round object that moves around a star, such as the Sun. Planets are cooler and smaller than stars. Even though some planets seem to shine, they do not give off their own light. A planet shines because light from the star it orbits reflects off the planet's surface.

Planets stay in their orbits because of gravity. Gravity is a force of attraction between objects. In the solar system, the Sun and each of the planets are attracted to each other because of gravity. The Sun has much more mass than the other objects in the solar system. The force of gravity between the Sun and a planet is large enough to move the smaller mass of the planet. Instead of moving in straight lines, gravity causes the planets to move in an ellipse around the Sun.

As shown in the diagram, the solar system has eight known planets. The four planets nearest the Sun are called the inner planets. The four planets farthest from the Sun are the outer planets. Other objects, such as dwarf planets, asteroids, and comets, also revolve around the Sun. You will learn more about these planets and objects in Lessons 3 and 4.

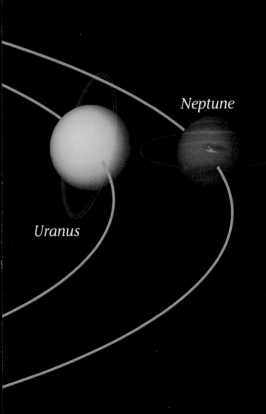

Neptune

Uranus

DIGITAL

Look for Active Art animations at www.pearsonsuccessnet.com

1. **√ Checkpoint** Identify the objects that make up the solar system.

2. What are two ways that planets are different from stars?

Gravity and the Moon

Have you ever looked at the Moon in the night sky? The Moon is a satellite of Earth. A **satellite** is an object that orbits another object in space. All of the planets in the solar system, except Mercury and Venus, have at least one moon.

Earth's Moon moves in an elliptical orbit around Earth. The Moon remains in this orbit because of the force of gravity. The Moon has much less mass than Earth. Therefore, gravity between the Moon and Earth keeps the Moon in orbit around Earth.

As you think about how Earth's gravity pulls on the Moon, you may wonder why gravity does not cause the Moon to crash into Earth. The reason is that the Moon is always moving forward. The forward movement of the Moon is balanced by the inward pull of Earth's gravity. Because of this balance, the Moon stays in a stable orbit around Earth.

Gravity keeps the Moon in its orbit around Earth while Earth orbits the Sun.

Orbiting the Sun

As the Moon is orbiting Earth, both the Moon and Earth are orbiting the Sun. The same thing happens with other planets and their moons. The planet-moon systems stay together as they orbit the Sun.

Gravity between a planet and its moons keeps the moons in orbit, and gravity between the planet-moon systems and the Sun keeps the systems in orbit around the Sun.

The Moon is a satellite of Earth. Astronauts have visited the Moon several times.

1. ✓Checkpoint What causes a planet to move in an ellipse around the Sun?

2. If the Moon is attracted to Earth by gravity, why doesn't it fall into Earth? Write a sentence for your answer.

263

Free Falling

Have you ever seen pictures of astronauts floating inside their space capsules? In such pictures, the astronauts are often described as being weightless. Weightlessness happens because the astronauts are in free fall. The astronauts are falling in space, along with their spaceship.

Remember that gravity on Earth pulls objects toward Earth's center. Suppose you throw a baseball straight out in front of you. The baseball moves forward, but it also curves as gravity pulls it down. If you throw the baseball harder, it moves forward farther and falls to the ground along another curved path. Now suppose you throw the baseball with a superhuman amount of force. The baseball would keep moving forward along a curved path that goes all the way around Earth. It would never hit the ground! This is what happens when a spaceship orbits Earth. The spaceship falls all the way around Earth in an orbit.

Now, suppose that you are riding on a roller coaster. As you move down a steep hill, you feel as if you could separate from your seat. This feeling happens because you and the roller coaster are falling at the same rate. Gravity still pulls you down, but you could float away from your seat if you were not held in. The same thing happens in a spaceship orbiting Earth. The ship and the astronauts are falling around Earth. Gravity pulls on the ship and the astronauts, but they do not feel the effect. The astronauts are weightless inside the ship.

Gravity causes a thrown ball to follow a curved path.

Much like the ball example above, gravity causes the Moon to follow a curved path all the way around Earth.

✔ Lesson Review

1. Why are astronauts in a spaceship weightless?

2. What keeps the Moon in orbit around Earth?

3. ✎ **Writing in Science** **Narrative** Write a journal entry about what it would be like to be an astronaut aboard the space shuttle as it orbits Earth. Explain what you would probably see and feel during your mission. Include details about what you would see as you look toward Earth and what you might see as you look farther into space.

Feeling Weightless

This plane is used by NASA's Reduced Gravity Research Program to prepare astronauts for free-fall conditions in space. After flying high into the atmosphere at a steep incline, the plane quickly dives back toward Earth. For about 20 seconds, people inside the plane are free falling and feel weightless. Airsickness can be a side effect of this experience, earning the plane the nickname of "Vomit Comet."

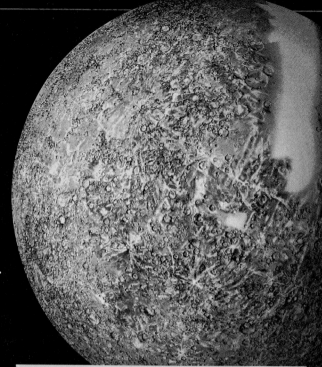

What are the inner planets?

The four planets closest to the Sun are known as the inner planets. Mercury, Venus, Earth, and Mars are all small, rocky planets.

Mercury

Mercury is the planet closest to the Sun. It is a small planet, a little bigger than Earth's moon. Mercury is covered with thousands of low spots. The low spots are shaped like bowls and are called craters. Craters were made when meteorites crashed into Mercury's surface long ago. A meteorite is a rock from space that has struck the surface of a planet or a moon.

In 1973, scientists sent the *Mariner 10* space probe to visit Mercury. It finally reached the planet in 1974. A space probe is a vehicle that carries cameras and other tools for studying different objects in space.

Too Hot and Too Cold

Mercury has almost no atmosphere. Because it is so close to the Sun, Mercury is scorching hot during the day. Daytime temperatures are more than five times greater than the hottest place on Earth. But with no atmosphere to hold in the heat, Mercury is very cold at night.

Mercury Facts

Average distance from Sun
57,900,000 km (35,983,000 mi)

Diameter
4,879 km (3,032 mi)

Length of day as measured in Earth time
59 days

Length of year as measured in Earth time
88 days

Average surface temperature
117°C (243°F)

Moons
none

Weight of a person who is 100 lb on Earth
38 lb

Standards Focus 5ES5.0 The solar system consists of planets and other bodies that orbit the Sun in predictable paths. As a basis for understanding this concept: **5ES5.b** Students know the solar system includes the planet Earth, the Moon, the Sun, eight other planets and their satellites, and smaller objects, such as asteroids and comets.

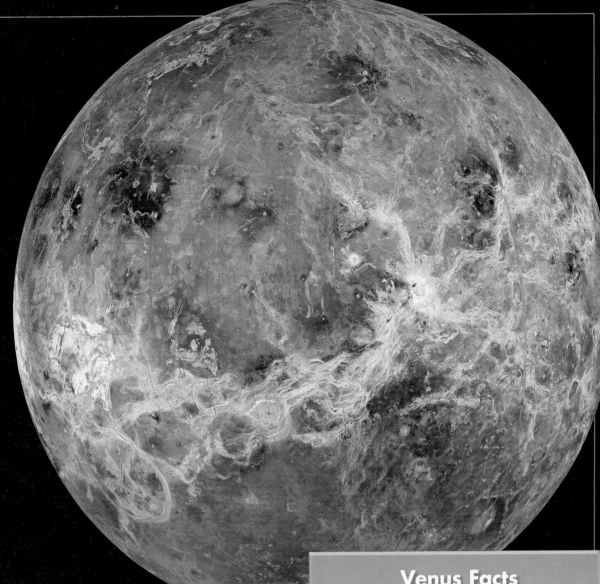

Venus

Venus is the second planet from the Sun. It is about the same size as Earth, but Venus rotates in the opposite direction. Like Mercury, Venus is very hot and dry. Unlike Mercury, Venus has an atmosphere made of thick, swirling clouds. The clouds of Venus are burning hot and poisonous! There are strong winds and lightning. The clouds also are good at reflecting the Sun's light. This makes Venus one of the brightest objects in Earth's night sky.

1. ✓Checkpoint What are some reasons people cannot live on Mercury or Venus?

Venus Facts

Average distance from Sun
108,200,000 km (67,200,000 mi)

Diameter
12,104 km (7,521 mi)

Length of day as measured in Earth time
243 days

Length of year as measured in Earth time
225 days

Average surface temperature
464°C (867°F)

Moons
none

Weight of a person who is 100 lb on Earth
91 lb

Earth

Earth, our home, is the third planet from the Sun. It is also the solar system's largest rocky planet. Earth is the only planet that has liquid water on its surface. In fact, most of Earth's surface is covered with water.

Earth is wrapped in a layer of gas that is hundreds of kilometers thick. This layer of gas, or atmosphere, makes life possible on Earth. It filters out some of the Sun's harmful rays. It also contains nitrogen, oxygen, carbon dioxide, and water vapor. Plants and animals on Earth use these gases. Earth is the only planet in the solar system known to support life.

Earth Facts

Average distance from Sun
149,600,000 km (93,000,000 mi)

Diameter
12,756 km (7,926 mi)

Length of day as measured in Earth time
24 hours

Length of year as measured in Earth time
365 days

Average surface temperature
15°C (59°F)

Moons
1

Weight of a person who is 100 lb on Earth
100 lb

The Moon

Remember that a satellite is an object that orbits another object in space. Moons are satellites of planets. Just as planets revolve around the Sun because of gravity, moons revolve around planets. The force of gravity between a planet and its moons keeps the moons in their orbits.

Earth has one large moon, which is about one-fourth the size of Earth. The Moon has almost no atmosphere. It has many craters that formed when meteorites crashed into its surface.

268

Mars

Mars is the fourth planet from the Sun. The soil that covers most of this rocky planet contains iron oxide. This is a reddish-brown material that makes up rust. This material is why Mars is sometimes called the "Red Planet." Mars has two deeply cratered moons.

The atmosphere of Mars does not have enough oxygen for plants or animals to live. Winds on Mars cause dust storms. These storms are sometimes large enough to cover the whole planet.

Mars has polar ice caps that grow in the winter and shrink in the summer. Mars has many volcanoes. It also has a canyon that is nearly 10 times longer than the Grand Canyon in Arizona.

Several probes have landed on Mars. The first, *Viking I,* landed on Mars in 1976. In 1997, a robot named *Sojourner* explored part of Mars. In 2004, two robot rovers, *Spirit* and *Opportunity,* landed. These rovers gathered information and sent it back to Earth. Scientists hope that the data will tell them about the rocks and soil on Mars and provide evidence that Mars has or once had water.

1. ✓Checkpoint What characteristics do Earth and Mars have in common?

2. ✏️ **Writing in Science**
Narrative Write what you think it would be like to live on Mars.

Mars Facts

Average distance from Sun
227,900,000 km (141,600,000 mi)

Diameter
6,794 km (4,222 mi)

Length of day as measured in Earth time
25 hours

Length of year as measured in Earth time
686 days

Average surface temperature
–63°C (–85°F)

Moons
2

Weight of a person who is 100 lb on Earth
38 lb

Mars rover

Asteroids

An **asteroid** is a rocky object up to several hundred kilometers wide that revolves around the Sun. Asteroids are sometimes called minor planets. Most asteroids orbit in the *asteroid belt*, which is between Mars and Jupiter. One ball-shaped object in the asteroid belt is named Ceres. It is a dwarf planet. Asteroids have uneven shapes. Some have smaller asteroids orbiting them. The smallest asteroids are pebble-sized. Most asteroids complete one revolution around the Sun in three to six Earth years.

Can Earth be hit by asteroids? It has happened, and you can still see some of the craters that formed. Such collisions are very rare. Fortunately, Jupiter's gravity holds most asteroids in the space beyond Mars.

Asteroid Ida

Ida is in the main asteroid belt between Mars and Jupiter. Ida is about 58 kilometers long and 23 kilometers wide.

Asteroid Eros

In 2001, Eros became the first asteroid to be orbited and landed upon by a spacecraft. Eros is 33 kilometers long and 13 kilometers thick. This image shows evidence of craters, boulders, and layers of rock.

Nucleus The nucleus of a comet is very small, often only a few kilometers across. Scientists describe the nucleus as a "dirty snowball." It is made of dust and ice—frozen water and frozen gases.

Comets

A **comet** is a frozen mass of different kinds of ice and dust that is in orbit around the Sun. Comets are much smaller than planets. Many comets come from parts of the solar system beyond Neptune and pass through the solar system along very elliptical paths. Several comets a year may circle the Sun. You may not be able to see them, though. Only the largest comets can be seen without a telescope.

NASA's Deep Impact Mission

Scientists think comets hold clues about how the solar system formed. One goal of NASA's Deep Impact Mission is to help find these clues.

An important part of the Deep Impact Mission took place on July 4, 2005. On that day, NASA crashed a small spacecraft into the comet Tempel 1. This spacecraft took pictures of the comet and sent them to Earth until moments before it hit. A second "fly-by" spacecraft took pictures of the collision from a distance. It also gathered data from the debris caused by the collision and the crater that formed.

Scientists are still studying the data from the Deep Impact Mission. So far, they have learned that the comet's surface is not like clean ice. They have also found that the dust of the comet is fine, like a powder.

Two Tails Outward moving particles from the Sun, called solar wind, always push the two tails in a direction away from the Sun. The tails may extend up to 80 million kilometers, making comets larger than asteroids.

Coma A giant cloud of dust and evaporated gases called the coma surrounds the nucleus. The coma gives a comet its bright, fuzzy appearance. The coma and tail form only when the comet gets close enough for the Sun to melt the nucleus.

✓ Lesson Review

1. Name the four inner planets. Identify one characteristic shared by these planets. Then, identify details about each.

2. Describe two differences between comets and asteroids.

3. **Make Inferences** What are two ways that comets and asteroids might affect Earth?

What do we know about the outer planets and beyond?

The outer planets are Jupiter, Saturn, Uranus, and Neptune. Their orbits are beyond the asteroid belt.

Jupiter

Jupiter, the fifth planet from the Sun, is the largest planet in the solar system. It is a gas giant. A gas giant is a very large planet made mostly of gases. Jupiter's atmosphere is mostly hydrogen and helium.

Jupiter has many moons. Four moons are shown here. In 1610, Galileo was the first person to see these four moons through his telescope.

Jupiter Facts

Average distance from Sun
778,400,000 km (484,000,000 mi)

Diameter
142,984 km (88,846 mi)

Length of day as measured in Earth time
10 hours

Length of year as measured in Earth time
12 years

Average surface temperature
–148°C (–234°F)

Moons
at least 63

Rings
yes

Weight of a person who is 100 lb on Earth
214 lb

Io has more active volcanoes than any other body in the solar system.

Europa has a frozen crust that may cover a liquid ocean beneath.

Ganymede is the largest moon in the solar system.

Callisto has more craters than any other object in the solar system.

Standards Focus 5ES5.0 The solar system consists of planets and other bodies that orbit the Sun in predictable paths. As a basis for understanding this concept: **5ES5.b** Students know the solar system includes the planet Earth, the Moon, the Sun, eight other planets and their satellites, and smaller objects, such as asteroids and comets.

The thousands of bright rings around Saturn are visible from telescopes on Earth.

Galileo Galilei (1564–1642) was an astronomer and mathematician. He used a telescope to observe the Sun, Moon, planets, and stars.

Saturn Facts

Average distance from Sun
1,426,700,000 km (885,900,000 mi)

Diameter
120,536 km (74,897 mi)

Length of day as measured in Earth time
11 hours

Length of year as measured in Earth time
29.4 years

Average surface temperature
–178°C (–288°F)

Moons
at least 47

Rings
yes

Weight of a person who is 100 lb on Earth
74 lb

Saturn

The sixth planet from the Sun, Saturn, is also a gas giant. Like Jupiter, Saturn's atmosphere is mostly hydrogen and helium. Saturn is very large, but it has a low mass compared with other planets.

When Galileo saw Saturn through his telescope, he was surprised. He saw what looked like a planet with handles! The "handles" were really the brilliant rings that orbit Saturn. The *Voyager* space probe studied these rings. It showed that the particles making up the rings vary in size from tiny grains to boulders. These particles are made of ice, dust, and rock.

1. **✔ Checkpoint** How are Jupiter and Saturn alike? How are they different?

William Herschel discovered Uranus in 1781. Uranus is the seventh planet from the Sun and the most distant planet you can see without a telescope. Uranus is a gas giant with an atmosphere of hydrogen, helium, and methane. The planet is so cold that the methane can condense into a liquid. Tiny drops of this liquid methane form a thin cloud that covers the planet, giving it a fuzzy, blue-green look.

Like the other gas giants, Uranus has rings and many moons. Unlike the rings of Saturn, Uranus's rings are dark and hard to see with Earth-based telescopes. The rings were discovered by a space probe in 1977.

Uranus rotates on its side. No one knows why Uranus has this odd tilt. Scientists think a large object may have hit the planet when the solar system was still forming. This bump may have knocked Uranus onto its side.

Uranus Facts

Average distance from Sun
2,871,000,000 km (1,784,000,000 mi)

Diameter
51,118 km (31,763 mi)

Length of day as measured in Earth time
17 hours

Length of year as measured in Earth time
84 years

Average surface temperature
−216°C (−357°F)

Moons
at least 27

Rings
yes

Weight of a person who is 100 lb on Earth
86 lb

Uranus is a gas giant with a large liquid core.

Neptune

Neptune is the eighth planet from the Sun. It is the smallest of the gas giants. Even so, if Neptune were hollow, it could hold about 60 Earths. Neptune is too far away to see without a telescope. Because Neptune is so far from the Sun, its orbit is very long. It takes more than one hundred Earth years for Neptune to orbit the Sun.

Neptune's atmosphere is like that of Uranus. Like Uranus, Neptune has a bluish color because of methane in its atmosphere. Neptune also has bands of clouds and storms like those on Jupiter. One huge storm on Neptune was called the Great Dark Spot. The storm was seen by the *Voyager 2* probe when it flew by in 1989. Five years later, the storm had vanished.

Astronomers discovered Neptune in 1846. A few days later, they saw Triton, Neptune's largest moon. Triton may be the coldest body in the solar system. Its surface temperature is about –235°C. Neptune has at least 13 moons.

1. **✓Checkpoint** How are Uranus and Neptune similar to the other gas giants?

2. What is similar about Uranus's and Neptune's atmospheres?

Neptune Facts

Average distance from Sun
4,498,300,000 km (2,795,000,000 mi)

Diameter
49,528 km (30,775 mi)

Length of day as measured in Earth time
16 hours

Length of year as measured in Earth time
165 years

Average surface temperature
–214°C (–353°F)

Moons
at least 13

Rings
yes

Weight of a person who is 100 lb on Earth
110 lb

Neptune's ring system

Neptune

Pluto

In 1930, Clyde Tombaugh discovered a small, rocky object whose orbit is sometimes beyond that of Neptune. This object is called Pluto. It is about the same size as Earth's moon. Until 2006, Pluto was considered a ninth planet. But Pluto is different from the eight planets in several ways. Now scientists refer to Pluto as a dwarf planet. A dwarf planet is a small, round or ball-shaped object that revolves around the Sun.

Pluto has a moon, Charon, that is only slightly smaller than Pluto. The planets that have moons are much larger than their moons. Pluto has at least two other moons, Nix and Hydra.

Clyde Tombaugh

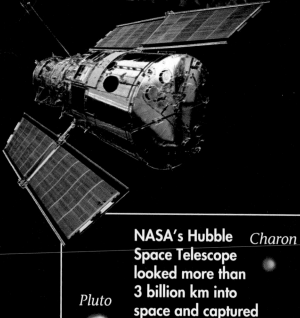

NASA's Hubble Space Telescope looked more than 3 billion km into space and captured this image of the small, icy Pluto.

Charon

Pluto

An Odd Orbit

Pluto has an odd orbit. The eight planets travel around the Sun at the same angle, while Pluto's orbit is tilted. During parts of its orbit, it is closer to the Sun than Neptune. This occurred from 1979 to 1999. The next time this will occur is in the year 2227.

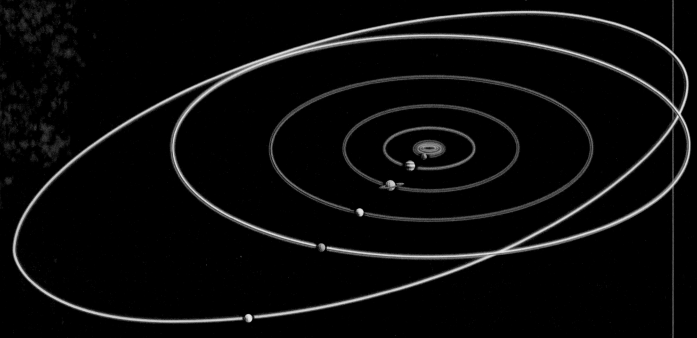

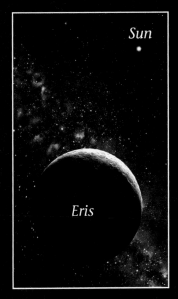

Sun

Eris

This is what the Sun might look like from Eris.

Other Dwarf Planets?

In 2005, scientists announced that they had found a dwarf planet that is a little larger than Pluto and at least three times farther from the Sun. It has at least one moon. This dwarf planet was called 2003 UB313, but in 2006, it was named Eris. Ceres, an asteroid outside the orbit of Mars, is also a dwarf planet.

Lesson Review

1. List the planets in order from smallest to largest.
2. **Make Inferences** Why did it take astronomers so long to see Eris?

TARGET

SKILL

Using Data About Planets

Each planet in the solar system has the shape of a sphere. The diameter of a sphere is the distance from one point on the surface of the sphere to a point on the opposite side, passing through the center. Think of digging a tunnel that passes through the center of Earth to the opposite side. The length of that tunnel would be Earth's diameter.

The table below gives the diameter in kilometers of each planet in the solar system.

Planet	Diameter
Mercury	4,879 km
Venus	12,104 km
Earth	12,756 km
Mars	6,794 km
Jupiter	142,984 km
Saturn	120,536 km
Uranus	51,118 km
Neptune	49,528 km

DIGITAL (e)

Standards Focus 5ES5.b Students know the solar system includes the planet Earth, the Moon, the Sun, eight other planets and their satellites, and smaller objects, such as asteroids and comets.

Copy the table on page 278. Add a third column, with the heading "Rounded Diameter."

1. Round each diameter to the nearest thousand kilometers. Write the rounded number in the table.

2. List the 8 planets with their rounded diameters in order from least to greatest. What is the median rounded diameter?

3. Which planet has a diameter about 10 times that of Venus?

4. Which planet has a diameter close to that of Venus?

Lab zone Take-Home Activity

Choose your favorite planet and do some research about it. Write a news article or a science fiction story about your planet.

Investigate How do space probes send images of the solar system?

You will use a graphic representation to model how space probe images are sent.

Materials

Image Receiving Grid and Image Sending Grid

black marker

What to Do

1. **Model** how space probes send images. Work with your back to your partner. You are the Sender. The Sender represents a space probe that is observing another planet. You change a camera image into a signal and send it to Earth.

2. Your partner is the Receiver. The Receiver represents the place on Earth that receives the signal from the space probe and changes the signal into an image.

3. The Receiver will say "A1." The Sender will look at square A1 on the Sending Grid and say "0" if that square is empty or "1" if the square is filled in. The Receiver will fill in the A1 square only if the Sender says "1." All squares are completely empty or completely filled in.

Do not let your Receiver see the Image Sending Grid.

The numbers spoken by the Sender represent signals sent by radio waves to Earth.

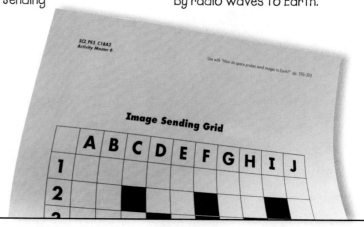

SCI PE5 C18A2
Activity Master 6

Use with "How do space probes send images to Earth?" pp. 592–593

Image Sending Grid

	A	B	C	D	E	F	G	H	I	J
1										
2										

DIGITAL Lab zone

5ES5.b Students know the solar system includes the planet Earth, the Moon, the Sun, eight other planets and their satellites, and smaller objects, such as asteroids and comets. **5IE6.g** Record data by using appropriate graphic representations (including charts, graphs, and labeled diagrams) and make inferences based on those data.

4 Continue with squares A2, A3, and so on. When finished with Column A, start Column B. Continue until all columns are complete.

Fill in a square when you hear "1."

The Receiver collects and organizes the data, re-creating the image that was sent by the Sender.

5 Compare the images. Are they the same? Explain.

Explain Your Results

1. How accurately was the signal received? Explain why the new image might not be perfectly accurate.

2. Based on the process you **modeled,** describe how the image is sent from a space probe.

3. **Infer** How do you think cameras on satellites orbiting Earth send images back to Earth?

Go Further

What would happen if you "sent" a partner a full-page picture drawn on a piece of graph paper with large squares and one drawn on a piece with small squares? Find out. Send both to a partner with matching graph paper. Does one take longer? Does one make a better picture?

The solar system is made up of the Sun, the planets, and other objects that orbit the Sun.

Lesson 1

What is the Sun?

- The Sun is an average star that is the central and largest body in the solar system.
- The Sun is made mostly of hydrogen and helium. Its energy comes from the fusion of hydrogen to form helium.

Lesson 2

Why do planets revolve around the Sun?

- A planet is held in its orbit around the Sun by the gravitational attraction between the Sun and the planet.

Lesson 3

What are the inner planets?

- The solar system consists of Earth, the Moon, other planets and their satellites, and smaller objects such as dwarf planets, asteroids, and comets that orbit the Sun.
- The four planets nearest the Sun—Mercury, Venus, Earth, and Mars—are the inner planets.

Lesson 4

What do we know about the outer planets and beyond?

- The planets farthest from the Sun—Jupiter, Saturn, Uranus, and Neptune—are the outer planets.
- All of the outer planets are gas giants.
- Pluto, once considered the ninth planet, is now called a dwarf planet.

Cross-Curricular Links

English–Language Arts

Building Vocabulary

Look again at pages 252–253. Identify the pictures behind the terms *star*, *satellite*, and *comet*. Write a paragraph about each term. Tell how each term relates to the picture and to the other terms.

Mathematics

The Distance from the Sun

At the closest point of its orbit, the dwarf planet Pluto is 4,436,820,000 km from the Sun. At the farthest point of its orbit, Pluto is 7,375,930,000 km from the Sun. What is the difference between Pluto's farthest location from the Sun and Pluto's closest location to the Sun?

Visual and Performing Arts

The Surface of a Moon

Draw a picture of what you think the surface of one of Jupiter's moons would look like.

Challenge!

English–Language Arts

Visiting Planets

Do research and use what you have learned to write about one of the planets in the solar system. Describe what it might be like to visit that planet. Include details about the planet's atmosphere, size and any moons it might have.

Use Vocabulary

asteroid (p. 270)	**satellite** (p. 262)
comet (p. 271)	**solar system** (p. 257)
ellipse (p. 260)	
planet (p. 261)	**star** (p. 257)

Fill in the blanks with the correct vocabulary words. If you have trouble answering a question, read the listed page again.

1. The _____ is made of the planets, moons, and other bodies that orbit the Sun.

2. A(n) _____ is a rocky object up to several hundred kilometers wide that revolves around the Sun.

3. A(n) _____ is a huge ball of very hot gas that gives off light energy.

4. A(n) _____ is a shape similar to an oval.

5. A(n) _____ is a frozen mass of different types of ice and dust that orbits the Sun.

6. A(n) _____ is an object that orbits another object in space.

7. A(n) _____ is a large, round object that moves around a star, such as the Sun.

Think About It

8. What is one way Mercury and Venus differ from the other planets in the solar system?

9. Explain why the pull of gravity keeps the Moon in orbit around Earth rather than pulling the Moon into Earth.

10. **Process Skills** **Make and Use Models** Make a model of Earth, the Moon, and the Sun. Show how these objects move relative to one another in space.

11. **Make Inferences** Read the paragraph. Then complete the graphic organizer to make an inference to answer this question: Why would a person have greater weight on Mars than on Mercury?

Weight is a measure of the pull of gravity on an object. Gravity is a force of attraction between any two objects. The strength of this pulling force is related to the masses of the objects. Objects with a greater mass exert a stronger force than objects with a smaller mass. For example, because Earth has much more mass than the Moon, people weigh much more on Earth than they would on the Moon.

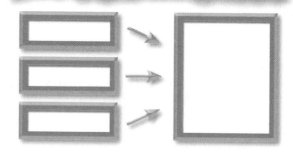

12. **Writing in Science**

Descriptive Suppose that you are an astronaut taking a trip to the Moon. Write a paragraph describing what you see when you arrive. Include what you see on the surface of the Moon and what you see in the sky.

California Standards Practice

Write the letter of the correct answer.

13. **What are the giant outer planets mostly made of?**

    A rocks

    B gases

    C minerals

    D water

14. **Which of the following is about the same size as Pluto?**

    A Earth

    B Jupiter

    C the Moon

    D Saturn

15. **What is the Sun mostly made of?**

    A methane

    B hydrogen

    C water

    D iron oxide

16. **What type of object is abundant between the orbits of Mars and Jupiter?**

    A planet

    B star

    C comet

    D asteroid

17. **What produces most of the Sun's energy?**

    A sunspots

    B fusion

    C boiling

    D methane

18. **About how many Earth-sized spheres could fit into a Sun-sized sphere?**

    A 1,000

    B 100,000,000

    C 1,000,000

    D 10

19. **So far, life in the solar system has been found on**

    A Jupiter and Earth.

    B Neptune and Venus.

    C Earth and asteroids.

    D Earth only.

20. **The chart shows the average distances of several planets from the Sun. Which of these planets takes the longest time to make one complete orbit around the Sun?**

Planetary Distances from Sun	
Planet	**Average Distance from Sun**
Venus	108,200,000 km
Earth	149,600,000 km
Mars	227,900,000 km
Saturn	1,427,000,000 km
Uranus	2,871,000,000 km

    A Uranus

    B Mars

    C Earth

    D Venus

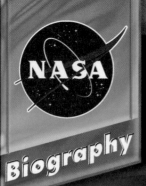

Jose Hernandez
MISSION SPECIALIST

Jose Hernandez was a high school student working in a farm field and listening to his radio. A news story about astronauts fascinated him. At that very moment, he decided to fly into space. "I was already interested in science and engineering," he remembers. "And that's something I've been striving for each day since then."

Jose did not speak English until he was 12 years old. He grew up in a family of migrant farm workers from Mexico. Every spring, the family traveled throughout California, picking fruits and vegetables along the way. They worked on the farms until December. Jose went to school during the week and worked on the farms on the weekends.

Jose's parents encouraged all their children to study hard and to go to college. Jose Hernandez graduated from college and went to a university to learn more about engineering. He then worked at a laboratory where he helped develop a tool to detect cancer.

Mr. Hernandez has also worked as an engineer for NASA. He has helped provide materials for the Space Shuttle and International Space Station. But now, he has reached a goal that he has been striving for since he was in high school. He is an astronaut, and is training to go to the Moon.

Lab zone Take-Home Activity

Write a TV news report about astronauts exploring the Moon. Include questions that a reporter on Earth might ask the astronauts. Include the astronauts' answers to the questions.

Unit C Summary

Chapter 5

How does water move through the environment?

- The water cycle is the continuous movement of water through the environment. Water is always moving on, through, and above Earth. The steps of the water cycle include evaporation, condensation, and precipitation.
- Most of Earth's water is the salt water of the oceans, which cover most of Earth's surface. Fresh water is located in rivers, lakes, underground sources, and glaciers. Fresh water is limited, so it must be used wisely.

Chapter 6

Why does the weather change?

- Energy from the Sun heats Earth unevenly, causing air movements that result in changing weather patterns. The oceans and water cycle also play a role in weather.
- Weather forecasters observe many variables to predict weather changes. These variables include temperature, moisture, cloud conditions, precipitation, wind speed, wind direction, and air pressure.

Chapter 7

What objects in space make up the solar system?

- The solar system includes the Sun, Earth and its moon, other planets and their satellites, and smaller objects, such as dwarf planets, asteroids, and comets.

Experiment What is one cause for the uneven heating of Earth?

Uneven heating of Earth causes air movements. The Sun heats some parts of Earth more than others. For example, the poles receive a smaller amount of heat than the equator. In this experiment, you use a model to learn more.

Materials

clay

3 thermometers

protractor and metric ruler

timer or clock with a second hand

lamp

Process Skills

Before beginning an **experiment,** clearly **identify** the independent and dependent **variables.** Make sure all other variables are **controlled,** or kept the same.

Ask a question.
How does the angle at which light shines on an object affect the amount of heat the object receives?

State a hypothesis.
If a light bulb shines on 3 thermometers at different angles, then will the temperature be greater the more directly the light shines on a thermometer, will it be less, or will the angle have no effect?

Identify and control variables.
The angle of the thermometer is the variable you change. The variable that you **observe** is the temperature of the thermometers after 3 minutes with the light on. Everything else must be controlled, or kept the same. Make sure you **measure** in the same way and use the same type of thermometers.

5ES4.0 Energy from the Sun heats Earth unevenly, causing air movements that result in changing weather patterns. **5ES4.a** Students know uneven heating of Earth causes air movements (convection currents). **5IE6.d** Identify the dependent and controlled variables in an investigation. **5IE6.e** Identify a single independent variable in a scientific investigation and explain how this variable can be used to collect information to answer a question about the results of the experiment. **5IE6.f** Select appropriate tools (e.g., thermometers, metersticks, balances, and graduated cylinders) and make quantitative observations. **5IE6.g** Record data by using appropriate graphic representations (including charts, graphs, and labeled diagrams) and make inferences based on those data. (Also **5IE6.b, 5IE6.c**)

Variables

An *independent variable* is what you change in an experiment.

A *dependent variable* is what you measure or observe.

A *controlled variable* is what could be changed but must not be changed for the experiment to be a fair test.

In this experiment, what is the independent variable? What is the dependent variable? What is the controlled variable?

Test your hypothesis.

1 Select the tools and supplies you need.

2 Place the thermometers in the clay. Use the protractor to place one thermometer at a 90° angle, one at a 60° angle, and one at a 30° angle. Do not move the thermometers once they are in place.

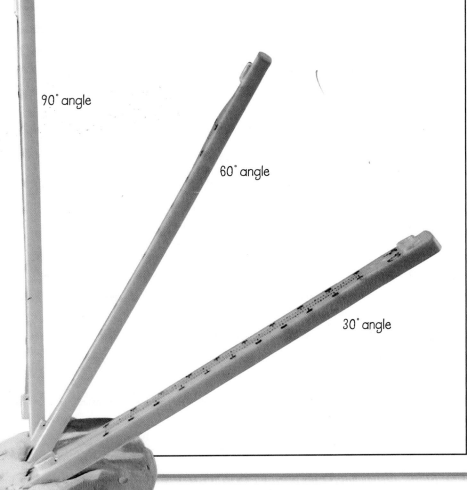

90° angle

60° angle

30° angle

3 Place the lamp 20 cm from the thermometers.

4 Turn on the lamp. Wait 3 minutes.

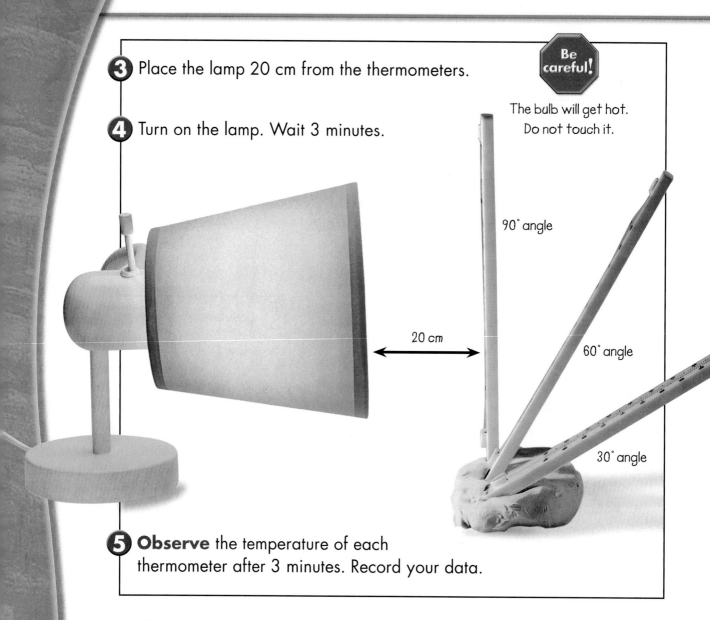

Be careful!

The bulb will get hot. Do not touch it.

90° angle

60° angle

30° angle

20 cm

5 **Observe** the temperature of each thermometer after 3 minutes. Record your data.

Collect and record your data.
Sometimes you show your observations with pictures or words. In this experiment you use numbers. Observations that use numbers are called quantitative observations.

Angle Measure	Starting Temperature (°C)	Temperature After 3 Minutes (°C)
30° angle	°C	°C
60° angle	°C	°C
90° angle	°C	°C

Interpret your data.

Examine how the final temperature (the dependent variable) varies with the angle of the thermometer.

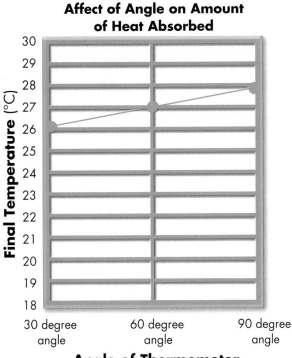

Affect of Angle on Amount of Heat Absorbed

State your conclusion.

How did the final temperature vary with the angle of the thermometer?

Compare your hypothesis and your results.

Communicate your conclusion.

Do you need further information to support your conclusion? Explain.

You collect information about the independent variable. Explain how this helped you answer the main question in the experiment.

Go Further

Does the Sun heat land and water the same? Plan and conduct a simple investigation to answer this question or develop a testable question of your own. Write clear instructions others could follow.

Show What You Know

Make a Mobile

Using any materials you like, make a mobile of the solar system. Show the Sun at the center of your mobile. Be sure to include the eight planets that orbit the Sun in their correct order from the Sun. Select a unique feature of each planet that you can illustrate in your mobile. For example, the craters of Mercury or the rust color of Mars could be shown. Label each planet with its name.

Gather Weather Data

Weather forecasters observe many variables to predict weather changes. These variables include temperature, moisture, cloud conditions, precipitation, wind speed, wind direction, and air pressure.

1. Develop a plan for setting up a weather station at your school. Choose a location for your station, and gather the tools you will need to collect weather data.

2. Set up your weather station. Use the tools you selected in Step 1 to gather weather data each day for one week. Record your data.

3. At the end of the week, draw conclusions from your data to describe the general weather patterns for the week.

Realistic Fiction

Write a realistic fictional story about traveling through space and exploring one of the planets in the solar system. Describe the planet and what happens on the planet. Remember to include the following elements in your story:

- Characters
- Plot
- Setting

Read More About Earth Sciences

Look for other books about Earth Sciences in the library-media center. Here is one you may want to read.

El Niño: Stormy Weather for People and Wildlife by Caroline Arnold

You may have heard of El Niño, a cycle of changing ocean surface temperature in the Pacific Ocean. How does El Niño affect people and wildlife? In this book, Caroline Arnold explores the effects of El Niño on Earth. El Niño can affect food chains, cause powerful storms, and even cause wildfires. Read more to find out how El Niño affects climate and organisms all over the world.

Discovery CHANNEL SCHOOL™ Science Fair Projects

Using Scientific Methods

1. Ask a question.
2. State a hypothesis.
3. Identify and control variables.
4. Test your hypothesis.
5. Collect and record your data.
6. Interpret your data.
7. State your conclusion.
8. Go further.

How do craters form?

The surfaces of Earth's Moon and of the planet Mercury are covered with craters. Craters are bowl-shaped low spots that form when chunks of rocks called meteorites crash into the surface of a moon or planet.

Idea: State a hypothesis about how the mass of a meteorite or the speed at which it travels affects the size of the crater it makes. Then, design and carry out an experiment to test your hypothesis.

How does fog form?

Fog is a cloud that forms near Earth's surface. Clouds form when water evaporates, then cools, and finally condenses to form droplets in the air.

Idea: Research to find out how to model cloud formation. Then design and carry out an experiment to model cloud formation.

How does a rain gauge work?

A rain gauge is an instrument used to measure how much rain falls at a given place. Rain gauges may be of different sizes or shapes. What effect do you think changing the size of the opening of the rain gauge has on the amount of rainfall the rain gauge collects?

Idea: Write a hypothesis to answer the question. Then, design and carry out an experiment to test your hypothesis. Share your results with the class.

Unit C California Standards Practice

Write the letter of the correct answer.

1. **Where is most of Earth's water located?**

   A rivers

   B lakes

   C glaciers

   D oceans

2. **What forms when liquid water evaporates?**

   A ice

   B clouds

   C water vapor

   D rain

3. **Which of the following must happen for water in clouds to fall as snow?**

   A Air temperatures must rise above the boiling point of water.

   B Air temperatures must cool below the freezing point of water.

   C Air temperatures must cool but remain above the freezing point of water.

   D Air temperatures must rise enough for water to evaporate.

4. **The picture below shows the water cycle. What process causes water vapor in the air to form clouds?**

   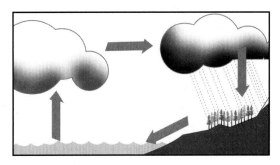

   A condensation

   B precipitation

   C runoff

   D evaporation

5. **Which of the following is not a source of fresh water?**

   A rivers

   B oceans

   C glaciers

   D groundwater

Unit C California Standards Practice

6. What is produced when gases or liquids rise and sink in a circular path due to termperature differences?

A air pressure

B anticyclone

C convection current

D warm front

7. The picture below shows a place where air currents will form as a result of the uneven heating of Earth.

In which direction will air currents at Earth's surface probably move?

A from the ocean toward the land

B straight up above the ocean

C straight up above the land

D from the land toward the ocean

8. Which of the following ocean features helps distribute heat around the world?

A ocean currents

B ocean waves

C marine animals

D water pressure

9. In what direction does air flow?

A from areas of high pressure to areas of low pressure

B from areas of low pressure to areas of high pressure

C from north to south in the Northern Hemisphere

D from north to south in the Southern Hemisphere

10. Where are hurricanes most likely to form?

A over deserts

B over cool ocean water

C over warm ocean water

D over mountains

11. A weather map on the local news shows a cold front approaching the area where you live. What weather conditions is this front likely to bring?

A warm, sunny weather

B cool, sunny weather

C light precipitation and increasing temperatures

D heavy precipitation and decreasing temperatures

12. Which of the following is true about atmospheric pressure?

A It increases with distance above Earth's surface.

B It decreases with distance above Earth's surface.

C It doesn't change with distance above Earth's surface.

D It is the same at all locations on Earth's surface.

13. Which of the following best describes the shape of a planet's orbit around the Sun?

A line

B triangle

C circle

D ellipse

14. The Sun's energy comes from collisions involving

A methane and oxygen.

B hydrogen and helium.

C water and oxygen.

D methane and hydrogen.

15. The diagram shows the Sun and the planets of the solar system. Which planet is shown at the letter _d_?

A Earth

B Saturn

C Mercury

D Mars

Unit C California Standards Practice

16. Which of these is a satellite of a planet?

A a star

B a comet

C an asteroid

D a moon

17. Between which two planets are most asteroids located?

A Earth and Venus

B Earth and Mars

C Mars and Jupiter

D Uranus and Neptune

18. What type of object is in the picture below?

A comet

B planet

C asteroid

D star

19. What keeps Earth in orbit around the Sun?

A the gravitational attraction between the Sun and Earth

B the gravitational attraction between the Moon and Earth

C the gravitational attraction between the Sun and the Moon

D the gravitational attraction between Earth and other planets

20. Which of the following best describes the Sun?

A The Sun is a giant star.

B The Sun is a supergiant star.

C The Sun is an average-sized star.

D The Sun is a small star.

California Science Content Standards, Grade 5

STANDARD SET 1. Physical Sciences

5PS1.0 Elements and their combinations account for all the varied types of matter in the world. As a basis for understanding this concept:

5PS1.a Students know that during chemical reactions the atoms in the reactants rearrange to form products with different properties.	pp. 6, 11, 17, **20, 21, 23,** 24, **25, 29, 34,** 36, 42, 45, **46, 47, 54, 55,** 56, 57, 58, 59, 60, 64, 65, 66, 67, 68, 70, 71, **75, 83**
5PS1.b Students know all matter is made of atoms, which may combine to form molecules.	pp. **12, 13, 20,** 21, **29, 34,** 36, 37, **75, 83,** 84
5PS1.c Students know metals have properties in common, such as high electrical and thermal conductivity. Some metals, such as aluminum (Al), iron (Fe), nickel (Ni), copper (Cu), silver (Ag), and gold (Au), are pure elements; others, such as steel and brass, are composed of a combination of elemental metals.	pp. 2, 11, **15,** 16, 17, **18, 19,** 22, 24, 34, 36, 37, 50, 55, 56, 74, **75,** 76, 77, 78, **79, 83, 84**
5PS1.d Students know that each element is made of one kind of atom and that the elements are organized in the periodic table by their chemical properties.	pp. 9, **12, 13, 14, 15, 16, 17,** 18, 19, 24, **29,** 30, 31, **34,** 36, **75, 84**
5PS1.e Students know scientists have developed instruments that can create discrete images of atoms and molecules that show that the atoms and molecules often occur in well-ordered arrays.	pp. **13, 20,** 34, 37, 84
5PS1.f Students know differences in chemical and physical properties of substances are used to separate mixtures and identify compounds.	pp. 10, 11, 20, **26, 27,** 28, **29, 32, 33, 34,** 36, 37, **60, 61, 62,** 63, 68, 70, 71, 83, 84, **85**
5PS1.g Students know properties of solid, liquid, and gaseous substances, such as sugar ($C_6H_{12}O_6$), water (H_2O), helium (He), oxygen (O_2), nitrogen (N_2), and carbon dioxide (CO_2).	pp. 20, **48, 49,** 50, 51, 52, 53, 54, 57, 71, **85**
5PS1.h Students know living organisms and most materials are composed of just a few elements.	pp. 9, 21, **34, 86**
5PS1.i Students know the common properties of salts, such as sodium chloride (NaCl).	pp. **21, 22, 23, 24, 34, 37,** 65, 80, **85, 86**

What It Means to You

Everything is made of atoms, which may be combined in compounds. Most of the items you use everyday are compounds.

California Science Content Standards, Grade 5

STANDARD SET 2. Life Sciences

5LS2.0 Plants and animals have structures for respiration, digestion, waste disposal, and transport of materials. As a basis for understanding this concept:

5LS2.a Students know many multicellular organisms have specialized structures to support the transport of materials.	pp. 92, 96, 98, **100, 101,** 116, 118, 119, 127, 128, 129, 130, 131, 132, 133, 134, 146, 148, 149, **153,** 161, 163
5LS2.b Students know how blood circulates through the heart chambers, lungs, and body and how carbon dioxide (CO_2) and oxygen (O_2) are exchanged in the lungs and tissues.	pp. 99, 100, **101,** 124, **127, 128, 129, 130, 131, 132, 133, 134, 135,** 142, 143, 144, 145, **149, 153,** 154, 155, 156, 157
5LS2.c Students know the sequential steps of digestion and the roles of teeth and the mouth, esophagus, stomach, small intestine, large intestine, and colon in the function of the digestive system.	pp. 99, 100, **136, 137, 138, 139, 146, 148, 149, 153,** 158, 162
5LS2.d Students know the role of the kidney in removing cellular waste from blood and converting it into urine, which is stored in the bladder.	pp. **100, 101, 140, 141, 146, 148, 149, 153,** 162, 163
5LS2.e Students know how sugar, water, and minerals are transported in a vascular plant.	pp. **102, 103, 104,** 105, **106, 107,** 116, 118, 119, **153,** 161, 163
5LS2.f Students know plants use carbon dioxide (CO_2) and energy from sunlight to build molecules of sugar and release oxygen.	pp. 97, 102, 104, **108,** 109, **111,** 114, 115, 116, 118, 119, **153,** 163, 164
5LS2.g Students know plant and animal cells break down sugar to obtain energy, a process resulting in carbon dioxide (CO_2) and water (respiration).	pp. 95, 96, **110, 111,** 116, 118, 119, 132, 148, 149, **153,** 158, 164

What It Means to You

Large organisms, such as trees and even humans are made of many different kinds of cells. These different cells make up structures that the organism needs to live. Trees have leaves to help them make food from sunlight, water, and carbon dioxide. Humans do not make their own food, but they do have structures to help them digest the food they eat.

California Science Content Standards, Grade 5

STANDARD SET 3. Earth Sciences (Earth's Water)

5ES3.0 Water on Earth moves between the oceans and land through the processes of evaporation and condensation. As a basis for understanding this concept:

5ES3.a Students know most of Earth's water is present as salt water in the oceans, which cover most of Earth's surface.	pp. **170, 173,** 174, 175, 200, 202, 203, 204, 287, 295
5ES3.b Students know when liquid water evaporates, it turns into water vapor in the air and can reappear as a liquid when cooled or as a solid if cooled below the freezing point of water.	pp. **188, 189, 190, 191,** 198, 199, **200,** 202, 203, 287, 295
5ES3.c Students know water vapor in the air moves from one place to another and can form fog or clouds, which are tiny droplets of water or ice, and can fall to Earth as rain, hail, sleet, or snow.	pp. **182, 190, 191, 192,** 193, 194, 195, 198, 199, 200, 202, 203, 250, 287, 295
5ES3.d Students know that the amount of fresh water located in rivers, lakes, underground sources, and glaciers is limited and that its availability can be extended by recycling and decreasing the use of water.	pp. **176, 177, 178, 179, 182,** 183, **184,** 185, 191, 200, 202, 203, 287, 295
5ES3.e Students know the origin of the water used by their local communities.	pp. **180, 181,** 182, 183, **186, 187,** 200, 202

What It Means to You

When you turn on the water in your home, do you ever think about where it comes from? In California, people use water from many sources. Fresh water is found in lakes, rivers, glaciers, groundwater, and precipitation. All of the fresh water you drink was once in the air as rain or snow. Whether your water comes from a well, a river, an aqueduct, or some combination of sources, everyone must take care to keep this limited resource available.

California Science Content Standards, Grade 5

STANDARD SET 4. Earth Sciences (Weather)

5ES4.0 Energy from the Sun heats Earth unevenly, causing air movements that result in changing weather patterns. As a basis for understanding this concept:

5ES4.a Students know uneven heating of Earth causes air movements (convection currents).	pp. 208, **214, 215, 216,** 217, 219, 222, 242, 243, **244,** 245, 246, 247, 287, 288, 289, 290, 291, 296
5ES4.b Students know the influence that the ocean has on the weather and the role that the water cycle plays in weather patterns.	pp. 188, 189, 190, 191, 192, **215,** 219, 228, **229, 230, 231, 244,** 246, 247, 248, 249, 287, 296
5ES4.c Students know the causes and effects of different types of severe weather.	pp. 218, 220, 221, **222, 223, 224, 225, 226,** 227, **228,** 229, 230, **244,** 246, 247, 287, 296, 297
5ES4.d Students know how to use weather maps and data to predict local weather and know that weather forecasts depend on many variables.	pp. 222, 226, 227, **232, 233,** 234, 235, **236, 237,** 238, 239, **244,** 246, 247, 287, 292, 297
5ES4.e Students know that the Earth's atmosphere exerts a pressure that decreases with distance above Earth's surface and that at any point it exerts this pressure equally in all directions.	pp. **211, 212, 213,** 222, **244,** 246, 247, 297

What It Means to You

Do you check the weather report before you get ready for school in the morning? Weather forecasters use data to help make predictions about the weather. These predictions make it easier for people to plan for the day or week. If the weather forecaster says it might rain, you might take an umbrella. Weather forecasters can also help you plan for severe weather. If there is severe weather in the area, a warning from the weather forecasters can help prevent injuries.

California Science Content Standards, Grade 5

STANDARD SET 5. Earth Sciences (Solar System)

5ES5.0 The solar system consists of planets and other bodies that orbit the Sun in predictable paths. As a basis for understanding this concept:

5ES5.a Students know the Sun, an average star, is the central and largest body in the solar system and is composed primarily of hydrogen and helium.	pp. **257,** 258, 259, **282,** 284, 285, 287, 297, 298
5ES5.b Students know the solar system includes the planet Earth, the Moon, the Sun, eight other planets and their satellites, and smaller objects, such as asteroids and comets.	pp. **260,** 261, 263, **266, 267, 268, 269, 270, 271, 272, 273, 274, 275, 276, 277,** 278, 279, 280, 281, **282,** 284, 285, 287, 292, 297, 298
5ES5.c Students know the path of a planet around the Sun is due to the gravitational attraction between the Sun and the planet.	pp. 254, **260, 261,** 262, **263,** 264, 268, **282,** 284, 285, 297, 298

What It Means to You

The Sun and all of the objects that orbit it make up our solar system. You live on one of these objects—Earth! Scientists have been looking to find out more about the other objects in our solar system, and objects even farther away. Some of the planets in our solar system are so far away, you need a telescope or another instrument to see them. Some are close enough to see without a telescope. They reflect light from the Sun and seem to shine like stars in the night sky.

California Science Content Standards, Grade 5

STANDARD SET 6. Investigation and Experimentation

5IE6.0 Scientific progress is made by asking meaningful questions and conducting careful investigations. As a basis for understanding this concept and addressing the content in the other three strands, students should develop their own questions and perform investigations. Students will:

5IE6.a Classify objects (e.g., rocks, plants, leaves) in accordance with appropriate criteria.	pp. 115, **158**
5IE6.b Develop a testable question.	pp. **157, 291**
5IE6.c Plan and conduct a simple investigation based on a student-developed question and write instructions others can follow to carry out the procedure.	pp. **33, 79,** 145, 157, 291
5IE6.d Identify the dependent and controlled variables in an investigation.	pp. **76, 77, 78, 154, 155, 288, 289, 291**
5IE6.e Identify a single independent variable in a scientific investigation and explain how this variable can be used to collect information to answer a question about the results of the experiment.	pp. **76, 77, 78, 79, 154, 155, 288, 289, 291**
5IE6.f Select appropriate tools (e.g., thermometers, metersticks, balances, and graduated cylinders) and make quantitative observations.	pp. **6, 42,** 66, **76, 79, 114, 115, 144, 145,** 154, 156, 157, 170, 198, 199, 242, 243, **288,** 289, **290, 291**
5IE6.g Record data by using appropriate graphic representations (including charts, graphs, and labeled diagrams) and make inferences based on those data.	pp. 28, 29, **33, 67,** 79, **92,** 142, 143, **145, 157,** 199, **208,** 254, 278, 279, 281, **290, 291**
5IE6.h Draw conclusions from scientific evidence and indicate whether further information is needed to support a specific conclusion.	pp. **6,** 42, **79, 145,** 157, 170
5IE6.i Write a report of an investigation that includes conducting tests, collecting data or examining evidence, and drawing conclusions.	pp. **79**

What It Means to You

You might plan and conduct a careful investigation to answer a question, such as, "Does the color of light affect plant's growth?" You could form and test a hypothesis, and then draw a conclusion from what you learned.

Glossary

The glossary uses letters and signs to show how words are pronounced. The mark ′ is placed after a syllable with a primary or heavy accent. The mark ′ is placed after a syllable with a secondary or lighter accent.

To hear these words pronounced, listen to the AudioText CD.

A

acid (as′ id) a substance that when combined with a base can form a salt (p. 23)

air mass (âr mass) a large body of air with similar properties all through it (p. 218)

air sacs (âr saks) the thin-walled sacs in the lungs where oxygen enters the blood and carbon dioxide leaves the blood (p. 132)

alloy (al′ oi) a metal made by mixing two or more metallic elements (p. 19)

altimeter (al tim′ ə tər) a tool that measures air pressure to show altitude (p. 213)

altitude (al′ tə tüd) the height above Earth's surface (p. 193)

anemometer (an′ ə mom′ ə tər) a tool that measures wind speed (p. 233)

aqueduct (ak′ wə dukt) a system of pipelines that carries water from a river or lake to the area where it is needed (p. 183)

aquifer (ak′ wə fər) the layer of rock and soil that groundwater flows through (p. 177)

array (ə rā′) an arrangement like a grid (p. 13)

artery (är′ tər ē) a blood vessel that carries blood away from the heart to other parts of the body (p. 128)

asteroid (as′ tə roid′) a rocky object up to several hundred kilometers wide that revolves around the Sun (p. 270)

atmosphere (at′ mə sfir) all of the air around Earth (p. 211)

atmospheric pressure (at′ mə sfir′ ik presh′ ər) the weight of air pushing down on an area (p. 211)

atom (at′ əm) the smallest particle of an element with the same properties of the element (p. 12)

atomic number (ə tom′ ik num′ bər) the number of protons in the nucleus of an atom; the single most important property of an element (p. 12)

atrium (ā′ trē əm) the upper part of each side of the heart; plural atria (p. 130)

B

balance (bal′ əns) a tool used to measure mass (p. 10)

barometer (bə rom′ ə tər) a tool that measures air pressure (p. 232)

base (bās) a substance that when combined with an acid can form a salt (p. 23)

bladder (blad′ ər) the sac that collects and stores urine formed by the kidneys (p. 140)

blood vessels (blud ves′ əls) the tubes in which blood flows throughout the body (p. 127)

boiling point (boil′ ing point) the temperature at which a liquid becomes a gas (p. 52)

brittle (brit′ l) breaks easily (p. 15)

bronchi (brong′ kī) the two tubes that lead from the trachea to the lungs; singular bronchus (p. 132)

bronchiole (brong′ kē ōl) a small tube in the lungs that carries air to air sacs (p. 132)

capillary (kap′ ə ler′ ē) the smallest kind of blood vessels (p. 128)

cell (sel) the basic building block of living things (p. 95)

cell wall (sel wȯl) a rigid structure surrounding a plant cell membrane that gives the cell support (p. 97)

cellular respiration (sel′ uyə lər res′ pə rā′ shən) the process by which cells break down sugar and oxygen to release energy, water, and carbon dioxide (p. 110)

chemical change (kem′ ə kəl chānj) a change in which one kind of matter changes into a different kind of matter with different properties (p. 45)

chemical equation (kem′ ə kəl i kwā′ zhən) a statement of chemical symbols that shows what happens during a chemical reaction (p. 54)

chemical property (kem′ ə kəl prop′ ər tē) any property of a material that describes how it changes into other materials (p. 11)

chemical reaction (kem′ ə kəl rē ak′ shən) when one or more substances change into other substances with different chemical properties (p. 45)

chlorophyll (klôr′ ə fil) a green substance that allows plants to make their own food (p. 108)

chloroplast (klôr′ ə plast) a structure in plant cells that stores chlorophyll (p. 108)

cilia (sil′ ē ə) the tiny hairlike structures on cells in the lining of many parts of the respiratory system (p. 133)

circulatory system (sėr′ kyə lə tôr′ e sis′ təm) the system of the body that transports nutrients and oxygen to cells and carries away cell wastes (p. 127)

classify (klas′ ə fī) to arrange or sort objects, events, or living things according to their properties (p. 80)

cold front (kōld frunt) the boundary between two air masses where the cold air mass is moving into the area (p. 220)

collect data (kə lekt′ dā′ tə) to gather observations and measurements into graphs, tables, charts, or labeled diagrams (p. 76)

colon (kō′ lən) a part of the digestive system that stores undigested food until it can be removed from the body (p. 138)

combination reaction (kom′ bə nā′ shən rē ak′ shən) a chemical reaction in which reactants come together to form new products (p. 56)

comet (kom′ it) a frozen mass of ice and dust with a tail up to 80 million kilometers long that is in orbit around the Sun (p. 271)

communicate (kə myü′ nə kāt) to use words, pictures, graphs, tables, charts, and labeled diagrams to share information (p. 79)

compound (kom′ pound) a kind of matter made of a chemical combination of two or more elements (p. 20)

conclusion (kən klü′ zhən) a decision reached after thinking about facts and details (p. 43)

condensation (kon′ den sā′ shən) the process by which particles leave a gas and become a liquid (p. 189)

conduct (kən dukt′) to let heat and electricity pass through (p. 11)

conservation (kon′ sər vā′ shən) the process of using a resource wisely so that it lasts longer (p. 184)

controlled variable (kən trōld′ vâr′ ē bəl) a variable that must not be changed in an experiment to have a fair test (p. 77)

convection current (kən vek′ shən kėr′ ənt) the rising and sinking of matter in a circular pattern caused by temperature differences (p. 214)

crystal (kris′ tl) a group of particles arranged in a regular pattern with flat sides (p. 22)

cyclone (sī′ klōn) a wind that spirals inward around an area of low pressure (p. 222)

decomposition reaction (dē′ kom pə zish′ ən rē ak′ shən) a chemical reaction in which reactants split apart to form products (p. 56)

dependent variable (di pen′ dənt vâr′ ē ə bəl) something you measure or observe in an experiment (p. 77)

details (di′ tālz) individual pieces of information that support a main idea (p. 171)

dew (dü) water vapor that condenses on cold surfaces during the night (p. 189)

diaphragm (dī′ ə fram) the muscle below your lungs that contracts to let air into the lungs and relaxes to push air out of them (p. 132)

digestion (di jes′ chən) the process that changes food into a form that the body can use (p. 136)

digestive system (di jes′ tiv sis′ təm) the system of the body that takes in food and breaks it down into a form cells can use (p. 136)

dissolve (di zolv′) to spread throughout a liquid (p. 23)

ductile (duk′ təl) able to be made into wires or hammered into sheets (p. 18)

dwarf planet (dwôrf plan′ it) small, round object that orbits the Sun (p. 276)

El Niño (el nē′ nyō) a cycle of changes in the surface temperature of the Pacific Ocean that brings especially wet and dry seasons to many places in the world (p. 248)

electron (i lek′ tron) the particle in an atom that has a negative charge (p. 12)

element (el′ ə mənt) one of more than 100 basic kinds of matter that cannot be broken into smaller pieces through physical or chemical processes (p. 9)

ellipse (i lips′) a shape like an oval (p. 260)

equator (i kwā′ tər) the imaginary line that separates the northern and southern halves of Earth (p. 216)

esophagus (i sof′ ə gəs) the tube that carries food from the mouth to the stomach (p. 136)

estimate and measure (es′ tə māt and mezh′ ər) to tell what you think an object's measurements are and then measure it in units (p. 154)

evaporation (i vap′ ə rā′ shən) the process by which particles leave a liquid and become a gas (p. 52)

excretory system (ek′ skrə tôr′ ē sis′ təm) the system of the body that removes waste (p. 101)

experiment (ek sper′ ə mənt) to use scientific methods to test a hypothesis (p. 76)

explore (ek splôr′) to study a scientific idea in a hands-on manner (p. 6)

fog (fog) a cloud at ground level (p. 193)

forecast (fôr′ kast) a prediction of what may happen in the future based on past patterns (p. 232)

front (frunt) a boundary between two air masses (p. 220)

frost (frŏst) water vapor that deposits as ice crystals on surfaces at temperatures below freezing (p. 189)

G

generalization (jen′ ər ə lə zā′ shən) an inference that applies the outcome of one situation to other situations (p. 93)

glacier (glā′ shər) a long stretch of ice that flows slowly downhill or spreads over a land area (p. 179)

glucose (glü′ kōs) a substance made during photosynthesis and used during cellular respiration; a type of sugar (p. 104)

groundwater (ground′ wô′ tər) rain or melted snow that seeps into the ground (p. 177)

H

hail (hāl) frozen rain that is repeatedly blown upward into a cloud gaining layers of ice until it is so heavy it falls to the Earth (p. 194)

heart chambers (härt chām′ bər) the parts of the heart (p. 130)

humidity (hyü mid′ ə tē) the amount of water in the air (p. 194)

hurricane (hėr′ ə kān) a dangerous cyclonic storm made up of swirling bands of thunderstorms with wind speeds of at least 119 km per hour that forms over warm ocean water (p. 228)

hydrologic cycle (hī′ drə lo′ jik sī kəl) the repeated movement of water through the environment in different forms; also called the water cycle (p. 188)

hydrosphere (hī′ drə sfēr) all of the waters of the Earth (p. 173)

hygrometer (hī grom′ ə tər) a tool that measures the amount of moisture in the air (p. 232)

hypothesis (hī poth′ ə sis) a statement of one possible way to solve a problem or answer a question (p. 76)

I

identify and control variables (ī den′ tə fī and kən trōl′ vâr′ ē bəlz) to change one thing, but keep all the other factors the same (p. 76)

independent variable (in′ di pen′ dənt vâr′ ē ə bəl) something you change in an experiment (p. 78)

infer (in fėr) to draw a conclusion or make a reasonable guess based on what you have learned or what you know (p. 7)

inference (in′ fər əns) a conclusion based on facts, experiences, observations, or knowledge (p. 7)

interpret data (in tėr′ prit dā′ tə) to use the information you have collected to solve problems or answer questions (p. 79)

investigate (in ves′ tə gāt) to solve a problem or answer a question by following an existing procedure or an original one (p. 32)

K

kidney (kid′ nē) one of a pair of organs that removes waste from the blood (p. 140)

L

large intestine (lärj in tes′ tən) a wider tube connected to the small intestine that removes water from undigested food and stores this waste until it is removed from the body (p. 138)

latitude (lat′ ətüd) a measure of how far a place is north or south of the equator (p. 216)

lightning (līt′ ning) a large electrical spark moving between areas of opposite charge (p. 225)

lungs (lungs) an organ of the respiratory system that contains bronchioles and air sacs (p. 132)

M

main idea (mān ī dē′ ə) the most important idea in a passage (p. 171)

malleable (mal′ ē ə bəl) can be bent and shaped without breaking (p. 18)

mass (mas) a measure of the amount of matter in an object (p. 10)

melting temperature (mel ting tem′ pər ə chər) the temperature at which a solid becomes a liquid (p. 50)

metal (met′ l) an element or combination of elements that are usually shiny, can be bent and shaped without breaking, can be made into wire, and conduct heat and electricity (p. 15)

metalloid (met′ l oid) an element that has some properties of both metals and nonmetals; also called semimetal (p. 15)

meteorologist (mē′ tē ə rol′ ə jist) a scientist who uses weather data to forecast the weather (p. 235)

mitochondria (mī′ tə kon′ drē ə) the parts of a cell where sugar is broken down to release energy in a process called cellular respiration; singular mitochondrion (p. 96)

mixture (miks′ chər) two or more substances combined while keeping their own properties (p. 26)

model (mod′ l) a sketch, diagram, or object that represents something else (p. 198)

molecule (mol′ ə kyül) the smallest part of a substance made from more than one atom that still has the properties of that substance (p. 13)

monsoon (mon sün′) a wind that changes direction with the seasons (p. 230)

mucus (myü′ kəs) a sticky, thick fluid which coats parts of the respiratory system trapping dust and germs (p. 132)

multicellular (mul′ ti sel′ yə lər) having many cells (p. 95)

neutron (nü′ tron) the particle in an atom that has no charge (p. 12)

nonmetal (non met′ l) an element that is usually brittle, does not conduct heat or electricity well, and cannot be made into wires or hammered into sheets (p. 15)

nucleus (nü′ klē əs) 1. the center of an atom containing protons and neutrons (p. 15) 2. the central part of a cell that directs the cell's activities and stores information to pass on to new cells (p. 96) 3. a mass of dust and frozen water and gases at the center of a comet (p. 270)

observe (əb zėrv′) to use your senses to find out about objects, events, or living things (p. 42)

organ (ôr′ gən) a group of different tissues that join together to form one structure (p. 98)

organ system (ôr′ gən sis′ təm) a group of organs and tissues that work together to carry out a life process (p. 99)

periodic table of elements (pir′ ē od′ ik tā′ bəl əv el′ ə mənts) a table containing all the elements organized by atomic number and chemical properties (p. 14)

phloem (flō′ əm) tubes that carry sugar from a plant's leaves to the rest of the plant (p. 103)

photosynthesis (fō′ tō sin′ thə sis) the process by which plants use water, carbon dioxide, and energy from sunlight to produce oxygen and sugar (p. 108)

physical change (fiz′ ə kəl chānj) a change in which matter keeps the same chemical properties; a change in size, shape, volume, or state of matter (p. 45)

physical property (fiz′ ə kəl prop′ ir tē) any property of a material that can be seen or measured without changing the material (p. 10)

planet (plan′ it) a large, round object that orbits the Sun and has cleared the neighborhood around its orbit (p. 261)

polar region (pō′ lər rē′ jən) area near the North or South Pole that is very cold (p. 217)

precipitation (pri sip′ ə tā′ shən) water that falls from clouds as rain, hail, sleet, or snow (p. 189)

product (prod′ əkt) a substance made by a chemical reaction (p. 54)

proton (prō′ ton) the particle in an atom that has a positive charge (p. 12)

radar (rā′ där) a technology used to collect weather data (p. 233)

rain gauge (rān gāj) a tool that measures the amount of rain that has fallen (p. 233)

reactant (rē ak′ tənt) a substance used in a chemical reaction (p. 54)

reclamation (rek′ lə mā′ shən) when wastewater from homes or businesses is treated and used again for purposes other than drinking (p. 185)

recycle (rē si′ kəl) to treat something so that it can be used again (p. 176)

replacement reaction (ri plās′ mənt rē ak′ shən) a chemical reaction in which the parts of one or more reactants switch places (p. 57)

reservoir (rez′ ər vwär) usually an artificial lake that forms behind a dam (p. 178)

respiratory system (res′ pər ə tôr′ ē sis′ təm) the system of the body that takes in oxygen and removes carbon dioxide (p. 132)

runoff (run′ ȯf) water moving downhill (p. 182)

salinity (sə lin′ ə tē) a measure of the amount of salt in water (p. 174)

salt (sȯlt) a compound formed by a chemical reaction between an acid and a base; often refers to sodium chloride (p. 22)

satellite (sat′ l īt) an object that orbits another object in space (p. 262)

scientific method (sī′ ən tif′ ik meth′ əd) organized ways of finding answers and solving problems (p. 76)

sea level (sē lev′ əl) the level of the surface of an ocean (p. 173)

sequence (sē′ kwəns) the order in which things happen (p. 125)

severe thunderstorm warning (sə′ vir′ thun′ der storm′ wôr′ ning) a message sent out to an area where severe thunderstorms have formed letting people know that they should get inside as soon as possible (p. 225)

severe thunderstorm watch (sə′ vir′ thun′ der storm′ wäch) a message sent out to an area where severe thunderstorms with high winds and hail might form (p. 225)

severe weather (sə vir′ weṯн′ ər) weather that can cause damage (p. 224)

sleet (slēt) frozen raindrops that fall as precipitation (p. 194)

small intestine (smȯl in tes′ tən) a narrow, winding tube where food is changed chemically and broken down into small particles that can be absorbed into the blood (p. 138)

solar system (sō′ lər sis′ təm) a system that includes the Sun and its planets, along with many moons, asteroids, and comets (p. 257)

solubility (sol′ yə bil′ ə tē) the amount of a substance that can be dissolved by a solvent at a certain temperature (p. 28)

solute (sol′ yüt) the substance that dissolves in a solution (p. 28)

solution (sə lü′ shən) a mixture in which substances are spread out evenly and will not settle (p. 28)

solvent (sol′ vənt) the substance in a solution in which the solute dissolves (p. 28)

star (stär) a huge ball of very hot gas that gives off energy (p. 257)

stationary front (stā′ shə ner′ ē frunt) the boundary between two air masses that does not move very much (p. 220)

sublimation (sub′ lə mā′ shən) the process by which a solid changes directly into a gas (p. 53)

telegraph (tel′ ə graf) a machine that allows people to send messages long distances (p. 234)

tempered (tem′ pərd) describes air that is warmed in winter and cooled in summer because it is near a large body of water (p. 230)

tissue (tish′ ü) a group of the same kind of cells that work together to do a job (p. 98)

tornado (tôr nā′ dō) a rotating column of air that extends from a thunderstorm to the ground (p. 226)

trachea (trā′ kē ə) the tube that carries air from the larynx to the lungs (p. 132)

urine (yur′ ən) the mix of waste and water taken out of the blood by the kidneys and stored in the bladder (p. 140)

vacuole (vak′ yü ōl) a part of a cell that stores water and nutrients (p. 96)

valve (valv) a part of the heart that opens and closes to make sure the blood flows in the right direction (p. 130)

vascular (vas′ kyə lər) describes the system of tubes in certain plants that transports water and minerals (p. 102)

vein (vān) a blood vessel that carries blood toward the heart (p. 128)

ventricle (ven′ trə kəl) the lower part of each side of the heart (p. 131)

villi (vil′ ī) the tiny finger-shaped structures that cover the walls of the small intestine (p. 138)

warm front (wôrm frunt) the boundary between two air masses where the warm air mass is moving into the area (p. 220)

water cycle (wȯ′ tər sī′ kəl) the repeated movement of water through the environment in different forms; also called the hydrologic cycle (p. 188)

water table (wȯ′ tər tā′ bəl) the top level of the groundwater in an aquifer (p. 177)

water vapor (wȯ′ tər vā′ pər) the gas form of water (p. 188)

watershed (wȯ′ tər shed) the area from which water drains into a river (p. 178)

weight (wāt) a measure of the pull of gravity on an object (p. 10)

wind (wind) convection currents in the atmosphere (p. 215)

xylem (zī′ ləm) tubes that carry water and minerals from a plant's roots to its leaves (p. 102)

Index

This index lists the pages on which topics appear in this book. Page number after a *p* refer to a photograph or drawing. Page numbers after a *c* refer to a chart, graph, or diagram.

L

M

Credits

Illustrations

10, 50, 54, 56, 60 Patrick Gnan; 71 Luciana Navarro Powell; 90-91, 96-97 Robert Ulrich; 91, 110, 180, 226 Tony Randazzo; 91, 102-103, 106-107, 123, 146 Jeff Mangiat; 96 Paulette Dennis AOCA, BScBMC, CMI; 98, 108, 110, 116, 190, 212, 214, 216, 218, 220, 222, 224, 228, 230, 232, 234, 236, 238 Sharon & Joel Harris; 100-101, 194, 211, 258, 260, 262, 266, 270 Peter Bollinger; viii, 122-123, 129-131, 133-135, 137, 139-141, 146 Leonello Calvetti; v, 168-169, 176, 188, 190, 200, 202, 206-207, 214-216, 219-221, 224, 237, 244 Studio Liddell; 169, 185-186, 207, 223 Matt Zang; 178 Clint Hansen; 195, 209, 217 Robert Kayganich; 253, 262, 264 Paul Oglesby

Photographs

Every effort has been made to secure permission and provide appropriate credit for photographic material. The publisher deeply regrets any omission and pledges to correct errors called to its attention in subsequent editions.

Unless otherwise acknowledged, all photographs are the property of Scott Foresman, a division of Pearson Education.

Photo locators denoted as follows: Top (T), Center (C), Bottom (B), Left (L), Right (R), Background (Bkgd).

Cover: (T) ©Craig Tuttle/Corbis, (C) ©John Giustina/Getty Images

Front Matter: ii ©DK Images; iii (TR, B) ©DK Images; vi (TL) ©Ryoichi Utsumi/Getty Images, (BC, CR) ©DK Images; vii ©Cees Van Leeuwen/Cordaly Photo Library Ltd./Corbis; viii ©Dr. George Wilder/Getty Images; ix ©Robert Llewellyn/Corbis; x (TL) ©Jeff Hunter/Getty Images, (BL) ©Scott Stulberg/Corbis; xi (TR) ©Nora Goods/Masterfile Corporation, (BR) ©Mark Garlick/Photo Researchers, Inc.; xii ©Royalty-Free/Corbis; xiii Frank Greenaway/©DK Images; xiv ©Gene Blevins/LA Daily News/Corbis; xv ©Tony Freeman/PhotoEdit; xix (TR, CL) Jupiter Images; xxiv Jupiter Images

Unit A – Opener: 1 ©Michael Simpson/Getty Images; 2 (TL) ©Luis Veiga/Getty Images, (Bkgd) ©Frithjof Hirdes/Corbis; 3 ©Ryoichi Utsumi/Getty Images; 4 (BL) ©P. Freytag/Corbis, (BR) ©Tony Freeman/PhotoEdit, (T) ©Connie Coleman/Getty Images, (C) ©Hulton-Deutsch Collection/Corbis, (T) ©Paul Silverman/Fundamental Photographs; 5 ©DK Images; 7 (CR) ©Roger Tully/Getty Images, (Bkgd) ©Connie Coleman/Getty Images; 8 (C) ©Connie Coleman/Getty Images, (BC) ©Hulton-Deutsch Collection/Corbis; 9 ©Neal Mishler/Getty Images; 10 (BR) ©P. Freytag/Corbis, (BR) ©Paul Silverman/Fundamental Photographs; 11

(TL) ©Tony Freeman/PhotoEdit, (TL) ©Scott Camazine/Photo Researchers, Inc., (TC) ©Diane Schiumo/Fundamental Photographs; 12 (BL) ©DK Images, (CL) Stephen Oliver/©DK Images; 13 (CR) ©Bernard Lang/Getty Images, (TR) Photo taken with Digital Instruments Nanoscope® SPM, courtesy of Veeco Instruments, Inc., Santa Barbara, CA; 15 (TR) ©Larry Stepanowicz/Visuals Unlimited, (L) ©David Samuel Robbins/Corbis; 16 ©Klaus Guldbrandsen/Photo Researchers, Inc.; 18 (TL, TCL, C, BCL) ©DK Images, (BL) Andy Crawford/©DK Images, (BL) ©Wally Eberhart/Visuals Unlimited, (BC) ©David Wrobel/Visuals Unlimited, (TL) Corbis; 19 (CR) Corbis, (BL) Getty Images, (T) Hemera Technologies, (BR) Jupiter Images; 21 (TC, BR) ©Richard Megna/Fundamental Photographs; 21 (TC) ©Andrew Syred/Photo Researchers, Inc.; 22 (TL, CR) ©DK Images, (TR) ©Paul Silverman/Fundamental Photographs; 25 (C, TC) ©Richard Megna/Fundamental Photographs, (TL, CR, TR) ©DK Images; 26 (TL) ©DK Images, (T) Jupiter Images; 28 (TR, CR, TL, BL) ©DK Images, ©David Taylor/Photo Researchers, Inc.; 29 (TC) Digital Vision, (TCC) ©Andrew Jaster, (CL) Getty Images, (CR) ©G. Tompkinson/Photo Researchers, Inc., (BC) ©Mark Schneider/Visuals Unlimited, (BL) ©Charles D. Winters/Photo Researchers, Inc., (BR) ©Astrid & Hanns-Frieder Michler/Photo Researchers, Inc.; 30 Getty Images; 34 (Bkgd) Getty Images, (BR) ©DK Images, (BL) Jupiter Images; 36 Jupiter Images; 38 Getty Images, (BR) ©Stephen Welstead/Corbis; 39 ©Cees Van Leeuwen/Cordaly Photo Library Ltd./Corbis; 40 (BC) ©Paul Seheult/Eye Ubiquitous/Corbis, (T) ©Geoff Higgins/Photo Library; 41 ©Charles D. Winters/Photo Researchers, Inc.; 43 (Bkgd) ©Geoff Higgins/Photo Library, (CR) Getty Images; 44 ©Geoff Higgins/Photo Library; 46 (TL, BL, BR) ©DK Images; 47 (BL) ©DK Images, (R) ©Richard Megna/Fundamental Photographs; 48 (TL) ©Floyd Dean/Getty Images, (R) ©Tom Schierlitz/Getty Images; 50 ©Runk/Schoenberger/Grant Heilman Photography; 51 (CL, TR, CR) ©DK Images, (TL) ©Floyd Dean/Getty Images; 52 (TR) Getty Images, (CR) ©Paul Seheult/Eye Ubiquitous/Corbis; 53 ©Charles D. Winters/Photo Researchers, Inc.; 54 ©DK Images; 55 (TR) Andy Crawford and Tim Ridley/©DK Images, (CR, BR) ©Richard Megna/Fundamental Photographs, (BL) ©DK Images, (BC) Dave King/©DK Images; 56 ©DK Images; 57 (L, CR) ©DK Images; 58 (TL) PhotoLibrary, (R) ©Julian Calder/Corbis; 59 ©Richard Megna/Fundamental Photographs; 60 ©Michael Rosenfeld/Getty Images; 61 ©1996 Richard Megna/Fundamental Photographs; 62 (BC, BL, BR) ©DK Images, (TL) ©Julie Toy/Getty Images; (CL) ©Lars Klove/Getty Images; 63 (BR, TL, TCL, TCR, TR, BL) ©DK Images; 64 (Bkgd) Digital Vision, (BL, CR) ©Scott Camazine/Photo Researchers, Inc.; 65 ©Scott Camazine/Photo Researchers, Inc.; 68 (TL) ©Geoff Higgins/Photo Library, (B, BL, BR, CL) ©DK Images, (TCL,

CL) ©Tom Schierlitz/Getty Images, (BCL, CL) ©1996 Richard Megna/Fundamental Photographs, (Bkgd) ©Astrid & Hanns-Frieder Michler/Photo Researchers, Inc.; 70 Getty Images; 72 (Bkgd) ©Roger Ressmeyer/Corbis, (CL) GRC/NASA Image Exchange, (CL) ©MSFC/NASA Image Exchange; 73 (T, B) GRC/NASA Image Exchange; 74 (BL) JPL/NASA, (BCL) ©Cris Cordeiro/PhotoLibrary, (TL) Kennedy Space Center/NASA; 75 (TL) ©Ryoichi Utsumi/Getty Images, (CL) ©Cees Van Leeuwen/Cordaly Photo Library Ltd./Corbis, (B) ©Frithjof Hirdes/Corbis; 81 ©David Vintiner/zefa/Corbis; 82 (BL) ©Dick Patrick/Getty Images, (TR) Getty Images; Unit B – Opener: 87 (Bkgd) ©Joseph De Sciose/Getty Images, (C) ©Premium Stock/Getty Images; 88 (Bkgd) ©Larry Brownstein/Ambient Images, Inc., (Inset) ©PhotoEdit/PhotoEdit; 89 ©Dr. George Wilder/Getty Images; 90 (BL) ©Carolina Biological/Visuals Unlimited, (BR) ©SIU/Visuals Unlimited; 93 (CR) ©NCI/Photo Researchers, Inc., (Bkgd) ©Michael Webb/Visuals Unlimited; 94 ©Michael Webb/Visuals Unlimited; 95 ©Dr. Fred Hossler/Visuals Unlimited; 98 (TL) ©Michael Webb/Visuals Unlimited, (BL) ©Biophoto Associates/Photo Researchers, Inc., (CR) ©Carolina Biological/Visuals Unlimited; 99 (CR) ©Alfred Pasieka/Photo Researchers, Inc., (C) ©SIU/Visuals Unlimited, (BC) ©DK Images, (BR) ©Jack Wilburn/Animals Animals/Earth Scenes; 102 Neil Fletcher and Matthew Ward/©DK Images; 103 Jupiter Images; 104 Clive Streeter/©DK Images; 106 (TR, TL) ©DK Images, (BR) ©P. Dayanandan/Photo Researchers, Inc.; 108 (TR) ©DK Images, (BL) ©Dr. Jeremy Burgess/Photo Researchers, Inc.; 110 ©P. Motta & T. Naguro/Photo Researchers, Inc.; 111 (TC) ©Bill Brooks/Masterfile Corporation, (CR) ©DK Images; 112 (Bkgd) ©Quest/Photo Researchers, Inc., (T) ©Dr. Fred Hossler/Visuals Unlimited; 116 (TL) ©Michael Webb/Visuals Unlimited, (TL, B) Neil Fletcher and Matthew Ward/©DK Images, (Bkgd) Getty Images; 118 Neil Fletcher and Matthew Ward/©DK Images; 120 (BL) Photo Researchers, Inc., (Bkgd) Getty Images; 121 (L) ©Robert Daly/Getty Images, (L) ©Robert Llewellyn/Corbis; 122 ©Lester Lefkowitz/Corbis; 125 (CR) ©Michael Webb/Visuals Unlimited, (Bkgd) ©Lester Lefkowitz/Corbis; 126 ©Lester Lefkowitz/Corbis; 128 (TL, TR, CR) ©Dr. Richard Kessel & Dr. Randy Kardon/Tissues & Organs/Visuals Unlimited; 130 ©Jean Claude Revy - ISM/Phototake; 132 ©Susumu Nishinaga/Photo Researchers, Inc.; 133 ©Susumu Nishinaga/Photo Researchers, Inc.; 135 ©Dr. Richard Kessel & Dr. Randy Kardon/Tissues & Organs/Visuals Unlimited; 136 ©Omikron/Photo Researchers, Inc.; 137 ©SPL/Photo Researchers, Inc.; 138 ©Susumu Nishinaga/Photo Researchers, Inc.; 140 ©Biophoto Associates/Photo Researchers, Inc.; 142 (Bkgd) ©BodyOnline/Getty Images, (BR) Getty Images, (CL) ©Tom Bean/Corbis, (BR) Digital Vision; 146 (Bkgd) ©Dr. Dennis Kunkel/Getty Images, (TL) ©Lester Lefkowitz/Corbis; 148 ©Susumu